Anthropological Ethics in Context

Anthropological Ethics in Context

AN ONGOING DIALOGUE

EDITED BY

Dena Plemmons
and Alex W. Barker

Walnut Creek, California

LEFT COAST PRESS, INC.
1630 North Main Street, #400
Walnut Creek, CA 94596
www.LCoastPress.com

Copyright © 2016 by Left Coast Press, Inc.

All rights reserved. No part of this publication may be reproduced, stored in a retrieval system, or transmitted in any form or by any means, electronic, mechanical, photocopying, recording, or otherwise, without the prior permission of the publisher.

ISBN 978-1-61132-879-0 hardback
ISBN 978-1-61132-880-6 paperback
ISBN 978-1-61132-881-3 institutional eBook
ISBN 978-1-61132-882-0 consumer eBook

Library of Congress Cataloging-in-Publication Data
Anthropological ethics in context : an ongoing dialogue / edited by Dena Plemmons and Alex W. Barker.
    pages cm
 Includes bibliographical references and index.
  ISBN 978-1-61132-879-0 (hardback : alk. paper) -- ISBN 978-1-61132-880-6 (pbk. : alk. paper) -- ISBN 978-1-61132-881-3 (institutional ebook) -- ISBN 978-1-61132-882-0 (consumer ebook)
 1. Anthropological ethics. 2. Anthropology--Methodology. I. Plemmons, Dena, editor. II. Barker, Alex W., editor.
 GN33.6.A46 2015
 174'.9301--dc23
                        2015022152

Printed in the United States of America

♾ The paper used in this publication meets the minimum requirements of American National Standard for Information Sciences—Permanence of Paper for Printed Library Materials, ANSI/NISO Z39.48–1992.

CONTENTS

Preface | 7

CHAPTER ONE | 9
Introduction: Ethics, Work, and Life—
Individual Struggles and Professional "Comfort Zones"
in Anthropology
Virginia R. Dominguez

CHAPTER TWO | 23
A Short History of American Anthropological Ethics,
Codes, Principles, and Responsibilities—
Professional and Otherwise
David H. Price

CHAPTER THREE | 39
Background and Context to the Current Revisions
Dena Plemmons and Alex W. Barker

CHAPTER FOUR | 75
Do No Harm
Katherine C. MacKinnon

CHAPTER FIVE | 91
Be Open and Honest Regarding Your Work
David H. Price

CHAPTER SIX | 107
Make Your Results Accessible
Alex W. Barker

CHAPTER SEVEN | 119
Obtain Informed Consent and Necessary Permissions
Robert Albro and Dena Plemmons

CHAPTER EIGHT | 145
Weigh Competing Ethical Obligations to Collaborators and Affected Parties
Nathaniel Tashima and Cathleen Crain

CHAPTER NINE | 167
Protect and Preserve Your Records
Alex W. Barker

CHAPTER TEN | 183
Maintain Respectful and Ethical Professional Relationships
Dena Plemmons

CHAPTER ELEVEN | 207
What's Different?
Alex W. Barker and Dena Plemmons

CHAPTER TWELVE | 213
On Professional Diversity and the Future of Anthropology
Laura A. McNamara

AFTERWORD | 231
Ethics as Institutional Process
Monica Heller

Index | 237

About the Editors and Contributors | 245

PREFACE

The contributions in this volume document the development of the most recent principles of professional ethics of the American Anthropological Association, the world's largest professional organization of anthropologists from all fields of practice. The AAA comprises forty different professional societies or sections representing different subfields or topics, geographical areas, and anthropological identities, and thereby brings these principles into the work of scholars studying all aspects of the human career. The contributions represent the viewpoints of different participants in the process of developing and debating the current ethical positions of the Association, reflecting their unique and sometimes conflicting personal perspectives on the complex and contentious topics involved.

An introductory chapter by the then-president of the AAA at the time the project began and an afterward by the AAA's current president help place the development of the current ethical statement into a broader institutional context. The book traces the historical development of the Association's ethics codes and the historical events which engendered their development, as well as the immediate social and political context in which the current statement was developed. Separate chapters address each of the individual principles and are written by participants in the discussions leading to their development and adoption. The two final chapters examine how the current statement differs from past statements or codes, and discuss the challenges of developing ethical expectations inclusive of anthropologists practicing in increasingly diverse and dissimilar contexts.

What the book does not represent is a complete and exhaustive discussion of every aspect of every principle. Such an enterprise is beyond both our ability and our inclination—anthropologists of good conscience can and should interpret these principles in different ways based on the unique circumstances of each situation, study, or project. An exhaustive explanation of how each principle should be viewed in all possible circumstances presupposes a static and unchanging document, which is quite different than our common intent in developing these principles.

Nor does the book represent positions in a unified or consistent manner. Each author approached these issues through their own subdisciplinary lenses and personal experience, and each of the participants perceived the discussion in somewhat different ways. Each chapter therefore reflects the individual opinion of its respective author(s).

—Dena Plemmons and Alex W. Barker

CHAPTER ONE

Introduction:
Ethics, Work, and Life—Individual Struggles and Professional "Comfort Zones" in Anthropology

Virginia R. Dominguez

As a recent past president of the American Anthropological Association—and the president during whose tenure most of the work of the AAA Task Force for Comprehensive Ethics Review was done—I am especially pleased to help introduce this book and launch it as a reflection and articulation of this deep, difficult, thoughtful, and inspiring project.

Most scientists, as Thomas Kuhn aptly argued in his now classic book *The Structure of Scientific Revolutions* (1962), work with paradigms, patterns, and habits that he called the workings of "normal science." It is what I have recently called our professional "comfort zones and their dangers" (Dominguez 2012). They are those ideas, practices, discourses, and questions that get to be so much a part of a scientific discipline or profession at any one time that they often get learned and adopted more than reflected upon or questioned.

This book reminds us of how important it is to reflect on our "comfort zones," their dangers, and the paradigms, patterns, and habits that become second-nature, at times so much so that they are to the detriment of the practitioner and the people or places s/he studies. I am not saying that thinking about ethics is new to anthropologists. It isn't. I am saying that the ethical questions are so central to the practice of anthropological life and work that they must be spotlighted and not just added to the training of new anthropologists or the awareness of professional anthropologists.

Anthropological Ethics in Context: An Ongoing Dialogue, pp. 9-21. © 2016 Left Coast Press, Inc. All rights reserved.

I am also saying that delving into matters of ethics means plunging into the struggle it entails. It is a struggle that is personal and professional, never-ending and open-ended, and crucial but without simple answers. It is that sense of worthwhileness and necessity, struggle and everydayness that is highlighted in this book. The AAA Task Force for Comprehensive Ethics Review had predecessors. The AAA has had principles and statements on ethics, and even resolutions on ethics, at various points in its long history (since the turn of the twentieth century) (see Chapter 2). What this book does is to highlight what has been learned from the past and what the current struggles are. It offers the background and conveys the urgency of the matter. It offers reflections and descriptions of the process of the AAA's deliberations and its "conclusions." It does not provide a simple answer, or even a simple formula, but it does go far toward keeping anthropologists (and their fellow travelers) from staying too much in their "comfort zones" of their own work and lives (both in their fields of research and in their everyday institutional places of work).

There is myopia in all walks of life. There are tacit agendas that don't even get noticed. There are ideas, behaviors, values, and practices that are reproduced more than noticed and questioned. These include the profession of anthropology itself—including, but not limited to, the profession in the U.S. That the work of the AAA Task Force for Comprehensive Ethics Review (from 2008 to 2011) can result in further scrutiny of the profession, its assumptions, its aporia, its strengths, and its potential is obvious to me, but this book makes it possible for it to be chewed on by many others, turned upside down, debated, consulted, expanded, and explored. It is one of this book's greatest strengths, a point this introductory chapter frames but only as a point of departure.

The Range

Let me begin with the matter of range. Anthropologists have long noticed many of the difficult questions that arise when we do research in the field. People have worried about inequality in our encounters, because so much of the research is extremely well-meaning but still entails a person with two or three university degrees doing research on a topic or issues that concern many people often less socially, economically, and even politically privileged (and indeed frequently far less privileged in the world). Anthropologists usually acknowledge that difference but also seek to temper its significance. The question is how well we succeed and whether the effort actually produces the results we seek. Consider friendship. After months, often years, living with and among people whose lives or struggles the anthropologist is studying, it is common for the anthropologist to get closer to some people than to others. But what does that mean? So central is the anthropologist's relationship to people in fieldwork that it warrants thinking—indeed, thinking long and hard—about what one does, the extent to which one uses, works with, collaborates with, but possibly exploits people in such settings when pursuing answers to specific questions in the field. Anthropologists may change the terms they use for the people from whom we learn the most in the field (from informant to interlocutor to friend), but do we also change the nature of our relationship with those people over the course of a lifetime or career? I have no doubt that the great majority of anthropologists come to care deeply for people whose lives they set out to study, but these feelings are far from simple and they entail deep and long-lasting ethical struggles for most of us. What are the implications of coming to see someone as a friend, as a partner, as a lover, as family? And what are the implications of coming to be seen as a friend, a partner, a lover, or a member of a family? These are central issues, struggles, and doubts, and indeed are usually aspects of fieldwork that become second-nature but also worrisome to the anthropologist in the field and after fieldwork.

Consider this further. When an anthropologist befriends someone while doing fieldwork, is that relationship more equal than others? Is it more mutual than others? Or might it actually lead to that relationship being more utilitarian than others because one comes to rely more on that person? And would the ethical thing to do then be to not befriend anyone in the field? For some time anthropologists have worried about tacit, unwitting, or de facto exploitation of the "researched" by the "researcher," perhaps because we (and our profession) care so much about making the world a better place for all, regardless of people's position in a geopolitical or socioeconomic hierarchy. For professionals who actively seek to include all of humanity into their data-gathering and theorizing about humanity (and not just, or not just primarily, have theories derived from research in prosperous countries or privileged sectors of those countries), the very idea that research/participant observation/fieldwork in less privileged or less powerful communities could exacerbate the problem of inequality is hard to swallow. But we must struggle with that issue and we must realize that much of our research is indeed fraught with ethical difficulties and not just epistemological ones.

But what exactly does this mean? I have had students encountering anthropology for the first time who appreciate much of the cultural, political, and economic critique they get from me as a teacher and from many other colleagues and the books they read, but who find themselves seriously asking themselves (and me) if the simple solution to the big anthropological research question isn't to stop doing it, that is, to never put oneself in the position of researching other people's lives. I understand the temptation but worry about its consequences, as I know colleagues on the Task Force have as well. For example, if anthropologists were to stop conducting research in places or locations frequently deemed marginal or powerless by richer and more dominant sectors of the world's population, I easily imagine two subsequent scenarios: (1) that many parts of the human experience of life on the planet would be ignored in the making of policies, the development of practices, and the elaboration of social theories as a consequence of discontinuing anthropological research; and (2) that other fields, other professions, other occupations would begin to do some of that work, but without the history of anthropologists doing the work and making mistakes, reflecting on those mistakes, and learning from them. This latter scenario worries me just as much as the first, because there is much to be said for the kind of serious engagement with the ethical struggles that are the bread and butter of now decades of anthropological fieldwork and practice.

Consider just a few of the issues that arise for all of us as anthropologists doing participant observation/fieldwork.

1. Intention versus results: We typically seek to make things better for people, or at least not to make them worse. Hence, the Task Force's first principle of doing "no harm." But Derrida (1980) was correct when for years he called attention to the fact that we don't really control the effect our presence has on a group of people or how they respond. So we face the quandary of having intentions that may be laudable but results with which we ourselves are not comfortable. We may, for example, give nicer presents to some people than others (let us say, those we befriend or come to see as members of our family). If those acts of generosity then lead to an improvement in material conditions, life expectancy, educational opportunities, or even migration opportunities of those individuals or families over others, thus exacerbating or altering social relations we did not seek out to alter, our intentions might have been perfectly understandable but the actions we took caused trouble for people we care about and also for ourselves.

2. Knowledge basis and sufficiency: We set out to learn a great deal in the course of doing fieldwork, but do we ever know enough to make decisions about what is best for a group of people? Again, "do no harm" is great, but when do we know enough to make a decision about what is best, for whom, and against what likely or expected results? Doubts arise about how much we know even after several years of research. Even worse, people often ask us for help, but the longer we stay in a place and know people personally, the more we realize that in helping "some" we are not necessarily helping all. We find ourselves taking sides, seeing imbalances and inequalities—for example, seeing bullying, domestic violence, degradation, upward mobility, downward mobility, resignation, and resistance. When people ask us for help and we realize that we would like to help, part of the anthropological dilemma is assessing what we know and how much we know so that we might knowingly anticipate a range of likely responses.

3. Part-time members of a "community" versus full-time members: No matter how immersed we are in a location or the lives of a group of people, anthropologists typically do not live "there" full-time. We have a way out, a life away from what we research, even if we make a point of continuing to do anthropological research with the same group of people over many years. At best we are friendly outsiders, but at worse we might be "slumming" or voyeurs or "snowbirds," with options and commitments elsewhere. No anthropologist I know likes admitting that. Many make a point of frequently visiting the people (or community) they worked with earlier in their careers. Yet few of us move to those communities full-time and most of us earn a living elsewhere, not as anthropologists in the field but as salaried employees of an educational institution, an NGO, a governmental organization, a company, or a health provider service. This built-in inequality is among the hardest ethical dilemmas for most anthropologists I know. Sometimes the anthropologist feels guilt, sometimes extra commitment, sometimes familial responsibilities, and sometimes downright sadness.

4. Material conditions and our responses to them: We may not enter a research site with a great deal of money, but we frequently have more money than many of the people among whom we do our research. Moreover, we typically have better living conditions than most. We often have far higher levels of formal schooling than most, and we often carry passports and nationalities from countries that

are more geopolitically and economically influential in the world—or at least higher socioeconomic classes in countries that may see themselves as "poor," "small," or at least "postcolonial." Of course, there are a good number of anthropologists, especially these days, who study "sideways" or "up" and these differences in material conditions do not hold. However, the majority of anthropologists, even when studying in their own country, a country like the United States, the United Kingdom, Canada, or Brazil, study the lives of the less economically privileged, the lives of poorer communities or marginalized groups, and these inequalities in existing and long-term material conditions do hold.

5. Equality as desire vs. geopolitical inequality: Implicit in many of these points is the largest issue of all and it pertains to our desire for equality and our understanding that there is much inequality in the world. Consider how frequently we strive for equality and how frequently anthropologists like to advocate for the "underdog." Yet, as an anthropologist gets to know a group, a community, the people who work in a work setting, or those who live in close quarters, one of the disturbing but recurring facts we discover is that there is always friction. There are power imbalances. There are always differences—in views, likes, dislikes, and even social hierarchies—that were not readily evident from the outside. In such settings, what then are the more and less ethical actions we can take? When we talk more to some people than to others or we find ourselves deeming some people more trustworthy than others, are we not participating in the social setting in ways that carry ethical and not just epistemological implications?

The range of ethical dilemmas is palpable, constant, and wide-ranging in fieldwork, and this Task Force for Comprehensive Ethics Review did well to concentrate on fieldwork in a good deal of what it debated, examined, and explored. But the range covered by the Task Force—a range for which I am personally quite grateful—also included matters outside the experience of anthropologists conducting fieldwork. Indeed, other matters, which we may not always perceive as ethical, nevertheless haunt us and cannot be ignored. Some may get less attention in ethical discussions because they may appear to pertain to many people and not just to anthropologists. Others get less attention because they occur more "at home," and still others may get less attention because they pertain to the profession at large and not to individual anthropologists.

But do not all of these entail ethical quandaries, ethical struggles, and ethical choices? I think so, and this volume goes far to remind us of those professional responsibilities and struggles outside "the field." Part of the struggle here (and for the Task Force) has been how to relate to those matters as well as to the basic principle of aiming to do no harm when we do our research and writing. Some of them are institutional matters, some are inherited ones, and many are matters within the larger society/ies in which we normally conduct our professional work. The range of issues that the Task Force contemplated is large and greatly exceeds the issue of anthropologists' responsibilities to the people whose lives they research or among whom they conduct short-term or long-term fieldwork.

Anthropological Lives

Consider the institutions that pay our salaries, or have us on staff as paid or even unpaid interns. Those institutions may be in the country in which the anthropologist tends to conduct fieldwork, but they often are not. Ethical issues populate our lives in those institutions, organizations, and societies just as much as elsewhere. When we see systemic consequential inequalities in those institutions—inequalities that go against our social and professional ideals—are we supposed to ignore them just because we are not doing fieldwork on them? I do not think so. And when laws concerning research, privacy, employment, gender, inequality, sexuality, health care, property, and inheritance exist in the country in which we are paid and/or the country in which we conduct our research, do we examine them, challenge them, or work to change them, or do we just abide by them? As many anthropologists have long known, those laws often do not meet anthropological standards or they are shaped by considerations and professions other than anthropology, its past, and its intentions. Colleagues in certain countries—South Africa perhaps most significantly—have long histories of seeing much of their work as research and advocacy, but even there it has not always been that easy to decide which laws to challenge, which legal systems to seek to change, and which future to aim for.

Moreover, many other anthropologists live in countries whose legal and political systems are less egregiously objectionable than apartheid South Africa (cf. Ross 2005). In those cases, it might be easier to say that our primary ethical quandary concerns our research and not our everyday lives as employees, managers, citizens, and participants, but should we not actually focus on the overall ethical responsibilities and struggles of anthropologists, rather than just our ethical dilemmas "in the field"? Anthropologists often believe that they are the most progressive or liberal or open-minded group of people on the planet (or at least as a profession), and it is often the case that anthropologists complain about the bureaucracy, regulations, and practices of their own societies. But is this the extent of our engagement with ethical questions, struggles, and quandaries in the societies/institutions in which we tend to live? Is there a simple answer? No, there isn't. Must anthropologists just be contrary? No, of course not. Must all anthropologists be first and foremost advocates, public interest anthropologists, politicians, and promoters of change? Of course, there's change and there's change, and there are differences to consider regarding changes to pursue, when to pursue them, and how to pursue them.

But it is also a matter of extending one's range of thought, one's range of responsibility, and thinking of the anthropologist's range of ethical processes, practices, and dilemmas as including all aspects of one's life, and not just of one's research "in the field." The fact is, that for many anthropologists, abiding by certain rules, laws, and regulations of the state/government in which they live and/or in which they conduct fieldwork is far from simple.

Numerous examples come to mind. When a government granting agency requires a signature stating that the grantee swears allegiance to the country and government making the grant, what can or do most anthropologists do? My sense is that most frown but sign the form because the proposed research is expensive and s/he deems the planned research project to be of higher ethical value or potential and, therefore, necessary. When a university requires its faculty members to uphold high moral standards or risk losing their jobs, anthropologists I know struggle in deciding whether some form of civil disobedience could cause them to lose their jobs. When a museum has the physical remains of people excavated by prior archaeologists, and the museum actually seeks to repatriate the remains but the country's laws include loopholes that do not make it necessary for the remains to be repatriated, which imperative is invoked? In all of these cases, the matter is not simple, and that is the point. Ethical dilemmas entail struggle. They also rarely entail just one possible solution, resolution, or decision. I wish they did, but they don't. The question is how best to address the matters, not how to hide them, pretend they fail to exist, or whitewash them.

Consider, for example, those physical remains I just mentioned. The law may express an intention, a necessity, an effort, and a process, and the anthropologist may find it too limiting, but what if the matter isn't clear and it is not readily obvious to whom the remains should go when there is no current named group of people who can readily be identified as their descendants? Or consider that older term—moral turpitude—in use in the U.S. academy for years to name actions and behaviors deemed by an academic employer so unacceptable that a tenured faculty member can lose tenure if charged with moral turpitude. Moral turpitude (and the general concept behind it) indexes some sense of morality, that is, some system of morals (often implicit rather than explicit but whose system of morality it reflects and whose ethical standards it privileges). In my experience, this charge has been invoked when someone breaks the law, especially when the matter is sexual or financial or leads to a felony arrest and conviction, but I also know of many cases of sexual harassment, racial harassment, borderline negligence of duties, and even apparent mismanagement of funds that have not led to a termination of tenure at a university in the United States. Often the cases are complex, and lawyers decide how best to handle the matter, especially when weighing the cost of litigation and the likelihood of winning or losing a trial. However, many of them affect anthropologists at least as much as they affect other colleagues, and they entail big and small questions of ethics. For example, does the invocation of "moral turpitude" get invoked enough? If not, do we not have ethical obligations to try to change those practices? And when we spot a practice or action that seems ethically wrong, are we sure we act ethically upon that knowledge?

Sadly, there are anthropologists who plagiarize (and not just first-year students who have not yet learned how to quote others, attribute work to others, and credit others). Sadly, there also are anthropologists who engage in sexual harassment and anthropologists who handle grants and fellowships in questionable ways, and sometimes these problems are handled "in-house" and sometimes they are not handled at all. When other anthropologists spot these matters, is it always clear when the proper response is whistle-blowing? I do not think so. Indeed, we have issues entailing our own human resources, our own relations between anthropologists, between men and women, between younger and older scholars, between colleagues in more prestigious anthropological departments or institutes and anthropologists in less well-known or more teaching-intensive locations. Here I ask if ethical questions do not also pertain to those relations, and I note with appreciation that the AAA Task Force for Comprehensive Ethics Review contemplated all of this as part of its mandate. It is, in other words, part of the range of issues in a profession, and certainly within the anthropological profession.

The Larger Context

Clearly the issue is not just that anthropologists seek to do no harm when they conduct anthropological fieldwork or research. As the Task Force said, anthropologists must "be open and honest regarding [their] work," "obtain informed consent and necessary permissions," "balance competing obligations," "make [their] results accessible," and "protect and preserve [their] records." Anthropologists must also "maintain respectful and ethical professional relationships." As I see it, the issue is how to live ethical lives more broadly (ethical lives that include all aspects of the work we do) and how to address the dilemmas that come up in any part of our professional anthropological lives. This book is a terrific exploration of many of those issues—from secrecy and privacy to navigating legal systems that seem unjust and choosing sides in cases that concern people "in the field" or even students and colleagues far from "the field."

It also explored the larger context in which the profession exists and operates. Anthropologists, indeed, tend to see themselves as the most liberal or progressive of the professions, certainly of the social sciences and, frequently, of all professions. Anthropologists worry about the ethical conduct of their students, coworkers, and colleagues, and certainly about their own decisions. Anthropologists worry about the societies in which they live and frequently about the societies in which they work. Sometimes anthropologists want to be advocates and public figures but hold back because they are not sure if they will be heard, or if they have all the facts, or if they know how best to approach legal, governmental, or societal transformations. Anthropologists frequently fear that others dismiss them or fail to understand them and, hence, that their own society is too conservative to understand anthropological critique and open-mindedness. We have many decades of experience, as a group, teaching against sexism, racism, prejudice, inequality, and cultural assertions of superiority, but many anthropologists would also say that we have many decades of not making much of a dent in the societies in which we live. That many anthropologists end up discouraged or unable to imagine having much power to change unjust laws and unequal systems is part of the larger picture. And it is in that larger context that many of the ethical struggles dealt with in this book ought to be contemplated.

In my November 2011 Presidential Address to the AAA, I chose to talk about comfort zones and their dangers. I did so because I am convinced that the anthropological profession is (at least in the United States) simultaneously full of self-doubt and replete of a sense of cultural or political superiority. It is quite common to find anthropologists who decry the lack of influence anthropologists have in the world, even when one can show that anthropology is not in decline across the board, as some fear and believe. But it is a two-edged sword with deep ethical implications. Decrying lack of influence only works if one is convinced that one (or a profession more generally) has the right ideas, ideals, and ethical stances and that they are better than other people's, other professions', or other communities' ideas, values, practices, and stances. This book shows us that there clearly is great anthropological interest in thinking about ethics and trying to live ethical lives, and that the profession takes this matter quite seriously. But this book also shows that there are rarely simple formulas to follow, even within the anthropological profession.

I am a big fan of the way the 2008-2011 AAA Task Force for Comprehensive Ethics Review chose to approach this matter. Not everyone was so keen. Some wanted to have clear and unequivocal clauses; some wanted the AAA to institute an investigatory and adjudicatory process leading to the possibility of condemnation and censure. The original document on this subject (AAA 1971) looked like a Code and was called Principles of Professional Responsibility. It had many sections, specific statements and clauses, and wording that were periodically debated and even replaced in the decades between its official adoption and the fall 2012 adoption by the AAA membership (by vote) of the Task Force's work (only slightly modified by the AAA Executive Board over the course of 2012). To some that 1971 Code was sufficient; to others it was weak; and to still others it was unworkable in the environment in which they worked. I often referred to the 1971 Code, especially when teaching, but I realize that, like many others, it did not help me that much in making my own decisions about research, writing, teaching, and collegiality. It simply couldn't. That Code could not help me decide whether to "out" someone in my research site who was acting unethically, in my view. I had to weigh various factors and decide on my own. That Code could not help me decide whether to "out" a colleague involved in a romantic relationship that seemed consensual but involved significant power difference. I had to weigh various factors and decide on my own. That Code could not help me decide what to do about a colleague who published material under his name alone, when I knew that much of the data had been gathered by students he had, not all of them employed by him as research assistants. I had to weigh various factors and decide on my own. That Code covered a range of work and relations that matter to any anthropologist, whether in training or post-training, but at times it made things look a bit too clear when they really weren't.

That is the reason I am such a fan of the results of the 2008-2011 AAA Task Force for Comprehensive Ethics Review. They recognized that ethical quandaries entail struggle and decisions and are not usually just a matter of applying a formula or statement. They came up with seven principles to help anthropologists think and act when presented with ethical dilemmas. And they came up with numerous supplementary materials and cases to help anthropologists see options, assess consequences, and understand the pros and cons of any decision they take. Compared to the earlier Code, the new Principles of Professional Responsibility strike me as more realistic, more usable, and a better characterization of what "ethics" means, especially "ethics" as a process, as a form of practice or, as I might also put it, as what ethics entails when one's goal is living an ethical life.

Not all anthropological societies around the world have official codes of ethics. It is not because they don't think about ethics but, rather, because there are indeed different ways to approach this question of how to engage with ethics as process or ethics as practice or ethics as struggle. The Task Force on Ethics of the World Council of Anthropological Associations (WCAA), established in August 2010, for example, has tried to gather the existing codes and statements on ethics of the now dozens of anthropological societies around the world that belong to the WCAA. But, not surprisingly, one of the issues it deals with is the variety of approaches to the writing of statements, codes, and principles or guidelines for anthropologists, whether in training or post-training. That there is that kind of variety in approach reflects the difficulty I try to capture here, and especially the difficulty encountered by the AAA Task Force for Comprehensive Ethics Review as it wondered what would be most helpful and how to undertake that work. This book is one wonderful result of their effort and I, for one, am honored to be included in it.

REFERENCES

American Anthropological Association
1971 "Principles of Professional Responsibility," Code of Ethics. Archived at www.aaanet.org.

Derrida, Jacques
1980 Writing and Difference. Chicago: University of Chicago Press. Original edition published in 1967 in Paris by Editions du Seuil.

Dominguez, Virginia R.
2012 Comfort Zones and Their Dangers: Who Are We? Qui sommes-nous? American Anthropologist 114(3):394-405.

Kuhn, Thomas
1962 The Structure of Scientific Revolutions. Cambridge: Harvard University Press.

Ross, Fiona, ed.
2005 Anthropology Southern Africa. Theme Issues on Ethics, 28(3-4).

CHAPTER TWO

A Short History of American Anthropological Ethics, Codes, Principles, and Responsibilities— Professional and Otherwise

David H. Price

American anthropology developed as a discipline with only occasional and informal attention paid to what we now recognize as questions of research ethics. This informality was a natural condition of a field first developed and populated by a mix of amateur enthusiasts and scholars with training in other fields, and later by an emerging class of professionally trained ethnographers, archaeologists, and biological, linguistic, and cultural anthropologists.[1]

During the discipline's earliest days, this lack of focused attention on and recognition of the ethical dimensions of the work betrayed an academic culture[2] privileging the goals of scientific enquiry over other human concerns. Regardless of whatever admiration and respect anthropologists held for the individuals and cultures they studied, these anthropologists at times misrepresented the nature of their work, harmed research participants, or pressured individuals to reveal information they would not have otherwise disclosed. Some of this early history perhaps reads as shameful prologue, but these instances of what would now be viewed as inappropriate anthropological conduct not only clarify the importance of integrating ethical concerns into all stages of anthropological research, but they also illuminate ongoing temptations facing researchers to sidestep what can be seen as bothersome research hurdles, in order to collect interesting and informative cultural data. While many ethical problems remain

Anthropological Ethics in Context: An Ongoing Dialogue, pp. 23-38. © 2016 Left Coast Press, Inc. All rights reserved.

within anthropology today, we now have disciplinary language, structures, and awareness for identifying and trying to cope with these issues that were absent during this earlier period.

During the late nineteenth and first half of the twentieth century, American anthropologists had no guidelines governing the conduct of their research outside of legal statutes, standards of scientific conduct, and their personal consciences. Under such conditions, it was not uncommon for individuals to loot native graves—with disciplinary ancestors such as Frank Hamilton Cushing or Franz Boas covertly sneaking off to steal skeletal remains from Indian burial sites for scientific study (Washburn 1985; Thomas 2001:59). Boas' involvement in the staging of a sham burial before Mink, the surviving son of an Inuit who died after being brought by Robert Peary to New York City in 1897, and the displaying of this man's skeletal remains in a case at the American Museum of Natural History illustrates the early discipline's general lack of attention given to disclosure and other ethical principles (Harper 1986). It is but one of many episodes illustrating tragic outcomes fostered by scientific pursuits disengaged from ethical considerations that give primacy to disclosure, consent, avoiding harm, and including research participants in the planning and conduct of research. This and other ethically problematic actions by early anthropologists were not undertaken with ill intent, yet arguably good intentions masked issues that raise ethical concerns today. Early anthropologists engaging in salvage ethnographic work at times let feelings of desperation override standards of dignity, resulting in disturbing episodes such as when John Peabody Harrington sent a telegraph asking that a dying Indian informant be dosed with morphine in order to sustain life until Harrington could arrive and complete more linguistic research (Walsh 1976:16).

Up into the mid-twentieth century, field ethnographers relied on uneven standards of research practices to collect cultural information. Some ethnographers at times paid informants to reveal sacred secrets, under false promises that this information would not be widely distributed, while others, like James Mooney, respected privacy in ways that would meet contemporary ethical expectations of research. Yet there were few standards of practice. To get some sense of the broad range of variation of what was considered ethical practice during the pre-war years, consider that when Margaret Mead and her then husband Reo Fortune conducted fieldwork on the Omaha Reservation, the couple developed significantly different standards for protecting the identities of their research subjects. When Mead published a monograph based on this work in 1932 she did not identify either the tribe or reservation, instead writing that, "it is presented anonymously here, under the pseudonym of the Antler Tribe, to shield the feelings of the individuals and to give no affront to the tribal pride" (Mead 1932:16). Mead's husband simultaneously published, at the same press as Mead, his results without using pseudonyms, and his book exposed tribal secrets without a pseudonymic veil sheltering the Omaha from the literate world at large and identified the town where he conducted his research (Fortune 1932:7).

It's not that anthropologists working in a pre-ethics code world did not care for the wellbeing of research participants; they appear to have generally done so, but with tendencies to "other" these populations as objects of study, the discipline had no developed notions of consent, no overarching framework of avoiding direct or indirect harm, and no shared basic understanding of responsibilities to others. Further, the seductive demands of accumulating scientific knowledge (at times, collecting such knowledge under conditions of perceived urgency) made it easy to develop field practices championing the collection of information over concerns about the impacts this work had on those whose lives were intertwined with and inseparable from these "data."

War and Postwar SfAA Code, and Postwar AAA Ethical Actions at the AAA Business Meeting

It was the Second World War, or more accurately, reconsiderations of wartime experiences during the postwar period, that produced the first modern human research ethics codes. The 1947 Nuremberg Code's directives mandating voluntary informed consent, disclosure, and not harming those researched were a byproduct of war crimes tribunals, but these directives broadly impacted all the human sciences.

The Society for Applied Anthropology (SfAA) approved its first ethics code in the aftermath of the Second World War; the SfAA's 1948 code stressed anthropologists' responsibilities to both sponsors and studied populations, the importance of honesty, to not bring about harm, to share knowledge, and to "take the greatest care to protect...informants, especially in those aspects of confidence which...informants many not be able to stipulate for themselves" (Mead et al. 1949). Because during the war, anthropologists working in wartime applied capacities had been pushed to undertake a broad range of activities with no ethical guidelines, it makes sense that the *applied* society (rather than the AAA) developed this first code as a consequence of its members' wartime experiences (Price 2008:272-277).

After the war, the AAA did not establish a professional ethics code, and this would not occur for another quarter century. However, even as the SfAA was establishing the first ethics code for American anthropologists, at the AAA 1948 annual council meeting the Fellows adopted the following resolution addressing some limited ethical concerns:

Be it resolved: (1) that the American Anthropological Association strongly urge all sponsoring institutions to guarantee their research scientists complete freedom to interpret and publish their findings without censorship or interference; provided that

(2) the interests of the persons and communities or other groups studied are protected; and that

(3) in the event that the sponsoring institution does not wish to publish the results nor be identified with the publications, it permit publication of the results, without use of its name as sponsoring agency, through other channels. (American Anthropologist 1949 51:370)

While not an ethics code, this resolution expressed postwar American anthropology's commitment to assuring freedom for anthropologists to make their research publicly available, a decision that made these results at least theoretically available to studied populations. This insistence that "the interests of the persons and communities or other groups studied are protected" was a sentiment at the core of the AAA's first ethics code, which was completed in 1971. Other postwar resolutions expressed, in a piecemeal fashion, members' concern with a host of ethical issues ranging from advocating for the interests of native groups (AA 1947 19(2):365), supporting racial equality (AAANB 1(3):1), guarding against the dangers of nuclear weapons (AA 1946 48(2):319), and championing academic freedom (AAANB 1949 3(1):I; AA 1949:370), but the Association avoided codifying a Code of Ethics until concerns over military uses of anthropology during the 1960s and '70s forced the Association to develop a code.

The 1967 Statement on Problems of Anthropological Research and Ethics

With revelations in 1964 and 1965 that anthropologists and other social scientists were being recruited to join Project Camelot, a Pentagon program developing counterinsurgency and insurgency strategies for the stabilization or destabilization of foreign governments, many

AAA members reacted with focused concerns. The AAA responded to Camelot by appointing anthropologist Ralph Beals, in concert with the Executive Board, to report on the extent of the anthropologists' activities with military and intelligence agencies, and further, to identify key ethical issues facing all anthropologists conducting research.

As a result of Beal's post-Camelot inquires, in July, 1966, the AAA's Executive Board adopted Ralph Beals' *Statement on Government Involvement in Research* as the AAA's interim statement. This AAA statement clarified that "except in times of clear and present national emergency, universities should not undertake activities which are unrelated to their normal teaching, research, and public service functions, or which can more appropriately be performed by other types of organizations" (FN1966 7(8):1). Clandestine research and research that did not disclose sponsorship were condemned, and the report declared that the "gathering of information and data which can never be made available to the public does not constitute scientific research and should not be so represented" (FN 1966 7(8):1-2).

In November 1966, Beals submitted his *Statement on Problems of Anthropological Research and Ethics* to the AAA Council. The statement was amended during a "spirited" floor discussion, and was adopted by a vote of 727 to 59, and later adopted by the AAA Fellows as a referendum (FN 1967 8(4):1).[3] The Beals Report focused on three primary areas: "anthropology and government," "sponsorships of anthropological research," and "research in foreign areas" (FN 1967 8(1):3). The Executive Board worried that anthropologists' links to governmental agencies would limit American anthropologists' safety and abilities to conduct fieldwork in other countries (FN 1967 8(1):3). Beals received a lot of feedback from AAA members: some were outraged by anthropologists' increasing interactions with intelligence agencies, whereas others believed decisions to work with military or intelligence agencies should be a matter of personal choice (FN 1967 8(1):4). Today, it is difficult to appreciate the range of opposition to establishing a Code of Ethics within the AAA—opposition that transcended political orientations. When Beals wrote Leopold Pospisil, requesting his assistance in his work on his report, Pospisil declined, writing that he was flattered by the request but that life in Nazi and Communist occupied Czechoslovakia left him opposed to external standards governing individual ethical decisions (RB 76, LP to RB 3/15/66).

In March 1967, AAA Fellows adopted the *Statement on Problems of Anthropological Research and Ethics* (SPARE), a statement of core values from the Beals Report. SPARE's condemnation of covert research made the national news, and the *Washington Post* and other newspapers covered the membership's approval of SPARE (Reistrup 1967). SPARE fell short of being a formal ethics code, but it embraced standards of ethical practice championing the freedom to conduct research and clarifying that anthropologists must disclose to research participants "their professional qualifications and associations, their sponsorship and source of funds, and the nature and objectives of the research being undertaken." The statement proclaimed that:

> Constraint, deception, and secrecy have no place in science. Actions which compromise the intellectual integrity and autonomy of research scholars and institutions not only weaken those international understandings essential to our discipline, but in so doing they also threaten any contribution anthropology might make to our own society and to the general interests of human welfare. (American Anthropological Association 1967)

Interestingly, however, SPARE was more concerned about the damage that might be done to anthropology's disciplinary reputation than the wellbeing of research participants. The word "harm" appears nowhere in the statement, and the only use of "damage" appears in a warning about damages to anthropology's international reputation by false anthropologists (American Anthropological Association 1967).

The 1969 Report of the Ad Hoc Committee on Ethics

After the U.S Navy ran an advertisement in the August 1968 issue of the *American Anthropologist*, a group calling itself "a committee of concerned anthropologists" used a mail campaign to gather signatures and funds that were used to publish, in the February 1969 issue of *American Anthropologist*, an advertisement protesting the military ad.[4] In an effort to address issues specifically raised by military ads in AAA publications and growing concerns over intelligence agencies seeking anthropological knowledge, the Executive Board appointed the AAA's first Committee on Ethics, as an ad hoc committee.[5] As its first act, the committee issued a statement proclaiming that "the AAA will not accept advertisements or notices for positions involving research or other activities the products of which cannot be made available to the entire scholarly community through accepted academic channels of communication" (FN 1969 10(3):1).

During a single weekend meeting in January 1969, the ad hoc Committee on Ethics drafted their proposed Code of Ethics. Their draft code drew heavily on the AAA's SPARE document, and incorporated ethical guidelines developed by the American Psychological Association, the American Sociological Association, and the Society for Applied Anthropology. The committee recommended to the Board that the membership immediately elect a standing Committee on Ethics (FN 1969 10(4):3; Berreman 2003). The four categories of issues addressed in the draft code were "relations with those studied," "responsibilities to the discipline," "responsibilities to students," and "relations with sponsors" (FN 1969 10(4):4-5). Much of the language in this draft remained in the Principles of Professional Responsibility that would be adopted two years later.

The draft report generated opposition from a vocal minority of anthropologists, who argued in the *Fellows Newsletter* that the proposed Code attempted to "legislate a socio-ideological system" that was akin to the sort of controlling mechanism used in Nazi Germany, a totalitarian tactic, similar to tactics in Orwell's *Animal Farm*, while some derisively referred to the Ethics Committee as the "Censorship Committee," or the "Ethical Surveillance Committee."[6] Some Executive Board members argued that the AAA membership should not vote on this draft code because the individuals who wrote the draft code had not been elected by the AAA membership. A standing Committee on Ethics was elected (with three individuals remaining from the original ad hoc committee) from the membership at large, and charged with drafting a Code of Ethics that would be presented to the Board (for changes) before being presented to the membership for a vote. This new committee, drawing on the existing draft code, presented their draft Code of Ethics to the Board in May 1970. Gerald Berreman wrote that "the Board promptly retitled it 'Principles of Professional Responsibility,' to soften the blow for members who did not want anyone to subject them to the constraints a 'code' seemed to imply" (Berreman 2003:57). This document was approved by the AAA membership in a May 1971 vote—a vote occurring in the shadow of revelations that anthropologists were working as advisors to U.S. military agencies in Southeast Asia (see Wakin 1992).

The AAA's First Code

The 1971 Principles of Professional Responsibility (PPR) opened by situating anthropologists' loyalties not with sponsors, but with research participants, clarifying that in matters of "research, anthropologists' paramount responsibility is to those they study." It advocated using pseudonyms to protect informants, condemned exploitation, and cautioned that "there is an obligation to reflect on the foreseeable repercussions of research and publication on the general population being studied" (PPR 1).

The condemnation of secret research had a central importance in the 1971 PPR, and the first three sections each contained clear language condemning secret reports (PPR 1(2)g, 2.a, & 3.a); it stated: "in accordance with the Association's general position on clandestine and secret research, no reports should be provided to sponsors that are not also available to the general public and, where practicable, to the population studied" (PPR 1(2)g). It identified responsibilities to the public, declaring that anthropologists should not falsify findings and that "anthropologists should not communicate findings secretly to some and withhold them from others" (2.a). It plainly stated that "anthropologists should undertake no secret research or any research whose results cannot be freely derived and publicly reported" (PPR 3.a).

The 1971 PPR showed great concern for protecting others from spying, the production of secret reports, and covert research; it also advocated for aligning anthropologists' interests with these populations, and disclosing research agendas. In hindsight it is striking that there was no discussion of obtaining voluntary informed consent from these same peoples (Fluehr-Lobban 2003b). With the exception of brief additions on plagiarism in 1974 (FN 1974 15(7):9) and in 1975, additions on workplace antidiscrimination language and clarification that guarantees of anonymity should never be made (FN 1975 16(2):1), and finally a 1976 removal of masculine pronouns, the 1971 PPR remained essentially unchanged until 1990.

Largely because the AAA's 1971 PPR was born from concerns over anthropology's uses for counterinsurgency and intelligence gathering, this initial code was conceived as an "enforceable" code, complete with a process for making accusations and investigating allegations of unethical conduct. This feature had a clear importance for many AAA members, though the meaning of such sanctions remained vague given the Association's status as a non-licensing, voluntary, professional association. While the intentions of establishing sanctions for unethical practices appear to have been to monitor and limit unethical research practices in the field, within a few years the majority of complaints filed with the AAA's Committee on Ethics involved not charges of inappropriate behaviors related to field research with members of cultures, but of alleged wrongdoing in university settings, most prominently including alleged sexual misconduct between professors and students, professors appropriating students work without attribution, workplace discrimination, and disputed outcomes in contentious university tenure and promotion battles (see Chapter 10). These investigations were expensive and worrisome for the Association, and at times required costly legal consultations. Within a decade and a half, many who had led the push for establishing an ethics code with sanctions were calling to abandon sanctions. In 1985 David Aberle, who had helped draft the original PPR, argued that the AAA should cease adjudicating ethical sanctions, "unless the Association makes obedience to the code a condition of membership" (Aberle 1985)—but the possibility of sanctions remained part of the PPR until 1995.

The 1980s Failed Effort to Revise the PPR

During the late 1970s and early 1980s, as more anthropologists found employment in applied settings outside of universities, increasing numbers of anthropologists were uncomfortable with the PPR's restrictions on such activities as writing "secret" reports, or even the code's prime directive that anthropologists' interests align with peoples studied. As applied anthropologists found themselves writing proprietary reports that studied populations could not access, there were increasing efforts to remove language in the PPR prohibiting the production of such reports.

In 1980 the AAA's Executive Board charged an ad hoc committee with revising the PPR as a new Code of Ethics.[7] In 1984 the ad hoc committee produced a brief draft code. At 1,000 words, it was a third of the length of the PPR, and once the Preamble and the statement on the "Role and Function of the Committee on Ethics" were removed, the entire code of ethics was reduced to only thirteen points, consisting of only about 400 words. The proposed code's points each consisted of only one or two sentences. The draft code reflected the 1980s human potential movement, with its opening EST-like insistence that anthropologists engage in self-reflection and assume "their own moral responsibility," urged openness, and cautioned that promises of confidentiality might not hold up in court proceedings. It advised anthropologists to not take actions that could jeopardize future researchers, and demanded honesty and high standards of academic freedom, disclosure of funding sources, and making data available to others (AN 1984 25(7):2).

Many anthropologists objected less to the specifics included in this proposed code than to what was *missing* from it. It removed the PPR's metanarratives of power and sanctions, and in their place recommended self-reflection. There were concerns about the removals of: a clear statement that anthropologists' primary responsibility was to those studied, sanctions (though there was increasing awareness of the problems these created), prohibitions against clandestine research, what had been a responsibility to engage in advocacy, and prohibitions on issuing secret reports (see Aberle 1985; Berreman 2003:64). Gerald Berreman later complained that these proposed changes were "a license for unfettered free-enterprise research; a charter for consulting and engineering disguised as anthropology, with the intent of employing the ethical reputation of the discipline to enable and facilitate a wide range of mission-oriented activities, including those of dubious ethical and even egregiously unethical nature" (Berreman 2003:64). The membership discussed the code, but it failed to generate enough support for adoption. The Association's inability to revise the PPR or address new concerns raised by new and old forms of anthropological fieldwork did not mean problematic practices stopped. As market forces shifted, increasing numbers of anthropologists entered applied anthropological workplaces with no new guidance for the issues they faced. Among the most famous accusations of ethically problematic research would later come from Patrick Tierney in his book *Darkness in El Dorado*, which accused Napoleon Chagnon with helping propagate measles epidemics, arming Yanomami, and encouraging warfare and other forms of lethal violence, and identified instances of other anthropologists and scientists harming the Yanomami (Tierney 2000; Ferguson 1995). The AAA's El Dorado Task Force found support for some, but not all, of the claims made by Tierney and others that Chagnon had engaged in ethically problematic research, but the final report by the Task Force was rejected by a vote of the AAA's membership, in part arguing that the AAA Task Force "violated the association's prohibition on ethics investigations" (AAA Resolution 2005).

The 1990s and post-9/11 Codes

In 1987 a new ad hoc committee was charged with revising the Principles of Professional Responsibility.[8] The committee's revised PPR was submitted in the Fall of 1988 to the AAA's Administrative Advisory Committee, which made some modifications before submitting it to the Executive Board (AN 1989:22).

While the revised PPR did not remove protections for those studied to the extent that the earlier 1980s un-adopted draft Code of Ethics had sought to do, it did remove references condemning secret and clandestine research. The revised PPR was discussed at the 1989 AAA meetings and was later adopted by a large majority of voting AAA members in March 1990 (Fluehr-Lobban 2003a:14). This was a period when American universities increasingly relied on Institutional Review Boards, or Human Subject Review Boards, as institutional clearinghouses used to protect these institutions from legal actions should claims be made against researchers (See Bosk 2007; Heimer and Petty 2010). These Boards seldom consulted the ethics codes developed by the AAA or SfAA.[9]

In the early 1990s a new ethics commission was formed and charged with reconsidering the Association's sanctions policy and its prohibition on secret reports—this second concern coming from applied anthropologists increasingly being asked to produce proprietary reports.[10] In May of 1995 "the AAA Executive Board, acting on the endorsement of the Section Assembly, unanimously accepted the recommendation that the purpose of the AAA Code is to educate and socialize AAA members in the discipline. The Board voted that the Association would not adjudicate claims of unethical behavior" (Anthropology Newsletter 1995:3). The reasons for discontinuing the grievance process included recognition of the impracticality of having sanctions for a voluntary, non-licensing, professional organization. One commission member, Carolyn Fluehr-Lobban, later lamented the decision to remove prohibitions against secrecy, arguing that distinctions between secret and proprietary research should have been made, yet for some, it remains difficult to conceive how such distinctions might be behaviorally differentiated (see Berreman 2003:77).

Because of disciplinary tensions, most obvious between applied/consulting anthropologists and university based colleagues following the increased uses of anthropologists by military and intelligence agencies in the years following the September 2001 terror attacks, in 2006, AAA President Alan Goodman established the Commission on the Engagement of Anthropology with the US Security and Intelligence Communities (CEAUSSIC) to study these interactions. In response to CEAUSSIC's 2007 report, Terence Turner introduced a resolution at the 2007 AAA Business Meeting calling for the reintroduction of the PPR's original language prohibiting anthropologists from producing secret reports (Redden 2007). The AAA Executive Board charged the Committee on Ethics, along with Board appointed ad hoc members, with producing language for the

Code of Ethics that would address Turner's intent of once again prohibiting secret reports (see Chapter 3). This revised language was approved by the membership and was added to the Code of Ethics in 2009. Simultaneous with the conclusion of the work of the ad hoc committee, a task force was appointed to consider revising the entire Code of Ethics.

The work produced by this task force is the current PPR, as edited by the AAA's Executive Board and adopted by the AAA membership in 2012, and as considered in this book.[11] These new Principles of Professional Responsibility proclaim shared disciplinary norms and strive to serve educational functions to assist anthropologists when facing ongoing ethical issues as they design, conduct, and evaluate research. Many of the principles identified here remain essentially unchanged from previous codes, some previously identified principles are no longer in the code, and some new principles are included.[12]

It is inevitable and proper that ethics codes are living documents—adapting to address the issues of an age, expressing old values in new ways, changing approaches to some issues, and identifying new concerns. Yet, as I argue elsewhere, in an essay titled "War is a force that gives anthropology ethics," from the mid-twentieth century to the present, anthropologists' mixed engagements with military and intelligence agencies have been a consistent dynamic forcing the discipline to codify, or revise, ethical standards for all forms of anthropological work (Price 2011:11-31). While the AAA ethical codes have been designed to address the broad range of activities undertaken by all anthropologists, there has been a recurrent pattern in which issues involving the militarization of anthropology have pressed the membership to develop and revise these codes. Under a dynamic that mirrors the forces that led the AAA to draft and adopt its first code, post 9/11 concerns over anthropologists writing secret military and intelligence reports began the chain of events that led to the AAA's most recent ethics revisions. But while the issues of military uses of anthropology have historically pushed the AAA to reconsider the ethical issues facing all anthropologists, future revisions may be pressed by other forces or other crises. In a society commodifying all facets of our lives, future code revisions may well be sparked by struggles other than warfare. Whatever the issues facing the discipline in the future, anthropologists grappling with framing the ethical practices of the discipline will find themselves focusing attention on establishing best practices for engaging with other anthropologists, research participants, sponsors, the public, data, and a future world seeking their records.

ABBREVIATIONS

AA   *American Anthropologist*
AAA   American Anthropological Association
AAANB   *American Anthropologist Association News Bulletin*
FN   *Fellows Newsletter of the American Anthropological Association*
RB   Ralph Beals Papers. National Anthropological Archives, Smithsonian Institution, Washington, D.C.

NOTES

1. Pels argues that the British ethnological tradition "emerged from moral concerns" expressed through the paternalistic views of the Aborigines Protection Society, which used moral frameworks to impose Western beliefs and practices on peoples imagined as "less advanced" (Pels 1999:104-106).
2. Today, the phrase "research participant" has replaced "studied populations," in part reflecting open forms of research and consent that make the use of the "research participants" for historical research relationships inappropriate.
3. The *New York Times* and international news coverage of Beals' reporting the findings of the Committee on Research Problems and Ethics renewed some international concerns about anthropologist spies. The *New York Times* reported Beals' warning that "secrecy and pressures by United States intelligence agencies were eroding the effectiveness and prestige of American scholarly research abroad" (Raymont 1966:1).
4. See *Fellows Newsletter* 1969 10(3):2 for a response by the Committee of Concerned Anthropologists. The members of the Committee of Concerned Anthropologists identified in the *Fellows Newsletter* were Harold Conklin, Morton Fried, Marvin Harris, Dell Hymes, Robert Murphy, and Eric Wolf.
5. This committee consisted of co-chairs David Schneider and David Aberle, and Richard N. Adams, Joseph Jorgensen, William Shack, and Eric Wolf.
6. The sources of these characterizations are as follows: "legislate a socio-ideological system" (Anthony Leeds, FN 1969); Nazi comparisons (Laura Thompson, FN 1969 10(7):4); totalitarian tactic (Esther Goldfrank FN 1969 10(7):4); *Animal Farm* (Otto von Mering, FN 1969 10(7):5); Censorship Committee" (Joe Pierce, FN 1969 10(8):2);"Ethical Surveillance Committee" (Igor Kopytoff, FN 1969 10(10):8).

7. The Ad Hoc Committee consisted of Karl Heider, Barry Bainton, Alice Brutes, Jerald Milanich, and John Roberts.
8. The committee was chaired by Robert Fernea, and consisted of J. Golbert, D. C. Anderson, C. Hughes, and M. L. Blakey.
9. These bodies developed different concerns from anthropological ethics codes; the institutional centrality of these bodies made them required bureaucratic stops for many university anthropologists, yet they seldom addressed the core ethical issues facing their work (Dingwall 2012).
10. This commission was chaired by James Peacock, and consisted of Barbara Frankel, Carolyn Fluehr-Lobban, Kathleen Gibson, Janet Levy, and Murray Wax (AN 1995:3).
11. This task force was chaired by Dena Plemmons, and consisted of Alec Barker, Charles Briggs, Laura McNamara, Katie Mackinnon, David Price, and Neil Tashima.
12. Among those principles removed was the principle that "anthropologists' paramount responsibility is to those they study" once viewed as a prime directive of anthropologists (see Nader 1999, for a critique of this directive), and the most striking new language is that which advises anthropologists of the dangers of compartmentalized research projects.

REFERENCES

Aberle, David
1985   The Proposed Code of Ethics. Anthropology Newsletter 26(4):28.
1984   Proposed Code of Ethics would Supersede Principles of Professional Responsibility. Anthropology Newsletter 25(7):2.

American Anthropological Association
2005   Resolution to Rescind AAA Acceptance of the El Dorado Report. www.aaanet.org/stmts/05ref_eldorado.htm, accessed July 8, 2015.

American Anthropological Association
1967   Statement on Problems of Anthropological Research and Ethics(SPARE) www.aaanet.org/profdev/ethics/upload/STATEMENTS-ON-ETHICS-1971-1986.docx, accessed April 20, 2013.

Anthropology Newsletter
1995   Ethics Commission Endorses education. Anthropology Newsletter 26(10):3.
1989   Proposed draft revision of the principles of professional responsibility. Anthropology Newsletter 30(11):22-23.

Berreman, Gerald D.
2003 Ethics Versus 'Realism' in Anthropology: Redux. In Ethics and the Profession of Anthropology: Dialogue for Ethically Conscious Practice. Carolyn Fluehr-Lobban, ed. Pp. 51-84. Walnut Creek: AlaMira Press.

Bosk, Charles L.
2007 The New Bureaucracies of Virtue, or When Form Fails to Follow Function. Political and Legal Anthropology Review 30(2):192-209.

Dingwall, Robert
2012 How Did We Ever Get Into this Mess? The Rise of Ethical Regulation in the Social Sciences. Studies in Qualitative Methodology 12:3-26.

Ferguson, R. Brian
1995 Yanomami Warfare: A Political History. Santa Fe: School of American Research Press.

Fluehr-Lobban, Carolyn
2003a Ethics and Anthropology 1890-2000: A Review of Issues and Principles. *In* Ethics and the Profession of Anthropology. Second edition. C. Fluehr-Lobban, ed. Pp. 1-28. Walnut Creek: AltaMira Press.
2003b Informed Consent and Anthropological Research: We are not Exempt. *In* Ethics and the Profession of Anthropology. Second edition. C. Fluehr-Lobban, ed. Pp. 159-177. Walnut Creek: AltaMira Press.

Fortune, Reo F.
1932 Omaha Secret Societies. New York: Columbia University Press.

Harper, Kenn
1986 Give me my Father's Body: The Life of Minik, the New York Eskimo. New York: Washington Square Press.

Heimer, Carol A., and JuLeigh Petty
2010 Bureaucratic Ethics: IRBs and the Legal Regulation of Human Subjects Research. Annual Review of Law and Social Science 6:601-626.

Mead, Margaret
1932 The Changing Culture of an Indian Tribe. New York: Columbia University Press.

Mead, Margaret, Eliot Chapple, and G. Gordon Brown
1949 Report of the Committee on Ethics. Human Organization, Spring, Pp. 20-21.

Nader, Laura
1999 CA Comments on Peter Pels' 'Professions of Duplexity.' Current Anthropology 40(2):121-122.

Pels, Peter
1999 Professions of Duplexity: A Prehistory of Ethical Codes in Anthropology. Current Anthropology 40(2):101-136.

Price, David
2011   Weaponizing Anthropology. Petrolia, CA: CounterPunch Books.
2008   Anthropological Intelligence. Durham: Duke University Press.

Raymont, Henry
1966   Spy Agencies Held Danger to Research. New York Times, Nov. 18, 1&2.

Redden, Elizabeth
2007   Secrecy and Anthropology. Inside Higher Ed, December 3rd. www.insidehighered.com/news/2007/12/03/anthro, accessed January 19, 2014.

Reistrup, J. V.
1967   Anthropologists Vote 12 to 1 to Oppose Joining in Secret Intelligence Work. Washington Post, April 21.

Thomas, David
2001   Skull Wars. New York: Basic Books.

Tierney, Patrick
2000   Darkness in El Dorado: How Scientists and Journalists Devastated the Amazon. New York: W. W. Norton.

Wakin, Eric
1992   Anthropology Goes to War: Professional Ethics and Counterinsurgency in Thailand. Madison: University of Wisconsin Center for Asian Studies, Monograph Number 7.

Walsh, Jane
1976   John Peabody Harrington: The Man and his California Indian Fieldnotes. Ramona, California: Ballena Press.

Washburn, Wilcomb. E.
1985   Ethical Perspectives in North American Ethnology. In Social Contexts of American Ethnology, 1840-1985. June Helm, ed. Pp. 55-64. Washington, D.C.: American Ethnological Society.

CHAPTER THREE

Background and Context to the Current Revisions

Dena Plemmons and Alex W. Barker

As the preceding chapter makes clear, the most recent revision of the American Anthropological Association's statement on ethics was developed in similar circumstances to those attending some of the prior code revisions in the Association's history. As before, concerns regarding the engagement of anthropologists with military and intelligence agencies cast a long shadow. In this most recent instance, we are given to understand that the Central Intelligence Agency posted an employment ad at the AAA job site, prompting member criticism and resulting in the formation of the Commission on the Engagement of Anthropology with the US Security and Intelligence Communities (CEAUSSIC).

CEAUSSIC drafted a report, submitted to the Executive Board (EB) in 2007, containing specific recommendations for action, including the following:

> The Commission recommends that emergent issues surrounding engagement with military, security, and intelligence be considered in the next revision of the Code of Ethics. Specifically, the language of the CoE[1] should be revisited or revised to include: Secrecy as a condition for funding, employment, research, written "products," or other applications of anthropology; the Ethics Committee or general membership should consider reinstating former language on secrecy from the 1971 CoE (sections 1.g, 2.a, 3.a, and 6).

Anthropological Ethics in Context: An Ongoing Dialogue, pp. 39-74. © 2016 Left Coast Press, Inc. All rights reserved.

The ensuing series of events, explained in the following open letter to the membership from then President Setha Low on behalf of the EB, is a relatively direct result of this recommendation in the CEAUSSIC report:

Dear AAA Member:

… At the Business Meeting conducted during the 2007 Annual Meeting, a resolution introduced by Terry Turner was passed by the membership.[1] This resolution directed the EB to restore sections 1.g, 2.a, 3.a and 6 of the 1971 version of the code of ethics. A related motion was introduced by John Kelly,[2] directing the EB to report to the membership if a decision was not made to restore, in total, the language proposed in the Turner motion. Both motions appear below.

The EB requested that the AAA Committee on Ethics draft, pursuant to the Kelly motion, a revised version of the ethics code that incorporated the principles of the Turner motion. The Committee on Ethics, supplemented with six invited guests, submitted a "Report to the AAA Executive Board on the Revision of the AAA Ethics Code" on June 16, 2008. This report contained majority and minority opinions about the changes in the code of ethics needed to comply with the Turner Motion.

The CoE report offered several reasons for rejecting incorporation of the Turner motion into the Code of ethics, namely:

"The majority of the working group express[es] concern that the 1971 language does not allow exceptions that both the working group and the framers of the resolution have acknowledged as valid, such as confidentiality regarding the location of archaeological resources or threatened populations of plants and animals. Further, they feel that if the purpose of the resolution is to prohibit anthropologists from abusing the trust placed in them by the people with whom they work and whom they study, then the language needs to be clarified to unambiguously allow confidentiality or restricted distribution of results in those cases where such restrictions are based on an anthropologist's primary ethical obligations to the people, species, and materials they study and to the people with whom they work."

An ad hoc subcommittee of the AAA Executive Board was constituted to consider the Committee on Ethics report, and prepared this document for consideration of the entire EB. This subcommittee consisted of T. J. Ferguson, Monica Heller, Tom Leatherman, Gwendolyn Mikell, and Deborah Nichols.

The AAA EB subcommittee, among its findings, agreed with the Committee on Ethics that the 1971 ethics language could not be reinserted verbatim into the AAA Code of Ethics, as proposed by Turner for the reasons outlined above. Furthermore the subcommittee also found that certain elements of the 1971 language fail to recognize valid but crosscutting ethical obligations and agreed that a new section of the ethics code be drafted regarding dissemination of research findings.

In sum, the AAA EB subcommittee recommended six changes to the Code of Ethics, and it is these changes we will be asking you to vote on shortly.

As a part of next steps, the EB has passed a motion to establish a Task Force to revise the entire Code of Ethics over a two year period to be completed by November 2010. Shortly, you will be asked for your direct input in updating and revising the entire Code of Ethics. For more information on this effort, please see http://www.aaanet.org/issues/policy-advocacy/Task-Force-Members-Named-for-Comprehensive-Ethics-Review.cfm.

We, the Executive Board, are committed to establishing the most responsible code of ethics for our discipline, and we ask that you join us in this effort by registering your vote and committing yourself to participation in this process.

Best,

The Executive Board of the American Anthropological Association

....

[1] While the resolution was passed by the membership, the action was considered "advisory" to the Executive Board because the resolution was not submitted at least 30 days prior to the start of the Business Meeting, as required by AAA bylaws.

[2] This resolution was considered advisory as well.

Behind this outcome, however, was a longer set of discussions and debates regarding how anthropology should address both the issue of engagement with military and security agencies and, at a more fundamental level, of how the discipline should view reports that were not intended for general distribution, regardless of whether these restrictions were due to classification or clandestine activity or restrictions imposed by clients, funders or others. Many of these debates are apparent in the report of that ad hoc committee, which follows.

Background

At the most recent AAA Annual Business Meeting, held in November of 2007, a resolution introduced by Terry Turner was passed by the membership. The resolution directed the AAA Executive Board to restore certain sections of the 1971 version of the code of ethics in order to, in the words of the sponsor, "[affirm] the importance of transparency and openness in anthropological research and the need for anthropological knowledge to circulate freely." The full text of the resolution appears below:

> WHEREAS the 1971 AAA Code of Ethics ("Principles of Professional Responsibility") contained clear language affirming the importance of transparency and openness in anthropological research and the need for anthropological knowledge to circulate freely (including to those studied); and
>
> WHEREAS this language was weakened in the 1998 AAA Code of Ethics; and
>
> WHEREAS the heightened involvement of anthropologists with U.S. military and intelligence institutions increases the danger that anthropological knowledge will be used to harm those we study and to impede the free circulation of anthropological knowledge; and
>
> WHEREAS the final report of the AAA Commission on the Engagement of U.S. Anthropology with the U.S. Security and Intelligence communities recommends that "the Ethics Committee or general membership should consider reinstating former language from the 1971 CoE (sections 1.g, 2.a, 3.a and 6)" (p.25);
>
> Be it moved that the AAA restore sections 1.g, 2.a, 3.a and 6 from the 1971 ethics code, to wit:
>
> 1.g "In accordance with the Association's general position on clandestine and secret research, no reports should be provided to sponsors that are not also available to the general public and, where practicable, to the population studied."
>
> 2.a "He should not communicate findings secretly to some and withhold them from others."
>
> 3.a "He should undertake no secret research or any research whose results cannot be freely derived and publicly reported."

6. "In relation with his own government and with host governments, the research anthropologists should be honest and candid. He should demand assurance that he will not be required to compromise his professional responsibilities and ethics as a condition of their permission to pursue research. Specifically, no secret research, no secret reports or debriefings of any kind should be agreed to or given. If these matters are clearly understood in advance, serious complications and misunderstandings can generally be avoided."

A related motion, introduced by John Kelly, directed the Executive Board to report to the membership if a decision was not made to restore, in total, the language proposed in the Turner motion. The full text of that motion appears below:

> Whereas we understand that the by-laws of our association do not require the Board of the AAA to respect our declared will in the matter of restoring the anti-secrecy clauses to our ethics code, as in other prior cases of motions without notice,
>
> be it resolved first, that we resent and resist any and all efforts to transform the call into a mere invitation to discuss the secrecy clauses,
>
> and second, that if the Executive Committee chooses any alterative to reinstating the 1971 secrecy language, we ask them to explain their anti-democratic decisions to us very carefully.

On January 20, 2008, the AAA Executive Board passed a resolution asking the Committee on Ethics to draft a revised version of the ethics code that "incorporates the principles of the Turner motion while stipulating principles…that identify when the ethical conduct of anthropology does and does not require specific forms of the public circulation of knowledge." The relevant portions of the EB ballot appear below:

> That the Committee on Ethics draft, for the consideration of the EB, a revised version of the Ethics Code that (i) incorporates the principle of the Turner motion while (ii) stipulating principles—themselves compatible with and/or following from the principles in Sections II and III in the existing Code of Ethics—that identify when the ethical conduct of anthropology does and does not require specific forms of the public circulation of knowledge.
>
> The Executive Board further requests that the Committee on Ethics, in preparing these draft revisions, give due attention to the

discussion of these issues in the report of the Ad Hoc Commission on Engagement of Anthropology in US Security and Intelligence Communities. The Executive Board further requests that the Committee on Ethics advise the EB on the effects of adopting such a proposal, with special focus on identifying for anthropologists what sorts of research and reporting practices would be considered unethical conduct if its draft proposal were incorporated into a revised Ethics Code. Finally, the Executive Board requests that the Ethics Committee prepare its response to this directive by April 1.

The Executive Board also passed a motion to add four invited guests to the Committee on Ethics to assist in the development of a revised version of the Code of Ethics; these four guest are Jeffrey Altschul, Agustín Fuentes, Merrill Singer, and David Price. [1] Another three guests were invited after the first conference call, Inga Treitler, Nathaniel Tashima, and Noel Chrisman.[2]

On March 7, the Committee on Ethics held its first teleconference to discuss how best to proceed on the Turner resolution and the subsequent charge from the Executive Board. Those participating from the Committee on Ethics included Alec Barker, Katie MacKinnon, Dena Plemmons, Dhooleka Raj [4], and those from the "ad hoc" advisory group of four included Jeff Altschul, Agustín Fuentes, Merrill Singer and David Price. A discussion of the process they agreed to follow in revising the Ethics Code was submitted to the Executive Board on May 3, 2007.[4]

During the course of the call it was agreed that the committee chair, Katherine MacKinnon, would create a Microsoft Word document and merge the 1971 and 1998 versions to facilitate comparison between the two codes in the specific areas outlined in the Turner motion.

During the initial teleconference, several potential concerns arose with incorporating the 1971 language:

Problems may arise, for example, if indigenous communities do not want certain information published in the public realm, if archaeological sites need to be protected, or if specific health issues and test results should not be published. Such cases may conflict with some of the 1971 language.

The committee should better define when secrecy may be permitted in anthropological work.

Notions of public access are becoming increasingly problematic, particularly for anthropologists doing multi-sited work, and the CoE[2] may need to tailor the ethics code to account for developments in this realm.

The Committee on Ethics surmised that once there is general agreement on the wording of the revised document, the committee will then discuss how best to advise the Executive Board on the effects of adopting such a proposal, with special focus on identifying for anthropologists what types of research and reporting practices would be considered unethical if the proposal were incorporated into a revised Code of Ethics.

Recommendations

The Committee on Ethics, including invited guests (hereinafter referred to as the working group), has met by teleconference on two occasions since May 7, 2008 and extensively discussed, debated and revised the proposed language through a series of emails. The working group is pleased to recommend the accompanying language, and offers this brief introduction to place our discussions in context.

There was unanimity that the precise language offered in the Turner resolution could not be implemented without revision of some kind, with the revisions needed ranging from the straightforward (it refers to all anthropologists as male; the language used to refer to those from whom we obtain our results isn't the most appropriate) to profound (it offers no exceptions for archaeological resources or client privilege and nondisclosure).

While the majority of the working group is sympathetic to what they took to be the primary goal of the Turner resolution, they express concern that the 1971 language does not allow exceptions that both the working group and the framers of the resolution have acknowledged as valid, such as confidentiality regarding the location of archaeological resources or threatened populations of plants and animals. Further, they feel that if the purpose of the resolution is to prohibit anthropologists from abusing the trust placed in them by the people with whom they work and whom they study, then the language needs to be clarified to unambiguously allow confidentiality or restricted distribution of results in those cases where such restrictions are based on an anthropologist's primary ethical obligations to the people, species, and materials they study and to the people with whom they work. Confidentiality regarding the location of archaeological resources fits into this framework, as does restricted distribution of certain kinds of culturally sensitive information regarding tangible and intangible cultural property or knowledge, certain categories of health or medical information, and information which, if disclosed, would unduly expose the study's participants to harm or threat.

For the majority of the working group, these cases represent clear ethical obligations. While recognizing the importance of making data available to the public and to participants in research projects, such distribution at the expense of the well-being of the population studied is unacceptable. If there are appropriate reasons results of research will not be made available to a study's participants, anthropologists must disclose this fact clearly to the participants. It is in this instance, the majority feels, that we most clearly meet one of the primary obligations of our profession: to protect the safety, dignity, and privacy of those with whom we work. The majority feels that our obligation to transparency and full disclosure is honestly and ethically met when constraints on sharing results are acknowledged at the outset of the research, and decisions about participation rest then where they should, with the participants.

Less clear is the permissibility of restricted access or distribution of results based on contractual obligations, or as a prerequisite to being given permission to conduct research. Anthropologists working with governments, corporations or NGOs may be asked to hold certain kinds of information or results in confidence. In some instances those stipulations may be required by the community or population being studied, as in cases of anthropologists working with tribal governments. Minority and vulnerable groups exist as part of larger groups, and often researchers are dealing with both the minority group and the larger group in relation to whom that group is defined. Are some research participants included in the distribution, but others not? Whether these restrictions in such cases are ethical must be determined on a case by case basis. A situation that evinces ambiguity regarding either disclosure or non-disclosure is not in its essence unethical; rather it places the onus for evaluation on the anthropologist, though guidance is provided by the Code's broad framework. Indeed, the preamble to our current code states:

> *In a field of such complex involvements and obligations, it is inevitable that misunderstandings, conflicts, and the need to make choices among apparently incompatible values will arise. Anthropologists are responsible for grappling with such difficulties and struggling to resolve them in ways compatible with the principles stated [in the Code].*

The majority feel that the principles currently added provide sufficient guidance to enable an anthropologist to make an informed and ethical decision.

Our Code also notes:

> *No code or set of guidelines can anticipate unique circumstances or direct actions in specific situations. The individual anthropologist must be willing to make carefully considered ethical choices and be prepared to make clear the assumptions, facts and issues on which those choices are based. These guidelines therefore address general contexts, priorities and relationships which should be considered in ethical decision making in anthropological work.*

It is felt by the majority that this ethical decision making rightly belongs with the individual anthropologist, aided by the principles in the Code and guided by expert opinion and advice from others in the profession. Relatedly, there is also the concern that the Turner resolution seems to remove this responsibility for anthropologists to consider the consequences of their actions; by broadly forbidding certain kinds of study it implicitly makes the remainder ethically acceptable, and thus without necessary examination, which is neither a valid nor a professionally acceptable outcome.

The working group's recommended language prohibits clandestine research, or research in which the purpose, character, intended results or sponsorship of the research is misrepresented.

The working group notes that this particular report, because of time constraints, is limited in scope and was unable to address the charge by the Executive Board to "[especially] focus on identifying for anthropologists what sorts of research and reporting practices would be considered unethical if its draft proposal were incorporated into a revised Ethics Code."

The working group recommends that the Executive Board establish a panel to come up with identifying such ethical dilemmas; such a panel would also provide, as needed, and on a case-by-case basis, opinion and guidance on ethically appropriate practices to AAA members and others in the discipline seeking such advice.

We note that the recommendations are unanimous with the exception of Section VI regarding dissemination of results. The majority of the working group understood it had been charged with recommending to the Executive Board a revised version of the Ethics Code that incorporated the intent of the Turner motion. We understood this to include stipulating principles compatible with those already in Sections II and III in the existing Code of Ethics that identified when the ethical conduct of anthropology does and does not require specific forms of the public circulation of knowledge. A dissenting view argued that the working group had no brief to consider anything other than the insertion of the Turner language guided by authorial intent, and that the concerns raised by other members of the working group undermined the will of the AAA membership in order to satisfy the concerns of special interest groups. A minority comment on the section in question will be submitted by those who hold these views.

Minority Commentary on the Turner Resolution of the 2007 AAA Business Meeting

We, the Committee's minority, concur with the Committee's majority in accepting the below three proposed common supplemental changes, relevant to the Turner Resolution, proposed to the AAA's Code of Ethics:

- III.A.2 (so that it reads: "Anthropological researchers must do everything in their power to ensure that their research does not harm the safety, dignity, or privacy of the people with whom they work, conduct research, or perform other professional activities, or who might reasonably be thought to be affected by their research.").
- III.B.4 (so that it reads: "Anthropologists should not work clandestinely or otherwise misrepresent the nature, purpose, intended outcome, distribution or sponsorship of their research.").
- III.C.2 (so that it reads: "In relation with his or her own government, host governments, or sponsors of research, an anthropologist should be honest and candid. Anthropologists must not compromise their professional responsibilities and ethics as a condition of permission to conduct research. Anthropologists should not agree

to conditions which inappropriately change the purpose, focus or intended outcomes of their research."

We agree with the majority on the above submitted language.

The minority's dissent focuses on section VI, "Dissemination of Results," of the proposed changes to the Code of Ethics relevant to the Turner Resolution. Below is the minority's recommended text for the revised Code of Ethics section VI on "Dissemination of Results." We have marked the language that must be struck from the majority's version, and marked our additional sentence to be added to VI.2 in italics:

VI. Dissemination of Results

1. The results of anthropological research are complex, subject to multiple interpretations and susceptible to differing and unintended uses. Anthropologists have an ethical obligation to consider the potential impact of both their research and the communication or dissemination of the results of their research on all directly or indirectly involved.

2. ~~It is generally expected that~~ Researchers will not withhold research results from the persons or communities studied when those results are shared with others. There are, ~~however,~~ specific instances in which confidentiality or restricted distribution of results is appropriate and ethical, particularly where these restrictions serve to protect the safety, dignity or privacy of participants, protect cultural heritage, tangible or intangible cultural property, or otherwise reflect valid but crosscutting ethical obligations. *The ethical responsibility of archaeologists and others to assist the preservation of cultural materials allows, and at times mandates, the production of reports that will have very restricted distribution.*

3. Anthropologists must weigh the intended and potential uses of their work and the impact of its distribution in determining whether limited availability of results is warranted and ethical in any given instance.

4. ~~If the results of studies will not be made available to the persons or communities being studied, this should be clearly disclosed at the outset to all concerned.~~

Our dissent rejects the majority's proposed language for Section VI because their language exceeds the Ad Hoc Ethics Committee's charge.

The majority did not adhere to the first portion (i) of the Executive Board's two-part charge, wherein it instructed the committee to:

> draft, for the consideration of the EB, a revised version of the Ethics Code that (i) incorporates the principle of the Turner Resolution while (ii) stipulating principles—themselves compatible with and/or following from the principles in Sections II and III in the existing Code of Ethics—that identify when the ethical conduct of anthropology does and does not require specific forms of the public circulation of knowledge.

In straying from the committee's charge of incorporating "the principle of the Turner Resolution" the majority language is so at odds with the original Resolution's principle that Professor Terry Turner and his co-drafter Professor Hugh Gusterson do not support it. As a point of procedure and for reasons of fundamental fairness, the majority's proposed language should be rejected.

During our first conference-call of March 7, 2008 the committee discussed our charge, and after one initial interpretation was presented suggesting that the committee should seek to alter core features of the Turner Resolution, the group agreed that our charge was to not undertake such a task, but to instead add the specified language cited by Professor Turner to the current Code of Ethics, to discuss how this related to the larger code, and to identify impacts of these changes by April 1, 2008. The committee undertook this task and in keeping with our charge, our chair eventually submitted different drafts of the Code that attempted to carry out these tasks. In April, the Executive Board asked the Ad Hoc Committee to continue working on integrating and analyzing the impact of Turner, but at no point did the committee's charge change to that of altering Turner's intent.

During our final two weeks of deliberations, some committee members made arguments that there were great difficulties in knowing Professor Turner's intent. These members argued against producing language that was starkly prescriptive, instead favoring a softened resolution stating general recommendations or expectations. The minority argued that Professor Turner meant to produce a prescriptive resolution and cited the prescriptive language used in the 1971 Code that is the basis of the Turner Resolution. Other arguments were made that Professor Turner intended to prohibit all forms of secrecy, including common practices used by archaeologists to protect cultural materials, the use of pseudonyms, or reports shared only with research participants. The minority countered these claims citing Turner's comments at the business meeting and his reliance on the AAA's Commission on the Engagement of Anthropology with the US Security and Intelligence Communities' 2007 report to frame and introduce his Resolution at the business meeting. On the advice of President Setha Low, David Price contacted Professor Hugh Gusterson (a co-drafter of Professor Turner's Resolution) and inquired whether the majority's proposed modifying-clause ("It is generally expected that") in the sentence at the heart of the division between the majority and minority nullified the intent of Professor Turner's resolution, and Professor Gusterson replied that it did. As a result of the query to Professor Gusterson, Price received a call from Professor Turner. Professor Turner was not thrilled that any changes were being made to his motion, but after some discussion he stated that he can live with the changes advocated by the minority, but he rejects those of the majority.

The majority's insistence on adding the clause, "it is generally expected that" to our statement that "researchers will not withhold research results from the persons or communities studied when those results are shared with others," fundamentally breaks with Professor Turner's intent. The majority's clause alters this sentence's intended meaning in the same way as would a translation of the Ten Commandments reading "It is generally expected that thou shalt not kill." Professor Turner's principle intent was to issue a strong injunction against such research, and the majority errs in replacing their intent for Turner's. As such, it does not incorporate the principle of the Turner Resolution as we are charged by the Executive Board under the charge's first stipulation to "incorporate the principle of the Turner Resolution."

The minority acknowledges that some inconveniences are created by reinstating language clarifying that it is unethical to produce secretive reports, but our first charge was to wordsmith the Turner Resolution so that its intention was intact, not to so reshape his intent so that it aligned with members who voted against the Turner Resolution at the business meeting. But this is the outcome that the majority achieved.

During deliberations, the majority advanced arguments claiming that many routine elements of anthropological research would be impinged by the minority's language. Arguments were made that our proposed language mandates that findings, published articles, books and other reports be somehow directly delivered to research participants; specific problems of getting results to poor, remote, off-line, or illiterate populations were frequently mentioned. The minority's language makes no such demand and such arguments distort what we have written and our intent. Our language does not insist that all research reports must be given to research participants. <u>We simply argue that reports provided to anyone other than research participants must not be sequestered under policies of secrecy, classification, or proprietary policies designed to make it impossible for research participants to access.</u> The minority's language will strengthen anthropologists' collective ability to negotiate improved conditions of the reporting of findings that will not exclude research participants.

The basic philosophy of Turner's resolution derives from the arguments made in sections of the 2007 final report of the AAA Commission on the Engagement of Anthropology with the US Security and Intelligence Communities in evaluating anthropological engagements with military and intelligence communities. Essentially, the commission decided that rather than focusing on specific agencies (e.g., CIA, NSA, DoD, etc.) as possibly presenting inherent problems for anthropologists' engagements, the commission decided to focus on potentially problematic ethical practices that anthropologists working in any setting might face. This approach advanced from a starting point that focused on ethical problems associated with specific practices rather than producing a list of agencies where anthropologists should not work. Issues surrounding secrecy and non-disclosure of research results were among the fundamental practices potentially raising ethical problems discussed by the commission (see section on "The role and interpretation of the AAA Code of Ethics," pp 15-17). Of particular relevance to Turner's resolution is a paragraph stating:

> *Anthropological ethics may be compromised by national security mandates that conflict with standards of full informed consent of participants in research. Pre-1986 versions of the [AAA Code of Ethics] offered more clarity on such interactions with the proviso that, "classified, or limited dissemination restrictions that necessarily and perhaps understandably are placed upon researchers do conflict with openness, disclosure, and the intent and spirit of informed consent in research and practice. Adherence to acknowledged standards of informed consent that conflict with conditions for engagement with national security agencies may result in a decision not to undertake or to discontinue a research project" (CoE 1971-1986). As discussed in the "Recom-*

mendations" section, the AAA Ethics Committee may wish to examine the possibility of reincorporating such language into the current [Code of Ethics]. (Final report of the AAA Commission on the Engagement of Anthropology with the US Security and Intelligence Communities 2007:16)

As Professor Turner clarified from the floor of the 2007 AAA business meeting, his resolution was linked to the commission report's discussion of issues relating to secrecy, and he specifically cited the report's concluding recommendation that some AAA body should consider reinstituting 1971 ethics language on secrecy (p. 25).

During our committee deliberations, the majority argued that the minority's proposed prescriptive language was out of keeping with the current Code of Ethics. This is not true. We find over a dozen instances of the code stating that anthropologists must do things like disclose funding sources and the potential impacts of work, strive to protect, gain informed consent, tell about possible impacts, not engage in clandestine research, be truthful, etc. Our proposed language simply clarifies that providing reports to external groups, while not making these reports accessible is but another of these ethical obligations that anthropologists must fulfill. This relates to the second charge that the Executive Board issued the Ad Hoc Ethics Committee stipulating that we should identify *"principles--themselves compatible with and/or following from the principles in Sections II and III in the existing Code of Ethics--that identify when the ethical conduct of anthropology does and does not require specific forms of the public circulation of knowledge."* To meet this charge, below we list prominent elements of the Code of Ethics that pertain to the minority's incorporation of Professor Turner's resolution:

- The Code of Ethics advocates that "In both proposing and carrying out research, anthropological researchers must be open about the purpose(s), potential impacts, and source(s) of support for research projects with funders, colleagues, persons studied or providing information, and with relevant parties affected by the research" (CoE III). Our proposed language is a natural extension of the code's commitment to sharing knowledge with research participants who are themselves the most "relevant parties affected by research." Our language strengthens and clarifies the duties of this core value and repairs inconsistencies created by the 1986 modifications of the Code.

- The Code of Ethics demands that anthropologists' primary duty be to those they study, yet the intentional generation of reports that these same people cannot access is counter to the spirit of the Code of Ethic's mandate that: "Anthropological researchers have primary ethical obligations to the people, species, and materials they study and to the people with whom they work" (CoE III A.1). As Turner Resolution collaborator, Hugh Gusterson, wrote to the committee in reply to a query from Price, "the purpose of the motion was not a crudely indiscriminate ban on any confidentiality, but a re-emphasis on anthropologists' primary obligation to those they study. Because anthropologists have a unique methodology that (unlike archival or survey work) generates information from relationships of trust with living people, we have a unique obligation of transparency and openness with the people who open their lives to us and, thus, make our work possible" (Gusterson to Price 6/12/08).

- The Code of Ethics states that anthropologists are obliged "to consult actively with the affected individuals or group(s), with the goal of establishing a working relationship that can be beneficial to all parties involved" (CoE III A.1). Our position is that active consultation is an ongoing process, and openness of reports and results is in accordance with this point, while intentionally inaccessible reports are in conflict with these core principles.

- Sharing research results has been traditionally accepted as a minimal means of reciprocating with people studied. The Code of Ethics states that anthropologists "should recognize their debt to the societies in which they work and their obligation to reciprocate with people studied in appropriate ways" (CoE III A.6). Our view is that not sharing reports with these "people studied" while sharing such information with others who have the power to keep these results secret risks the betrayal of this obligation of reciprocation.

- The code's directive that "anthropologists should not work clandestinely" (CoE III B.4) addresses the spirit of a directive declaring that anthologists will not selectively make information available to powerful sponsors, while withholding this information from those who generated this knowledge, and to whose lives it pertains.

These elements of the Code support the minority's argument that our proposed language is in keeping with the fundamental philosophy of the Code of Ethics. Our proposed changes clarify how the circulation of knowledge is tied to anthropologists' commitments to research participants, and it restores and clarifies the Code's historic

(1971-1986) statements on the ethically problematic nature of secrecy with greater clarity than the original code's statements.

The AAA membership needs to be allowed to vote on language that meets the principle intent of the Turner Resolution. When the Executive Board accepted and acknowledged Professor Turner's approved 2007 business meeting floor resolution by forming our Ad Hoc Committee, it committed the Association to a path that would advance Turner's resolution to the membership in a form properly articulated with the existing Code of Ethics. The minority's proposed language accomplishes this task. This Ad Hoc Ethics Committee's charge was not to negate Turner's intent. The majority's proposed language accomplishes this task. Our charge was not to decide the wisdom or folly of the Turner Resolution, that decision must lie with the Association's membership. Obviously both the majority and minority maintain strong feelings on these issues, and it is exactly because such strong feelings are present that the Executive Board must maintain the rule of order by following established procedures and not allowing the committee to exceed its charge. We ask the Executive Board to hold this committee to its charge, and in so doing we believe it will find with the minority.

....

[1] After the first set of conference calls held in March, Merrill Singer was not able to participate in subsequent conference calls or email discussions.

[2] Noel Chrisman was unable to participate in any way.

[3] K. Sivaramakrishnan and Pamela Bunte, both elected Committee on Ethics members, have been unable to participate in any of the calls; K. Sivaramkrishnan has communicated by e-mail on few occasions.

[4] "Report to the AAA Executive Board on the Activities of the Committee on Ethics," submitted by Damon Dozier, May 3, 2008.

As was noted in the preceding open letter from the EB, the EB convened a subcommittee to review the recommendations of this ad hoc committee, and after further revisions to the code, put forth those revisions for a vote. The revisions were approved in 2009 (and can be found at www.aaanet.org/issues/policy-advocacy/upload/AAA-Ethics-Code-2009.pdf), while at the same time the newly formed (in Fall of 2008) Task Force for Comprehensive Ethics Review (hereafter referred to as the Task Force) was beginning its own work.

As stated on the AAA website:

> As the membership is aware, there have been recent revisions to the AAA's Code of Ethics, in response to a motion put forward at the business meeting of the AAA in 2007. The revisions, on which the membership will vote next week, were specific to only a few sections of the code, and consisted of a very few sentences. In light of the specificity of those revisions, the Executive Board has determined that a more comprehensive review of the entire Code of Ethics is warranted. The EB has convened a task force to undertake such a review over the next two years. The official charge is:
>
>> The Executive Board recommends the formation of a Task Force to review and propose revisions to the AAA Code of Ethics, which: (a) will consist of three (3) members of the Committee on Ethics and five (5) additional members to be chosen by the President in consultation with the Executive Board and the Task Force Chair; (b) be authorized to review the Code of Ethics for a period of no longer than 18 months, and (c) consult extensively over a period of no less than six months with relevant AAA committees and commissions, the Section Assembly, the membership at large and others through presentations and panel discussions at the 2009 annual meeting and articles and reports in Anthropology News. The new code is subject to approval by the Executive Board before being submitted for approval to the AAA membership by email ballot. This Task Force will issue its final report to the Executive Board by Nov. 15, 2010.[3]

The Task Force, comprised of members of the then standing Committee on Ethics and of others jointly chosen by the Chair of the Task Force and the AAA President, set out to be as open and transparent as possible in the process of crafting a code, or set of principles, for the Association. From the beginning, we paid keen attention to both our process and the hoped for outcome. We knew we wanted an interactive engagement with the membership and an iterative process with the materials. And, rather than establishing detailed codes, which by implication allow whatever is not specifically proscribed, we wanted to develop principles which focused on values that all anthropologists must employ to assess appropriate action in any given situation. We wanted to emphasize that while there may be situations in which obligations under different principles must be weighed one against another, there are *no* situations in which the principles themselves do not apply, and *no* actions that can be justified as ethical simply by saying they are not expressly forbidden. At the end of the three year process, we wanted to have an online and living document, threaded through with active links to other resources, to academic articles and opinion pieces, to work that both supported and challenged what was written for any given principle, and we wanted those links to be updated frequently. We based our process, in part, on that previously used by the Linguistic Society of America, and this book—with its individually signed chapters representing unashamedly different viewpoints and opinions on specific principles and processes—is an expression of those values. The recent revelations of the involvement of members of the American Psychological Association in the interrogation programs of the CIA and, more damning, the complicity of high ranking members of the APA in twisting their Association's Code of Ethics to allow that practice are in stark contrast to the AAA's approach to crafting this latest version of our code. Laura Stark (2015), in an article in *Inside Higher Ed*, writing about this APA debacle, and some of the history of the creation of the first APA code of ethics, concludes:

> The APA's current ethics mess is a problem inherent to its method of setting professional ethics policy and a problem that faces professional organizations more broadly. Professions' codes of ethics are made to seem anonymous, dropped into the world by some higher moral authority. But ethics codes have authors. In the long term, the APA's problems will not be solved by repeating the same process that empowers a select elite to write ethics policy, then removes their connection to it.
>
> All ethics codes have authors who work to erase the appearance of their influence. Personal interests are inevitable, if not unmanageable, and it may be best for the APA—and other professional groups—to keep the link between an ethics policy and its authors. Take a new lesson from the Hippocratic oath by observing its name. The APA should make its ethics policies like most other papers that scientists write: give the code of ethics a byline.

We think it's important to note that the Task Force was identified to the membership from its creation, and our names were on the final report submitted, along with the draft code, to the EB in 2011. This naming of task force and committee members who have worked on our codes and principles of professional responsibility has been true of our Association since our first code was written, and continues to be part of our deliberate approach to not just the construction of this text, but also our broader conversations and investigations into the ethical implications of our practice.

The Task Force began its work by disseminating a survey to assess members' perceptions of codes of ethics in general and solicit opinions about the AAA's code specifically, both about what the then code contained and what it was missing. We convened discussions at the AAA meetings of 2009 and 2010 of students and section assembly leaders and, through email, telephone, and personal contact, frequently solicited engagement with the membership in these conversations. As we drafted the principles for the revised code, we posted them on a blog accessible to members and to the public, and used comments left there in an iterative fashion as we continued to write. The Task Force met face to face for each of the three years that it was doing its work. In the fall of 2011, the Task Force submitted to the EB the draft revised code and our report of the process along with recommendations. We include that report here.

Final Report of The Task Force for Comprehensive Ethics Review

In early 2009, the AAA membership voted on revisions to the AAA's Code of Ethics, in response to a motion put forward at the business meeting of the AAA in 2007. Those revisions were specific to only a few sections of the code, and consisted of a very few sentences. In light of the specificity of those revisions, the Executive Board determined that a more comprehensive review of the entire Code of Ethics was warranted. Consequently, the EB convened a task force in late 2008 to undertake such a review over a three year period [1], with a final report to be submitted to the Executive Board in November, 2011. We respectfully submit this report along with our suggested revisions to the AAA Code of Ethics.

The Task Force's Approach

The Task Force began their work, a review of the Code of Ethics with the purpose of proposing revisions, in early 2009 by creating a survey which was disseminated to the entire membership. The survey was meant to be both a broad examination of perceptions of codes of ethics in general—what they should do, what they cannot do—and an assessment of opinions about the AAA code of ethics and its specific content. We wanted to know if and how the membership used the code in practice and in teaching, and if there were ways to make the code more relevant to our work. Several of the Task Force members entered into informal conversations with colleagues and with anthropologists who were not members of the AAA to examine their uses of the code and how they go about making ethical decisions.

At the same time, Task Force members began consulting with other sections of the AAA as well as organizations outside the AAA, and we also began a comprehensive review of the codes of ethics of these other organizations. We used all of this information, along with the results of the survey, to inform the agenda for our first face to face meeting in September of 2009, held in Washington DC.

From the survey results and our own conversations at this meeting, we first identified several purposes of a code of ethics: to state clearly that anthropologists are responsible for engaging in an on-going process of ethical thinking and practice that grapples with dilemmas that necessarily emerge in conducting research and other aspects of our professional lives; to assist faculty members and their students in teaching and learning about ethical dimensions and laying foundations on which anthropologists can continue to build throughout their careers; to be of real and immediate value to anthropologists in the actual contexts in which they make ethical decisions. Finally, we recognized that a code must be flexible enough to adapt to diverse circumstances and adjust to the wide range of contexts of anthropological practices, while providing core principles informing ethical practice in real-world situations.

In addition to discussions about the purposes of the code, we created several workgroups to focus on the major concepts or issues of practice which we saw as central to our code of ethics; the task of these workgroups was to make clear all the dimensions of these issues so that we would have a simultaneously clear and nuanced picture. Because of the breadth of anthropology as a discipline, it was crucial to deliberately and systematically explore a range of viewpoints and approaches. The workgroups examined relevant resources from a broad range of sources, as well as soliciting cases from anthropologists which helped contextualize the concepts with which we were working. Throughout the process, we continuously connected our work back to the current code of ethics. We continued soliciting comments and feedback from the membership through an intentionally wide range of approaches, ranging from broadcast discussions, such as columns in Anthropology News, and a series of face-to-face events at the AAA annual meetings of 2008, 2009, and 2010 to allow members multiple opportunities to express views, concerns and criticisms. These included specific roundtables to address student concerns and specific invitations and roundtables for the AAA's section leadership and committee members to address their individual needs.

Members of the Task Force met again in September of 2010 at Fort Burgwin on the SMU in Taos campus. Taking the workgroup documents, which had been informed by survey results, codes of other organizations, conversations with colleagues and students, and a wide array of resources—both anthropological and not—the Task Force members began the process of distilling all of the material into basic principles, which we thought would best represent the concerns of the code and of the members in a new way. We wanted to take what was latent in the current CoE and make it more evident/explicit and easier to remember in the form of principles, with preliminary explanatory text [2]. Framing of these principles was informed by three additional goals:

1. To create easily remembered phrases which summarized key principles, and could inform the day to day decision making of anthropologists, increasing the immediacy and relevance of the code to all AAA members;

2. To revise the code in ways that reflected the breadth of sub-disciplines and contexts of practice, and thus addressing concern expressed by some respondents that the current code seemed to privilege certain kinds of approaches or contexts of practice; and

3. To employ a layered or nested approach in which broad principles were supported by framing discussions explaining and providing depth to the principles, and further supported by specific discussions or resources situating these principles within those different approaches or contexts of practice.

Our decision from the first meeting to reformulate the current code was not meant to imply that the current code is necessarily deficient. We did and still do think, however, that any effective and meaningful code needs to be periodically revised and restated to keep current with the ways in which ethical issues, however timeless, are encountered, discussed and debated in the field. Our intent has not been to suggest a completely new code that will stand without further revision, but to make the current code more immediately relevant. We hope and expect that it will be revisited and revised again on a regular basis, not just in the event of a disciplinary crisis, but as a living and evolving document with member input in the revision process. This is the precise process the Task Force began with this current revision, and we recommend that this process be returned to in the next instance of review.

Critical Questions for Review

During its three-year tenure, the Task Force examined a set of issues that have been salient in AAA member discussions over the past decade. We summarize these issues and our views on them below.

- **Primary Responsibility:** Past codes specifically stated that anthropologists owe their primary ethical obligation to the people they study. While the members of the Task Force were sympathetic to this view, it became increasingly clear that it reflected a cherished anthropological value rather than an actual principle of ethical practice. Anthropologists "studying up," studying those in power, do not owe a greater ethical obligation to powerful individuals than to those vulnerable to that power. Nor is that value equally applicable to all kinds of anthropologists without either broad exclusions or special pleading (e.g., archaeologists, paleoanthropologists). While acknowledging the problematic nature of this previous principle, the Task Force nevertheless did discuss concerns that its removal weakens what had traditionally been perceived to be clear guidance for anthropologists caught in conflicting positions between the needs of research participants, sponsors, and other populations. We wish to note that this was a difficult issue for the Task Force, and we were never able to reach unanimity. The new code does place responsibility for one's actions squarely on the anthropologist, however. It requires her/him to consider the impacts of the work and its potential to cause harm. The Task Force is keenly aware that the Do No Harm principle is also complex and problematic, yet we feel this more directly and immediately addresses the ethical imperative informing the older "primary responsibility" statement, while recognizing that anthropologists study all kinds of individuals and institutions, some of whom do not necessarily command our primary allegiance or obligation. As was the case with the 1998 revisions to the Code, this topic demanded much energy and emotion. We think the intense investment in this discussion—as we witnessed it among ourselves and in the wider membership through comments left on the blog—is a strength of our Association, and we assume attention to and investment in this topic will continue among our members for the foreseeable future.

- **Accessibility of Results:** Recent challenges to the existing Code of Ethics focused on the accessibility of results, and particularly whether there are cases where it is appropriate for results to be shared with some and not others, especially when those "others" are the subjects of the research. In addressing this topic the Task Force attempted a more complex approach, one which recognized that, in general, such sharing is expected, but that our research collaborators should also be accorded the right to make informed decisions on this topic for themselves. It has always been recognized that blanket requirements of accessibility do not apply (e.g., location of endangered study populations or archaeological sites), and the new principles provide greater guidance regarding how and why access should instead be limited and/or facilitated. We believe this provides more nuance than a broader statement that calls for sharing of research data and/or results, with implied exceptions.

- **Clandestine Research:** The problematic nature of clandestine research has long been recognized by the discipline. The Task Force draws a distinction between clandestine research in which *informed consent could not possibly, by design or context, be adequately and fairly given* and other kinds of research in which participants may not have full access to all information but are honestly and adequately informed regarding the nature, scope and sponsors of the research and have freely consented to their role. This more nuanced approach focuses on ethical considerations of anthropological practice instead of labels (e.g., "secret") whose meanings vary by context. We feel this approach more fully recognizes previous work by AAA task forces addressing these topics.[3]

- **Adjudication:** The Task Force discussed the issue of the AAA again having an adjudication process in cases of allegations of unethical conduct by anthropologists. When we gathered information from the membership at the start of our process, we learned that they have a range of opinions concerning the advisability of reinstating adjudication procedures. Like the AAA membership at large, the Task Force is composed of members representing the full range of views concerning the possible reinstatement of sanctions for ethical violations. While we discussed these issues, as a group we concluded that it should be considered separately from revising the ethics code. We recommend that if the Executive Board wishes to pursue an adjudicative code as a possibility, it should appoint a committee to consider this matter only after the EB has determined if it is in a position to make a financial and philosophical commitment to this process.

From our discussions of this matter, we believe that such a committee would need to answer at least the following questions in considering this possibility:

1. What, exactly, would be the process for defining something to be an ethical violation, and from whom/what sources would those definitions arise? How would the Association reliably differentiate behavior that might more appropriately be considered unprofessional from that which is unethical?
2. Who hears complaints? How are those persons chosen? By what criteria and what credentials? Are those individuals indemnified by the Association?
3. What would the process be to change definitions of what constitutes an ethical violation—member vote? Committee? If the latter, would definitions/sanctions then be influenced by current committee membership, and how would the Association control for consistency?
4. Would you need to determine different levels of severity for violations, and then different sanctions for those different violations? And who would be making these decisions? What could the possible range of sanctions be, given that we aren't licensed or credentialed practitioners?
5. How would the code be a part of this process? Would it become a legal document then? How would the current code need to be re-written to be a part of a sanctioning process? Would new members have to make an attestation that they are legally bound to the code?
6. What about ethical violations committed by non-members? Can members being investigated for potential malfeasance simply withdraw their membership to avoid sanction?
7. From where would the funds come for the considerable expenditures necessary for ensuring due process and addressing issues of liability [personal/association]?
8. How would the Association reliably differentiate ethical concerns from political concerns, agendas, and interests which, however appropriate *and laudable, should not be confused with what is or is not ethical?*

The Task Force would like to point out that even though the AAA has no formal sanctioning process, there are nevertheless legitimate and viable means within the Association for addressing ethical issues of concern. In addition to the standing Committee on Ethics and the ad hoc advisory group Friends of the Committee on Ethics, there are such avenues as Association wide discussions of particular incidents, roundtable sessions at the AAA, case-based AAA sessions, special events at the AAA meetings, etc. The Task Force would encourage AAA leadership to institutionalize these means of purposefully addressing ongoing ethical education.

Communicating the Proposed Principles

Beginning just after that September 2010 meeting, the first of the principles was posted to a blog site on the AAA website, with principles being posted one at a time, through May of 2011. In addition to publicly posting these principles for comment, we also drew attention to these posts through communication with international anthropological organizations, section leaders and anthropology departments throughout the country. We chose this sequential method of dissemination for two reasons: first was to allow members to focus on each individual principle in turn, which we hoped would encourage deliberate and substantive discussion on the merits of each as a meaningful and relevant principle <u>on its own</u>, and second, and equally important, this was meant to be part of an iterative process in which ongoing discussion by the membership would determine both how each draft principle should be revised and how many additional principles might be needed to adequately address the concerns identified from discussion by the membership.

At the end of June 2011, all of the principles which had been drafted and re-drafted by the Task Force over the previous 9 months were posted on the blog, in one document; this draft document represented a series of carefully vetted and debated principles, each able to stand alone, which we then asked the membership one last time to review and discuss, and to provide suggestions and comments that would help ensure that the complete document adequately and coherently addressed key areas and concerns. Members of the Task Force then reviewed every comment, concern and posting, summarizing key viewpoints, concerns and opinions for discussion by all members of the Task Force to help revise both the individual principles and to identify any areas not adequately addressed in the existing principles.

In September of 2011, the Task Force met for a final time to review these summaries, all of the comments and suggestions left on the blog after posting of the complete set of principles, as well as additional comments solicited by e-mail from committees and section leaders. Taking those comments and concerns into consideration, we did final editing of the principles, 7 in all; drafted a code preamble, and began the process of collecting the supporting documents and resources that would be linked from the specific principles. It was our plan from the outset to present the principles with other resources; those other resources include additional codes of ethics, articles, cases, and additional text and interpretation. It is our hope that the code of ethics of the AAA and supporting materials be seen as the primary resource, but among many, that the members can turn to for guidance in determining ethical practice and that it will be consulted by AAA members in those contexts in which they must make ethical decisions.

Recommendations

Along with this final report and our recommendation to the Executive Board to adopt the proposed changes to our Code of Ethics, we conclude with recommendations from the 1996 Commission to Review the AAA Statement on Ethics, recommendations which remain relevant and important, and which still require our attention as a discipline and a professional Association:

The AAA should produce and periodically update a publication of case studies of ethical dilemmas anthropological researchers, teachers and practitioners might face, suitable for use in graduate training, post-doctorate training, and continuing education.

The AAA should provide to departments technical assistance in establishing educational offerings in ethics.

The AAA should conduct ethics training workshops at annual meetings and during the year.

The AAA should seek a joint grant with one or more other social science organizations to develop a basic ethics teaching module, which could be used by all social sciences, calling on resources from across the campus, and which would be supplemented with department training specific to the discipline.

The AAA should seek a joint grant with one or more social science organizations to develop a common basic statement of teaching ethics.

The AAA should develop broad guidelines to help departments determine the appropriate minimum of ethics training which should be offered to different levels of students.

Respectfully submitted –

The Task Force for Comprehensive Ethics Review

Dena Plemmons, Chair

Alec Barker

Charles Briggs

Laura McNamara

Katherine C. MacKinnon

David Price

Niel Tashima

....

[1] The initial charge:

The Executive Board recommends the formation of a Task Force to review and propose revisions to the AAA Code of Ethics, which: (a) will consist of three (3) members of the Committee on Ethics and five (5) additional members to be chosen by the President in consultation with the Executive Board and the Task Force Chair; (b) be authorized to review the Code of Ethics for a period of no longer than 18 months, and (c) consult extensively over a period of no less than six months with relevant AAA committees and commissions, the Section Assembly, the membership at large and others through presentations and panel discussions at the 2009 annual meeting and articles and reports in Anthropology News. The new code is subject to approval by the Executive Board before being submitted for approval to the AAA membership by email ballot. This Task Force will issue its final report to the Executive Board by Nov. 15, 2010.

While the Task Force was initially given a two-year period in which to conduct its review and suggest revisions, given the scope of the review process and plans for membership involvement in the revision process, the Task Force requested, and was given, a third year

[2] We used the codes of ethics of the American Public Health Association (www.aspher.org/pliki/pdf/ethics_phls.pdf) and the International Society of Ethnobiology (http://ethnobiology.net/code-of-ethics/code-inenglish/) as exemplars.

[3] The Commission on the Engagement of Anthropology with the United States Intelligence and Security Communities (CEAUSSIC) dealt with this topic in both the 2007 report examining general issues related to the practice of anthropology in the context of "security," as well as the 2009 report discussing the Commission's findings on the Human Terrain Systems program. The revisions of the code in 2009 also addressed this issue somewhat tangentially.

Accompanying that report were the draft principles as developed by the Task Force, as included here.[4]

I. Preamble

Anthropology—that most humanistic of sciences and scientific of humanities—is an irreducibly social enterprise. Its practitioners work in the widest variety of contexts studying all aspects of the human experience, and face myriad ethical quandaries inflected in different ways by the contexts in which they work and the kinds of issues they address. What is presented here is intended to reflect core principles shared across subfields and contexts of practice.

These core principles are expressed as concise statements which can be easily remembered for use by anthropologists in their everyday professional lives. Each principle is accompanied by brief discussions placing that principle in a broader context, with more detailed examinations of how each affects or may be helpful to anthropologists in different subfields or work contexts. These examinations are accompanied by resources to assist anthropologists in tackling difficult ethical issues or the new situations that inevitably arise in the production of knowledge.

As a social enterprise, research and practice always involve others—colleagues, students, research participants, employers, clients, funders, among others—and anthropologists must be sensitive to the power differentials, constraints, interests and expectations characteristic of all relationships. In a field of such complex rights, responsibilities, and involvements, it is inevitable that misunderstandings, conflicts, and the need to make choices among apparently incompatible values will arise. Anthropologists are responsible for grappling with such difficulties and struggling to resolve them in ways compatible with the principles stated here. These principles provide anthropologists with tools to engage in developing and maintaining an ethical framework for all stages of anthropological practice—when making decisions prior to beginning projects, when in the field, and when communicating findings and preserving records.

No principles can anticipate unique circumstances or direct actions in specific situations. The individual anthropologist must be willing to make carefully considered ethical choices and be prepared to make clear the assumptions, facts and issues on which those choices are based. These principles address general circumstances, priorities and relationships, and also provide helpful specific examples, that should be considered in anthropological work and ethical decision making.

Ethics and morals differ in important ways. The complex issues that anthropologists confront rarely admit to the simple wrongs and rights of moral dicta, and one of the prime ethical obligations of anthropologists is to carefully and deliberately weigh the consequences and ethical dimensions of the choices they make—by action or inaction. Similarly, ethical principles and political positions should not be conflated; their foci of concern are quite distinct. Finally, ethics and law differ in important ways, as well, and care must always be taken in making these distinctions; making ethical and legal decisions involves different processes. While moral, political, legal and regulatory issues are often important to anthropological practice and the discipline, they are not specifically considered here. These principles address ethical concerns.

While these principles are primarily intended for Association members, they also provide a structure for communicating ethical precepts in anthropology to students, other colleagues, and outside audiences, including sponsors, funders, and Institutional Review Boards or other review committees.

The American Anthropological Association does not adjudicate assertions of unethical behavior, and these principles are intended to foster discussion, guide anthropologists in making responsible decisions, and educate.

Do no harm

Avoidance of harm is a primary ethical obligation shared by all anthropologists. It is imperative that, before any anthropological work be undertaken—in communities, with non-human primates, at archaeological and paleoanthropological sites—each researcher think through the possible ways that the research might cause harm. This includes not only the avoidance of direct and immediate harm but implies an obligation to weigh carefully potential consequences and inadvertent impacts of an anthropologist's work. This primary obligation can supersede the goal of seeking new knowledge and can lead to decisions not to undertake or to discontinue a project when this primary obligation conflicts with other responsibilities. Determining harms and their avoidance in any given situation is complex and must be sustained throughout the course of projects.

Anthropologists may choose to move beyond research to a position of advocacy. While anthropologists welcome work benefiting others or increasing the well-being of individuals or communities, determinations regarding what is in the best interests of others or what kinds of efforts are appropriate to increase well-being are complex and value-laden and should reflect sustained discussion with those concerned. Such work must similarly reflect deliberate and thoughtful consideration of both potential unintended consequences and long-term impacts on individuals, communities, identities, tangible and intangible heritage and environments.

Be open and honest regarding your work

Anthropologists should be clear and open regarding the purpose, methods, outcomes, and sponsors of their work. Anthropologists must also be prepared to acknowledge and disclose to participants and collaborators all tangible and intangible interests that have, or may reasonably be perceived to have, an impact on their work. Transparency, like informed consent, is a process that involves both making principled decisions prior to beginning the research and encouraging participation, engagement, and open debate throughout its course.

Compartmented research that by design will not allow the anthropologist to know the full scope or purpose of a project is ethically problematic, since by definition the anthropologist cannot communicate transparently with participants, nor ensure fully informed consent. Researchers who mislead participants about the nature of the research and/or its sponsors; who omit significant information that might bear on a participant's decision to engage in the research; or who otherwise engage in clandestine or secretive research that manipulates or deceives research participants about the sponsorship, purpose, goals or implications of the research, do not satisfy ethical requirements for openness, honesty, transparency and fully informed consent.

Anthropologists have an ethical obligation to consider the potential impact of both their research and the communication or dissemination of the results of their research. Anthropologists must consider this issue prior to beginning research and throughout the research process. Explicit negotiation with sponsors/clients about data ownership and access, and dissemination of results, may be necessary before deciding whether to begin research.

Obtain informed consent and necessary permissions

Anthropological researchers working with living human communities must obtain the voluntary, prior and informed consent of research participants. Minimally, informed consent includes sharing with potential participants the research goals, methods, funding sources or sponsors, expected outcomes, anticipated impacts of the research, and the rights of research participants. It must also include establishing expectations of anonymity and credit. Researchers must present to research participants the possible impacts of participation, and make clear that despite their best efforts, confidentiality may be compromised or outcomes may differ from those anticipated. Anthropologists have an obligation to ensure that research participants have freely granted consent, and must avoid conducting research in circumstances in which consent may not be truly voluntary or informed. In the event that the research changes in ways that will directly affect the participants, anthropologists must revisit and renegotiate consent. The informed consent process is necessarily dynamic, continuous and reflexive. Anthropologists should initiate this process as a part of project design and continue through implementation as an ongoing dialogue and negotiation with research participants. Informed consent does not necessarily imply or require a particular written or signed form. It is the quality of the consent, not its format, which is relevant.

Anthropologists working with biological communities or cultural resources have an obligation to ensure that they have secured appropriate permissions or permits prior to the conduct of research. Consultation with groups or communities affected by such research should be an important element of the design of such projects and should continue as work progresses or circumstances change. It is explicitly understood that defining what constitutes an affected community is a complex, dynamic and necessary process.

Balance competing ethical obligations due collaborators and affected parties

Anthropologists must balance competing ethical obligations to research participants, students, professional colleagues, employers and funders, among others.

These varying relationships may create conflicting, competing or crosscutting ethical obligations, reflecting both the relative vulnerabilities of different individuals, communities or populations, asymmetries of power implicit in a range of relationships, and the differing ethical frameworks of collaborators representing other disciplines or areas of practice.

Anthropologists have an obligation to distinguish the different kinds of interdependencies and collaborations their work involves, and to consider the real and potential ethical dimensions of these diverse and sometimes contradictory relationships, which may be different in character or change over time. When conflicts between ethical standards or expectations arise, anthropologists need to make explicit their ethical obligations, and develop an ethical approach in consultation with those concerned. Anthropologists must balance these competing ethical obligations while recognizing their obligation to avoid harm to those they study. Anthropologists should not agree to conditions which inappropriately change the purpose, focus, or intended outcomes of their research, nor should they mislead sponsors or collaborators about the nature of the work or its outcomes. Anthropologists remain individually responsible for making ethical decisions.

Collaborations may be defined and understood quite differently by the various participants. The scope of collaboration, rights of the various parties, and issues of credit, acknowledgment and data access should be openly and fairly established at the outset. Collaborations normally involve compromise, and anthropologists must be sensitive to relationships of power and whether such compromise is freely given.

Make your results accessible

The generation of knowledge presumes that results of anthropological research will be made accessible in a timely fashion. These results are complex, subject to multiple interpretations, and susceptible to differing and unintended uses. In some situations, limited dissemination may be appropriate where such restrictions will protect the safety, dignity, or privacy of participants; or protect cultural heritage and/or tangible or intangible cultural or intellectual property.

Limited dissemination poses significant risks. There may be equally great risks associated with dissemination itself. Once information is disseminated, even in a limited sphere, there is great likelihood that it will become widely available. Thus, anthropologists should consider situations where preventing dissemination may be the most ethical decision.

Anthropologists should not normally withhold research results from research participants when those results are shared with others. Restrictions on disclosure may be appropriate and ethical, however, such as where participants have been fully informed and have freely agreed to limited dissemination. Proprietary, classified or other research with limited distribution raises complex ethical questions which must be resolved using these ethical principles. Anthropologists must weigh the intended uses of their research and work to evaluate potential uses of their research and the impact of its dissemination now and in the future.

Protect and preserve your records

Anthropologists have an ethical responsibility for ensuring the integrity, preservation, and protection of their work. An anthropologist's ability to protect and use the materials collected may be contingent upon complex issues of ownership and stewardship.

Researchers have an ethical responsibility to take precautions that collected data and materials will not be used for ends other than those specified at the time the data were collected. These issues are not always clear at the time of data collection, but the researcher is responsible for considering and communicating likely or foreseeable uses of collected data and materials as part of the process of informed consent or obtaining permission. Researchers are also responsible for consulting with research participants regarding their views of generation, use and preservation of research records. This includes informing research participants whether data and materials might be transferred to or accessed by other parties; how they might be transformed or used to identify participants; and how they will be stored and how long they will be preserved.

Researchers have a responsibility to use appropriate methods to ensure the confidentiality and security of field notes, recordings, samples or other primary data and the identities of participants. Ethical decisions regarding the preservation of research materials must balance obligations to maintain data integrity with responsibilities to protect research participants against future harmful impacts. Given the multiple constituencies for and new uses that are often made of anthropological research, such as by heritage communities, the interests of preservation ordinarily outweigh the potential benefits of destroying materials for preserving confidentiality. Researchers generating object collections have a responsibility to ensure the preservation and accessibility of the resulting materials and/or results of analyzed samples, including associated documentation.

In the absence of other agreements or obligations, an anthropologist is presumed to own her/his notes and records, and has an ethical responsibility to ensure their integrity and continued accessibility after the anthropologist's death. Other factors (source of funding, employment agreements, or negotiated agreements with collaborators, among others) may impact ownership of records. Anthropologists should determine record ownership relating to each project and make appropriate arrangements accordingly as a standard part of ethical practice. Researchers should be aware that records may be subject to legal claim based on applicable laws and jurisdictions.

Maintain respectful and ethical professional relationships

There is an ethical dimension to all professional relationships. Whether working in academic or applied settings, anthropologists have a responsibility to maintain respectful relationships with colleagues. In mentoring students, interacting with colleagues, working with clients, or supervising staff, anthropologists should comport themselves in ways that promote a supportive and sustainable workplace environment.

In their capacity as researchers, anthropologists are subject to the ethical principles guiding all scientific and scholarly conduct. They must not plagiarize, nor fabricate or falsify evidence, or knowingly misrepresent information or its source. They must also be alert to the potential of bias to compromise the integrity of anthropological work; anthropologists may gain personally from their work, but they must not exploit individuals, groups, animals, or cultural or biological materials. When they see evidence of research misconduct, they are obligated to report it. They must not obstruct the scholarly efforts of others when they are carried out responsibly.

> In their role as teachers and mentors, anthropologists are obligated to provide instruction on the ethical responsibilities associated with every aspect of anthropological work. They should facilitate, and encourage their students to engage in, dialogue on ethical issues, and discourage their participation in ethically questionable projects. Anthropologists should appropriately acknowledge student contributions to their research and writing, and compensate students justly for any assistance they provide. They are obligated to give students appropriate credit for the authorship of their ideas, and encourage the publication of worthy student work.

This draft was then sent on to a subcommittee of the EB, who spent more time in consultation with the membership and in revision, before submitting their version to the membership for a vote in 2012, which was adopted by a wide margin. The principles included in this volume and about which we are writing are the principles accepted by the membership.

We thought it necessary to situate this specific revision in its particular time and context, and provide some of the many textual materials generated throughout this process. It is our hope that our current PPR will be reviewed thoughtfully, at regular intervals, as both our practice and the many landscapes in which we practice change rapidly.

NOTES

1. Editors' note: Code of Ethics
2. Editors' note: Committee on Ethics
3. Editors' note: The Task Force asked for and was granted another year to complete the comprehensive review and revision.
4. For the sake of clarity what we have included here in this chapter are the principles as originally submitted by the Task Force for the consideration of the Executive Board; those accepted by the Executive Board and ultimately adopted by the membership are included elsewhere in this volume and on the AAA website, at http://aaanet.org.

REFERENCES

Stark, L.
2015   Why Ethics Codes Fail. Inside Higher Ed, July 21, 2015. www.insidehighered.com/views/2015/07/21/essay-why-scholarly-ethics-codes-may-be-likely-fail.

CHAPTER FOUR

Do No Harm

Katherine C. MacKinnon

A primary ethical obligation shared by anthropologists is to do no harm. It is imperative that, before any anthropological work be undertaken—in communities, with non-human primates or other animals, at archaeological and paleoanthropological sites—each researcher think through the possible ways that the research might cause harm. Among the most serious harms that anthropologists should seek to avoid are harm to dignity, and to bodily and material well-being, especially when research is conducted among vulnerable populations. Anthropologists should not only avoid causing direct and immediate harm but also should weigh carefully the potential consequences and inadvertent impacts of their work. When it conflicts with other responsibilities, this primary obligation can supersede the goal of seeking new knowledge and can lead to decisions to not undertake or to discontinue a project. In addition, given the irreplaceable nature of the archaeological record, the conservation, protection and stewardship of that record is the principal ethical obligation of archaeologists. Determining harms and their avoidance in any given situation is ongoing and must be sustained throughout the course of any project.

Anthropologists may choose to link their research to the promotion of well-being, social critique or advocacy. As with all anthropological work, determinations regarding what is in the best interests of others or what kinds of efforts are appropriate to increase well-being are value-laden and should reflect sustained discussion with others concerned. Anthropological work must similarly reflect deliberate and thoughtful consideration of potential unintended consequences and long-term impacts on individuals, communities, identities, tangible intangible heritage and environments.

> *Yet the ethics of anthropology is clearly not just about obeying a set of guidelines; it actually goes to the heart of the discipline; the premises on which its practitioners operate, its epistemology, theory and praxis. In other words, what is anthropology for? Who is it for?* (Caplan 2003:3)

Introduction

Anthropological practice has always necessitated a reflective discourse on our responsibility to the people, communities, and animals with whom we work. There are no simple definitions or answers, nor should there be. Philosophically inherent in discussions of ethics are questions of definition, inclusion/exclusion, history and relativity. As such, the most recent AAA Task Force for Comprehensive Ethics Review was certainly not a new endeavor—the AAA has grappled with providing a solid statement on working with complex, nuanced ethical issues in our field since the early part of the twentieth century. Foundational to these discussions is the principle of *Do No Harm*, as in "Anthropologists should avoid doing harm to the individuals, communities or environments they study or that may be impacted by their work." Do no harm. Those three small words are central to all "code of ethics" documents, regardless of discipline, but what do they actually mean in a lived, working practice of anthropology? In this chapter I share my thoughts on the *Do No Harm* principle, which I reviewed during the Task Force project (2009-2011), and discuss aspects of the process I found particularly useful and which brought us to the most recent version of the AAA PPR, the subject of this volume.

How I Came to be Involved with the Task Force

I am a biological anthropologist specializing in field primatology, yet I consider myself first and foremost an *anthropologist*. My professional self-identity is in large part due to holistic undergraduate and graduate training, and also reflects my commitment to an anthropology that employs integrative methodologies and theory to help transect traditional boundaries. While in graduate school, I served as editor of the *Kroeber Anthropological Society Papers*, the oldest graduate student-run anthropology journal in the country, and was guest editor of *Behind Many Masks: Gerald Berreman and Berkeley Anthropology, 1959-2001* (MacKinnon 2003). Such experiences were formative, and the diverse interests of faculty and students during that time sparked a long-standing interest in anthropological ethics. In terms of my own practice, I conduct fieldwork in Central and South America, and more recently Zambia, and since receiving my Ph.D. in 2002 I have held a faculty position at the second-oldest Jesuit research university in the country, Saint Louis University.

As an active member in the AAA I feel strongly that we need continued representation from all subfields of anthropology. I have served on various AAA committees throughout the years, and as my particular stripe of anthropology tends towards the biological (as well as the general), I held the Biological Anthropology Seat for the Committee on Ethics (2005–2008), I chaired the Committee on Ethics (2007–2008), and was also Contributing Editor of the "Ethical Currents" column for *Anthropology News* (2007–2008). I also served as Program Chair of the Biological Anthropology Section (2012–2014), and was a member of the Task Force for Comprehensive Ethics Review (2008–2012), charged with overhauling the AAA Code of Ethics, which led to this volume. Currently, I serve on Friends of the Committee on Ethics (2009–present), a consultative body of the AAA, and I am President-Elect of the Biological Anthropology Section. In terms of a broader impact, the updated AAA document has also informed and influenced the construction of other ethical statements. For example, we recently published *Code of Best Practices for Field Primatology*, a document that was also five years in the making (see Riley et al. 2014; MacKinnon and Riley 2010, 2013), and the 2012 AAA PPR was one of several sources useful in guiding that process. Throughout these activities, I have been constantly reminded of the necessity to continue—and at times, jumpstart—the conversation on the role of ethical guidelines in anthropology, *particularly* for undergraduate and graduate student training (see MacKinnon 2014).

The First Principle: Do No Harm

Physicians and philosophers have been grappling with the *Do No Harm* position for centuries (and see a recent book review in *The New Yorker*, "Anatomy of Error: A Surgeon Recounts His Mistakes" by Joshua Rothman (2015), which critiques a memoir titled *Do No Harm* by the

London neurosurgeon Henry Marsh). Indeed, the original home of *Do No Harm* is medical ethics. Specifically, the idea of nonmaleficence is embodied by the phrase, *primum non nocere* or "first, do no harm." The principle of nonmaleficence, however, is not absolute, and has to be balanced with the corresponding principle of beneficence: doing good. *The Belmont Report: Ethical Principles and Guidelines for the Protection of Human Subjects of Research* (1974) is one of the first "official" places where the *Do No Harm* principle was proposed in order to protect research subjects in the United States; it remains an excellent reference when examining the nuances of the *Do No Harm* principle for any professional organization. Also, the *Declaration of Helsinki* was developed by the World Medical Association (WMA) as a set of ethical principles for the medical community regarding human experimentation, and is widely regarded as the cornerstone document of human research ethics (WMA 2000; Bošnjak and Tutin 2001; Tyebkhan 2003).

For anthropology, the revised code places responsibility for one's actions squarely on the anthropologist; it requires each of us to consider the impacts of our work and its potential to cause harm. The Task Force has been keenly aware that the *Do No Harm* principle is complex and problematic, yet we feel this specific phrase directly and immediately addresses the ethical imperative informing the older "primary responsibility" statement, while also recognizing that anthropologists study all kinds of individuals and institutions, some of whom do not necessarily command our primary allegiance or obligation.

Central questions that framed our thinking as we reviewed the first principle included: What are the ways in which research can cause harm, either tacitly or explicitly? What are important intersections of research projects and the communities they affect, either currently or in the future? How do we, as anthropologists, avoid both immediate and lasting harm to those people, communities, and nonhuman primates with whom we work? What are some unintended consequences and long-term impacts of our work that necessitate careful reflection and consideration of proper guidelines in place? We mulled over previous versions of the code of ethics and discussed what contexts and situations brought about subsequent modifications; we reviewed *Do No Harm* in other disciplines, which helped to highlight the unique position of anthropology in tackling complex and shifting definitions; and we consulted specific examples in order to update the language and pull in relevant case studies that might better resonate with a contemporary anthropological audience (i.e., for the anthropologists that will be using the code as a set of consultative guidelines). We worked diligently to craft a document that best represented the concerns and research of our broad membership.

Useful Activities during the Process

Two of the more useful endeavors we took part in during the multi-year process of updating the Code of Ethics were, first, a productive committee workshop in Taos, New Mexico (in 2011), where we hashed out specific wording—sometimes spending hours on a sentence or phrase—and clarified terminology and concepts and, second, soliciting comments from the AAA membership via an AAA blog. For me, these two undertakings stand out above and beyond the myriad conference calls and committee reports presented at the AAA annual meetings in terms of producing the most valued modifications to the document.

As with previous revisions to the Code, *Do No Harm* generated much emotional investment and many fruitful ideas from the membership in regard to solicited comments on the blog (see the following section: Soliciting Responses). Many of the concerns and comments were extremely useful in our reflections and re-wording of an appropriately contemporary set of "best practices" that could be referred to when undertaking anthropological research in our complicated present.

There is a plethora of case studies going back decades that are relevant for several components of this first principle. When thinking about our re-wording process, I found many of these particularly useful as a set of references against which to situate the first principle, and some of them are especially helpful in illustrating concepts for students. For instance, when thinking about ways that the intended/planned work might cause harm, historical and more contemporary cases can both be examined, such as the Tuskegee Study, 1932–1972 (e.g., Shavers et al. 2000; www.cdc.gov/tuskegee/), the Human Genome Diversity Project and the Genographic Project (e.g., TallBear 2007; and see Marks 1996, 2003), the exploitation of Native American and indigenous blood/genetic samples (e.g., Rasmussen et al. 2011; Reich et al. 2010; Reich et al. 2011), the possible exploitation of student genome samples (e.g., Scheper-Hughes 2010), and ethical problems in the Guatemala STD study (e.g., Lynch 2012). When considering avoidance of direct and immediate harm, *The Belmont Report* serves as a classic example, especially in terms of IRB protocols (e.g., Cassell 2000). When exploring how *Do No Harm* functions in light of a position of advocacy, the Native American Graves and Repatriation Act (NAGPRA) (Bruning 2006; www.nps.gov/nagpra/) is an excellent model for effective policy with meaningful resolutions for the affected parties involving ethical infractions. Similarly, a sustained discussion with those concerned can be illuminated by issues of conflict management (e.g., Castro and Nielsen 2001; Kierney et al. 2007). For exploring unintended consequences and long-term impacts, the role of embedded anthropologists during wartime (e.g., Human Terrain System) provides much needed insight into the complexities of ethical considerations when absolutes are relative and moralities are multiple (Albro et al. 2009; González 2012; Price 2014; www.aaanet.org/pdf/EB_Resolution_110807.pdf). Another set of case studies exists with pharmaceutical companies appropriating indigenous knowledge for profit and gain (Brush 1993; Greene 2004). Finally, in my own subfield of anthropological primatology, a recent piece by Karen Strier (2010) details the often-unforeseen impacts of long-term primatological fieldwork, both for the local human communities and economies, as well as for the animals themselves (also see MacKinnon 2014).

Several recent volumes highlight additional case studies and contexts for discussion of *Do No Harm* (see Caplan 2003; Evens 2008; Faubion 2011; Fluehr-Lobban 2003; Lambek 2010; MacClancy and Fuentes 2011; Ong and Collier 2008; Turner 2004). As just one example, the book *Ethics in the Field: Contemporary Challenges* (MacClancy and Fuentes 2013) provides readers with a rich array of topics from varying sub-disciplines and asks us to reconsider the nature, process, and outcomes of fieldwork. The chapters explore what is common throughout, and distinctive of, the diverse disciplines in anthropology, and a particular aim of the editors is to help develop a "trans-disciplinary" anthropology at the methodological level.

Soliciting Responses from the AAA Membership on The First Principle: Do No Harm

In late 2008 the Task Force was charged with updating the AAA's Code of Ethics, and over a 3-year period (2009-2011), we put the individual principles online and asked for membership feedback; we posted various sections in stages, in the hope that shorter pieces would be easier to digest and would facilitate more thoughtful commentary from AAA members.

The postings appeared in a blog format, and we conducted our conversation with the membership there, not through email. The Task Force specifically examined what was stagnant in the then current 1998 Code of Ethics, and worked to make these concerns more evident/explicit and easier to remember in the form of principles; we also addressed what was missing in the code, and updated sections accordingly. We presented these principles along with other professional ethical statements in order to better contextualize their purpose, reminding readers that the AAA Code of Ethics is but one resource among many that anthropologists should consult to help determine ethical practice. As we posted the principles, individually, to the blog, we asked readers to read each principle carefully, paying attention to the content, and to think about its relevance to their practice. We asked that people make pertinent comments and suggestions on the blog site in a timely manner, and specifically, to share personal stories, examples, and varying interpretations. We advised readers to pay attention to the ongoing conversations about the principles and to do background reading if they came late to a discussion of a particular topic. We also asked the membership to let us know their thoughts about the document as a whole after all the principles had been posted. The membership comments were an important part of the discussion and a critical component of the document re-working process.

We received more than 50 responses on the AAA website and predictably, replies varied considerably. One set felt strongly that Do No Harm is the core principle for our discipline, while others argued it is often too difficult to determine what would actually cause harm, and that the principle should instead read "intend no harm." We decided to stay with the original wording in order to avoid the inherent difficulties of framing ethical principles on intent (i.e., potentially allowing absolution based on purity of motive alone). Some also suggested that Do No Harm doesn't go far enough and that the principle should state that anthropologists' work should directly benefit the communities they study. This framed one of the more nuanced discussions the Task Force had, and we took to heart the many comments noting that if it is hard to know what might actually harm a community or individual(s), it is also difficult to determine what should be done by others on their behalf. In a related vein, some respondents questioned whether the principle is too vague (e.g., in some situations, harm to those benefitting from inequalities might be justified). We considered this very carefully as well, and concluded that the principle as worded still allowed for the intricacies of individual situations to be considered. There were several common themes that circulated, some more than others. For example, many of those commenting brought up *The Belmont Report*, which requires maximizing benefit and minimizing harm. Given that there are difficulties with requiring beneficence as a prerequisite of ethical anthropological research, we recommend researchers consider the following: 1) seek to avoid harm; 2) weigh carefully the potential positive and negative impacts of their work; and 3) recognize that determinations of "best interest" are multiple and value laden, requiring careful consultation with all affected parties. Overall, the blog comments were roughly split between noting that the *Do No Harm* principle requires too much knowledge in terms of the difficulties determining what might actually cause harm (along varying temporal scales as well), and that it requires too little advocacy and beneficence. Finally, as several respondents noted, this principle is intended as a call to consider the complexities of harm, and for anthropologists to accept responsibility for their actions. The devil is in the details, indeed (see the Appendix for the Task Force Committee's response to the membership on the First Principle).

After careful consideration of all the thoughtful points raised by the membership, we kept returning to our central goal of forming a set of principles that anthropologists may generally consider when assessing the ethical dimensions of their work, and can apply to new situations not previously encountered, rather than listing a set of simple cookie-cutter dicta to be followed without reflection. The AAA Ethics Blog, a forum sponsored by the Committee on Ethics, continues, and posts are made by the AAA membership on many topics (e.g., *Encountering Racism While 'Doing No Harm'* on 5 May 2015 http://ethics.aaanet.org/encountering-racism-while-doing-no-harm/).

Summary

Clear answers to ethical questions are not easy to come by, nor should we expect them to be. Complicated anthropological issues require nuanced understandings and interpretations of the events we find ourselves fully enmeshed in, are associated with, or examine from a distance. With valued input from the AAA membership, along with many online discussions, quarterly meetings via conference calls, AAA symposia, a committee workshop, and ongoing re-workings of the language, content, and context over the several years, we arrived at a version of the document we feel best represents—for now—the philosophical position of the AAA and our intellectual discipline. Not everyone will find it useful, not everyone will agree with our updates. Misunderstandings about the role of the Committee on Ethics exist, namely that the committee is an adjudicating body—it is not, and so cannot make a formal judgment or decision about a problem or disputed matter. What is especially important about the *Do No Harm* principle for anthropology? Given that the central, foundational tenet in our discipline involves trying to understand *what makes us human*, this undertaking naturally involves studying people, our ancestries, our biologies, and our cultures, not only in the present but throughout disparate temporal landscapes and also across species. *Do No Harm* means not hurting ourselves and others, and recognizing the complexities inherent in this endeavor requires a reflexive set of guidelines so that we may continue the conversation as we go forward.[1]

Appendix: Task Force Response to Membership Comments on the First Principle Do No Harm, AAA Ethics Blog (February 16, 2011)

Dear All –

Thank you all for your comments/suggestions/feedback. It's clear that responses to this principle vary considerably. One set of comments supports the proposal as the "core principle for our discipline." One set of responses argues that it is hard to determine what would actually cause harm, and that the principle should instead read "intend no harm." While we understand and are sympathetic to this viewpoint, it introduces a number of difficulties, among them the challenge of framing ethical principles based on intent, and potentially allowing purity of motive to absolve anthropologists of responsibility for their actions, however well intentioned. Another set of responses suggests that "do no harm" is inadequate, and instead the principle should require anthropologists to directly benefit the communities they study. Certainly anthropology serving those being studied is worthy, but we are not certain it is an imperative for all ethical anthropological work. In some cases determination of what is in the best interests of an individual or community may be problematic at best, and often more difficult to reasonably gauge than what is likely to cause harm. If we take seriously the concerns of a number of respondents that it is hard to know what may harm a community, it seems at least as likely that it will be as hard or harder to determine what should be done by others on their behalf. There are also venues for ethical anthropological inquiry in which this principle would be difficult to assess, such as many kinds of research not involving living human subjects.

In a related vein, several researchers treat the principle as broadly analogous to IRB guidelines, and suggest using the approach articulated in *The Belmont Report*, which follows "do not harm" with the requirement to maximize benefit while minimizing harm. As noted above, there are several difficulties with requiring beneficence as a prerequisite of ethical anthropological research, and we have instead recommended that anthropologist should: 1) seek to avoid harm; 2) weigh carefully the potential positive and negative impacts of their work; and 3) recognize that determinations of best interest are complex and value laden, requiring careful consultation with all affected parties. Most of the respondents appear to interpret *The Belmont Report* as expecting that research should benefit the individuals being studied, and some respondents stated that only research addressing questions of immediate interest and benefit to communities being studied should be allowed. Research may have a range of benefits at widely varying scales, however, and for many anthropologists the advancement of human knowledge is itself a real and tangible benefit.

Some respondents question whether the principle is too vague, since in some situations harm to those in power or to those benefiting from inequities might be justified. This is a valid concern, and has been discussed by the task force at some length during its deliberations. We believe that the principle as worded allows for the complexity of individual situations to be considered, and for anthropologists to responsibly consider the differential impacts of their work on different individuals or communities. Like many of the principles in this and previous codes, they may have different interpretations or ramifications when applied to individuals or to communities of differing scale. Hence our intent has been less to propose cookie-cutter solutions than to offer core principles which encourage discourse and reflection.

One respondent argued that we must all do harm, and the only question was to whom and why. Rhetoric aside, this view still presumes that there are more and less appropriate actions, and we feel that the logic of this principle, restated in accordance with this philosophical position, still offers meaningful guidance for ethical conduct.

On balance, the comments seem divided between feeling the principle requires too much knowledge in the face of difficulties in knowing what might cause harm, on the one hand, and too little advocacy and beneficence, taking actions on behalf of those studied, on the other.

Finally, as several respondents note, this principle is intended as a call to consider the complexities of harm, and for anthropologists to accept responsibility for their actions. We agree with one respondent that the devil is indeed in the details. We do not imagine these statements to be a series of simple dicta which can be followed without deliberate thought, but instead a set of principles which anthropologists may reasonably consider in assessing the ethical dimensions of their work, and apply to new situations not previously encountered.

We very much appreciate these comments, and consider this an on-going dialogue. Please continue to share your thoughts and perspectives with us over the next several months.

Best –

Task Force

NOTES

1. I would like to thank the members of AAA Task Force for Comprehensive Ethics Review for making the multi-year process of revising the code an intellectually stimulating and enjoyable experience—one that has prompted me to think more deeply about my own practice, my sub-discipline of biological anthropology, and our role as anthropologists writ large. I would particularly like to thank Dena Plemmons and Alex Barker for their tenacity with this book project, and for their patience, humor, and forbearance.

REFERENCES

Albro, Robert, James Peacock, Carolyn Fluehr-Lobban, Kerry Fosher, Laura McNamara, George Marcus, David Price, Laurie Rush, Jean Jackson, Monica Schoch-Spana, and Setha Low
2009   AAA Commission on the Engagement of Anthropology with the US Security and Intelligence Communities (CEAUSSIC): Final Report on The Army's Human Terrain System Proof of Concept Program. www.aaanet.org/cmtes/commissions/CEAUSSIC/upload/CEAUSSIC_HTS_Final_Report.pdf.

Bošnjak, Michael, and Tracy L. Tutin
2001 Classifying Response Behaviors in Web-based Surveys. Journal of Computer-Mediated Communication 6(3) doi: 10.1111/j.1083-6101.2001.tb00124.x.

Bruning, Susan. B.
2006 Complex Legal Legacies: The Native American Graves Protection and Repatriation Act, Scientific Study, and Kennewick Man. American Antiquity 71(3): 501-521.

Brush, Stephen B.
1993 Indigenous Knowledge of Biological Resources and Intellectual Property Rights: The Role of Anthropology. American Anthropologist 95:653–671.

Caplan, Patricia
2003 The Ethics of Anthropology: Debates and Dilemmas. New York: Routledge.

Cassell, Eric J.
2000 The Principles of the Belmont Report Revisited: How Have Respect for Persons, Beneficence, and Justice Been Applied to Clinical Medicine? Hastings Center Report 30(4):12-21.

Castro, Alfonso P. and Erik Nielsen
2001 Indigenous People and Co-management: Implications for Conflict Management. Environmental Science and Policy 4(4-5):229-239.

Evens, Terry M. S.
2008 Anthropology as Ethics: Nondualism and the Conduct of Sacrifice. New York: Berghahn Books.

Faubion, James D.
2011 An Anthropology of Ethics. Cambridge: Cambridge University Press.

Fluehr-Lobban, Carolyn
2003 Ethics and the Profession of Anthropology: Dialogue for Ethically Conscious Practice. 2nd ed. Walnut Creek: Altamira Press.

González, Roberto J.
2012 Anthropology and the Covert: Methodological Notes on Researching Military and Intelligence Programmes. Anthropology Today 28(2):21-25.

Greene, Shane
2004 Indigenous People Incorporated? Culture as Politics, Culture as Property in Pharmaceutical Bioprospecting. Current Anthropology 45(2): 211-237.

Kearney, John, Fikret Berkes, Anthony Charles, Evelyn Pinkerton, and Melanie Wiber
2007 The Role of Participatory Governance and Community-Based Management in Integrated Coastal and Ocean Management in Canada. Coastal Management 35(1):79-104.

Lambek, Michael
2010 Ordinary Ethics: Anthropology, Language, and Action. New York: Fordham University Press.

Lynch, Holly F.
2012 The Rights and Wrongs of Intentional Exposure Research: Contextualising the Guatemala STD Inoculation Study. Journal of Medical Ethics 38:513-515.

MacClancy, Jeremy and Agustín Fuentes, eds.
2013 Ethics in the Field: Contemporary Challenges. Oxford, UK: Berghahn Books.
2011 Centralizing Fieldwork: Critical Perspectives from Primatology, Biological Anthropology and Social Anthropology. Oxford, UK: Berghahn Books.

MacKinnon, Katherine C., guest editor
2003 Behind Many Masks: Gerald Berreman and Berkeley Anthropology, 1959-2001. Special edition of The Kroeber Anthropological Society Papers, vol. 89/90. University of California, Berkeley.

MacKinnon, Katherine C.
2014 Contemporary Biological Anthropology: Integrative, Connected, and Relevant. American Anthropologist 16(2):352-365.

MacKinnon, Katherine C., and Erin P. Riley
2013 Contemporary Ethical Issues in Field Primatology. In Ethics in the Field: Contemporary Challenges. Jeremy MacClancy and Agustín Fuentes, eds. Pp. 98-107. Oxford: Berghahn.
2010 Field Primatology of Today: Current Ethical Issues. American Journal of Primatology 72(9):749-753.

Marks, Jonathan
2003 What It Means to Be 98% Chimpanzee: Apes, People, and Their Genes. Berkeley: University of California Press.
1996 I'm Not Against the HGDP. Honest. Anthropology News 37(4):2-5.

Ong, Aihwa, and Stephen J. Collier, eds.
2008 Global Assemblages: Technology, Politics, and Ethics as Anthropological Problems. New York: John Wiley & Sons.

Price, David H.
2014 Counterinsurgency by Other Names: Complicating Humanitarian Applied Anthropology in Current, Former, and Future War Zones. Human Organization 73(2):95-105.

Rasmussen, Morten et al.
2011 An Aboriginal Australian Genome Reveals Separate Human Dispersals into Asia. *Nature* 334(6052):94-98.

Reich, David, Richard E. Green, Martin Kircher, Johannes Krause, Nick Patterson, Eric Y. Durand, Bence Viola, Adrian W. Briggs, Udo Stenzel, Philip L. F. Johnson, Tomislav Maricic, Jeffrey M. Good, Tomas Marques-Bonet, Can Alkan, Qiaomei Fu, Swapan Mallick, Heng Li, Matthias Meyer, Evan E. Eichler, Mark Stoneking, Michael Richards, Sahra Talamo, Michael V. Shunkov, Anatoli P. Derevianko, Jean-Jacques Hublin, Janet Kelso, Montgomery Slatkin, and Svante Pääbo
2010   Genetic History of an Archaic Hominin Group From Denisova Cave in Siberia. Nature 468:1053-1060.

Reich, David, Nick Patterson, Martin Kircher, Frederick Delfin, Madhusudan R. Nandineni, Irina Pugach, Albert Min-Shan Ko, Ying-Chin Ko, Timothy A. Jinam, Maude E. Phipps, Naruya Saitou, Andreas Wollstein, Manfred Kayser, Svante Pääbo, and Mark Stoneking
2011   Denisova Admixture and the First Modern Human Dispersals into Southeast Asia and Oceania. American Journal of Human Genetics 89(4):516-528.

Riley, Erin P.
2013   Contemporary Primatology in Anthropology: Beyond the Epistemological Abyss. American Anthropologist 115(3):411–422.

Riley, Erin P., Katherine C. MacKinnon, Eduardo Fernandez-Duque, Joanna M. Setchell, and Paul A. Garber
2014   Code of Best Practices for Field Primatology. Document hosted on the websites of the International Primatological Society and the American Society of Primatologists. www.asp.org/resources/docs/Code%20of_Best_Practices%20Oct%202014.pdf.

Rothman, Joshua
2015   Anatomy of Error: A Surgeon Remembers His Mistakes. The New Yorker Magazine, May 18th. www.newyorker.com/magazine/2015/05/18/anatomy-of-error, accessed May 24, 2015.

Scheper-Hughes, Nancy
2010   The Poisoned Gift: 'Fortune Cookie' Genomics at UC Berkeley. Anthropology Today 26(6):1-3.

Shavers, Vickie L., Charles F. Lynch, and Leon F. Burmeister
2000   Knowledge of the Tuskegee Study and its Impact on the Willingness to Participate in Medical Research Studies. Journal of the National Medical Association 92(12):563–572.

Strier, Karen B.
2010   Long-term Field Studies: Positive Impacts and Unintended Consequences. American Journal of Primatology 72:772–778.

TallBear, Kim
2007   Narratives of Race and Indigeneity in the Genographic Project. The Journal of Law, Medicine & Ethics 35(3):412-424.

Turner, Trudy, ed.
2004 Biological Anthropology and Ethics: From Repatriation to Genetic Identity. New York: State University of New York Press.

Tyebkhan, G.
2003 Declaration of Helsinki: The Ethical Cornerstone of Human Clinical Research. Research Methodology 69(3):245-247.

World Medical Association
2000 WMA Declaration of Helsinki—Ethical Principles for Medical Research Involving Human Subjects. www.wma.net/en/30publications/10policies/b3/, accessed on May 24, 2015.

SOURCES RELATING TO THE AAA'S TASK FORCE FOR COMPREHENSIVE ETHICS REVIEW

2012 Preamble. http://ethics.aaanet.org/ethics-statement-0-preamble/.

2012 Do No Harm. http://ethics.aaanet.org/ethics-statement-1-do-no-harm/.

2012 Executive Board Resolution. www.aaanet.org/pdf/EB_Resolution_110807.pdf.

Task Force for Comprehensive Ethics Review, American Anthropological Association. www.aaanet.org/cmtes/ethics/Proposed-Revised-Code-of-Ethics-for-Public-Review.cfm.

Friends of the Committee on Ethics, consultative body of the American Anthropological Association.

http://aaanet.org/cmtes/ethics/Friends-of-the-Committee-on-Ethics.cfm.

NIH Office of Human Subjects Research: The Belmont Report Ethical Principles and Guidelines for the protection of human subjects of research. http://ohsr.od.nih.gov/guidelines/belmont.html.

CHAPTER FIVE

Be Open and Honest Regarding Your Work

David H. Price

Anthropologists should be clear and open regarding the purpose, methods, outcomes, and sponsors of their work. Anthropologists must also be prepared to acknowledge and disclose to participants and collaborators all tangible and intangible interests that have, or may reasonably be perceived to have, an impact on their work. Transparency, like informed consent, is a process that involves both making principled decisions prior to beginning the research and encouraging participation, engagement, and open debate throughout its course.[1]

Researchers who mislead participants about the nature of the research and/or its sponsors; who omit significant information that might bear on a participant's decision to engage in the research; or who otherwise engage in clandestine or secretive research that manipulates or deceives research participants about the sponsorship, purpose, goals or implications of the research, do not satisfy ethical requirements for openness, honesty, transparency and fully informed consent. Compartmented research by design will not allow the anthropologist to know the full scope or purpose of a project; it is therefore ethically problematic, since by definition the anthropologist cannot communicate transparently with participants, nor ensure fully informed consent.

Anthropologists have an ethical obligation to consider the potential impact of both their research and the communication or dissemination of the results of their research. Anthropologists must consider this issue prior to beginning research as well as throughout the research process. Explicit negotiation with research partners and participants about data ownership and access and about dissemination of results may be necessary before deciding whether to begin research.

In their capacity as researchers, anthropologists are subject to the ethical principles guiding all scientific and scholarly conduct. They must not plagiarize, nor fabricate or falsify evidence, or knowingly misrepresent information or its source. However, there are situations in which evidence or information may be minimally modified (such as by the use of pseudonyms) or generalized, in order to avoid identification of the source and to protect confidentiality and limit exposure of people to risks.

On Being Open and Honest Anthropologists

"Secrecy is the enemy of science." —*Laura Nader (1996:267)*

This ethical principle stresses that as anthropologists, we need to tell those we encounter who we are, what we are doing, who funds us and why, and what we can reasonably expect to be done with our work. It also reminds anthropologists that regardless of how tempting it might be to conduct covert research, we should not do it. This principle declares we should be honest and forthright in our interactions with colleagues and the public. There are some significant differences between covert or clandestine research (in which researchers intentionally and programmatically fail to identify themselves as researchers making observations) and forms of proprietary research or other research that do not make the results of research available in public forms. Yet, to the extent to which these practices reduce or eliminate transparency and openness with research participants, they raise significant ethical issues.

The goal of being open and honest about research is obviously desirable, but the more one considers it, the more complicated it can become. While egregious examples of clandestine or covert research or misrepresentations of intended uses clarify the need for such standards, it is the more mundane instances of withholding certain information from research participants that mark just how complicated such an apparently straight-forward principle can become in application.

The ethical principle of being open and honest has significant overlap with principles of requiring informed consent and necessary permissions and stressing the importance of making results accessible. These principles share common themes of transparency and disclosure—who is undertaking the research, why they are doing it, who might use this research, and the anticipated products of this work.

Being open and honest about the purpose, methods, and sponsors of work might limit anthropologists' access to others with whom anthropologists work and study. But the purpose of ethical principles is not to make it easier to conduct research; inevitably ethical research complicates research methodologies, and arguably often reduces the reliability or validity of the data we collect. Instead, establishing and engaging in ethical research practices recognizes that the well-being, and informed voluntary participation of others in research has a greater value than whatever confounds (complicating research validity and reliability) may emerge as a result of these measures.

The principle of being open and honest articulates with all subfields of anthropology. The importance of openness, disclosure, and issues linked to future uses of collected data for biological anthropologists can be seen in the disputes arising with native peoples resisting efforts to have their DNA collected and analyzed by global projects seeking to catalog DNA (Harmon 2006), the fate of Henrietta Lacks' cells (Skloot 2010), or the disputes arising after the Havasupai Indian Tribe allowed geneticists from Arizona State University to use blood samples for diabetes research, only to later learn that these materials were being used for research projects for which tribal members had not consented (Marks 2010; see also Chapter 6).

Because the desires for naturalist observations are strong, cultural anthropologists routinely face the attractions of engaging in covert research, and at times have difficulties being forthright in sharing the nature of their research with participant populations. As applied anthropologists increasingly study consumer behaviors and undertake ethnographic studies, they sometimes face workplace conditions with differing standards of disclosure (notifying all participants that they are in fact research participants) from those generally found in purely academic settings (Barnes 2009; Wood 2013).

Linguists are acutely aware of the intervening relations of power and of the ways that speakers may alter their speech patterns when they are aware they being studied, and they use a number of techniques to try and mitigate these methodological issues in ethical ways. Linguistic anthropologists wishing to observe naturalistic interactions are at times drawn to conducting covert research, but such planned research practices can violate principles of openness and honesty.

Archaeologists also face delicate disclosure issues. Archaeologists' scientific reporting is often limited by needs to protect the precise locations of sites that could otherwise lead to the loss of valuable cultural materials. For archaeologists, this specific principle might mean that archaeologists working on cultural resources management contracts need to establish and maintain open relationships with descendant communities, regardless of whatever difficulties such relationships might entail. Archaeologists can face conflicting roles, responsibilities, or allegiances as they find themselves working *with* landowners or other groups with vested interests in the outcome of their work, while working *for* other interest groups. Sometimes this creates the need to compartmentalize specific pieces of knowledge, while in other instances archaeologists may need to protect broader knowledge (e.g., proprietary knowledge relating to a planned construction or development project) unrelated to archaeological artifacts. Archaeologists' openness at times may be constricted by who does and who does not have access to their reports. In instances where native communities review and play an approval role for proposed projects, archaeologists may be tempted to over-represent the possible benefits coming from a proposed project, or likewise, to downplay potential controversies embedded in this work. The principle's focus on being open and honest admonishes archaeologists and other anthropologists to do their utmost to make such claims as truthfully as possible, despite the negative consequences for such disclosures.[1]

Cultural anthropology's approach to duplicity marks disciplinary differences with psychology and sociology, whose more experimental orientation at times allows for minor deceptions designed to mitigate changes in natural behavior that may arise when research participants are cognizant of the true nature of a given study. While not denying these differences in disciplinary orientations, many anthropologists sometimes find themselves limiting the sort of analysis they share with the populations they study; at times this occurs because the theoretical questions being explored might appear bizarre to these populations, while at other times, the complete sharing of research questions could interfere with their work in ways similar to the fields of psychology or sociology. Yet, even with such complicating factors, anthropologists generally embrace the ethical principle of being open and honest about the work they are doing.

Secrecy

Secrecy has a dualistic presence in anthropological research. Anthropologists routinely use forms of secrecy to protect cultural information—whether deploying pseudonyms to disguise individuals or communities appearing in ethnographic research, or cloaking the location of archaeological research to protect against looting—and secrecy is used by ethnographers or their employers (either in forms of covert research or in producing inaccessible reports of the type criticized in the later section in this chapter entitled "Clandestine or Secretive Research") in ways that can threaten harm to research participants (see Redden 2007).

The specific nature of individual anthropologists' understanding of their ethical responsibility and loyalties to studied populations is in part revealed in the forms of secrecy they use. During the early twentieth century anthropologists developed traditions of using forms of secrecy such as pseudonyms to hide the identities of individuals and locations of ethnographic research. The use of pseudonyms evolved to protect the privacy and interests of studied populations, effectively shielding those studied from the outside world.

The concept of "secrecy" in anthropological research is complicated, and some uses of secrecy to protect research participants' identities has long been accepted as a requirement of ethical research, while issuing secret reports that participants cannot possibly access raises an ethical red flag. There is no single type of secrecy, and distinctions between secrecy, pseudonyms, proprietary and embargoed research can help identify important ethical issues. Anthropologists' use of secrecy to protect informants is rooted in the field's tradition of protecting the disenfranchised groups that anthropologists have traditionally studied. The AAA's original 1971 Principles of Professional Responsibility (PPR), as in other iterations of the AAA's Code of Ethics, advocated for the use of such ethnographic pseudonyms. This tradition of using discretion and pseudonyms to protect the research participants has become a standard of anthropological practice. Some anthropologists have at times confused the ethical requirements of using secrecy to protect individuals and groups studied with using secrecy to protect *employers*. But the application of secrecy in that instance is not rooted within the traditional ethical reasons that anthropologists use pseudonyms or other forms of secrecy.

Other forms of secrecy employed by anthropologists can raise different ethical issues; these primarily involve proprietary reports (reports written for employers that do not publicly circulate), embargoed reports (non-circulating reports that will be released at later dates), or secret reports (reports written for employers that by design cannot be accessed by studied populations). Behaviorally, there are not significant differences between proprietary and secret reports, but proprietary reports are most generally written for private sponsors, and secret reports are written for governmental or private agencies; proprietary reports are generally kept secret to protect information valued by a private business. While the reasons for producing these non-circulating reports varies, the inability of studied populations to possibly access these reports raises similar ethical issues linked to lack of transparency.

Anthropologists who publish results in academic journals or make their results available in other outlets are in keeping with the principle of being open and honest, yet some argue that difficulties for remote populations to access research hidden behind peer review journals' pay-walls diminish claims of accessible results. While these barriers are real, there is a fundamental difference between these secondary difficulties in accessing reports, and barriers of secret, embargoed, or proprietary reports, which are from the outset designed to be inaccessible by studied populations.

The 1971 PPR explicitly stated that "no reports should be provided to sponsors that are not also available to the general public and, where practicable, to the population studied" (AAA 1971 PPR 1.g), but this language was removed in the Code revisions of 1990, and as post-9/11 concerns about anthropologists contributing secretive reports to military and intelligence agencies arose, language was added to the Code and the new PPR, stating that "anthropologists should not withhold research results from research participants, especially when those results are shared with others" (see the later section entitled "Clandestine or Secretive Research") (see Glenn 2007).

While the use of pseudonyms is generally recommended to protect the privacy of individuals and groups, anthropologists also need to be aware that those we write about must have access to our writings, and thus may be able to identify themselves and others mentioned in our writings regardless of whatever measures are taken to camouflage identities.

On Considering Impacts of Anthropological Writing

The PPR urges anthropologists to consider the potential impacts of conducting research and of publishing or otherwise disseminating the result of their work; anthropologists are urged to consider these outcomes at all stages of planning and implementing research.

Sometimes the lines separating academic publications from reports of applied contract work and cultural appropriation are blurry, and in a world where everything is at risk of commodification, anthropologists need to negotiate appropriate uses of the information they gather from those who share their lives with them. Whether recording stories, musical performances, linguistic utterances, genealogies, or any other cultural information, anthropologists need to discuss plans for dissemination early in the research process.

At all stages of research and planning, anthropologists need to consider how research and reports resulting from this work could impact research participants and communities, and in some instances anthropologists may choose to not disseminate information should they become aware that the results of their work could have detrimental impacts on participants.

Anthropologists sometimes conflate the differences between secrecy and privacy, or have at times failed to adequately consider how decisions to not publish research are distinct from secret research. In describing political problems faced by those engaging in interracial marriage in New Guinea in the 1970s, Cyril Belshaw defensively recounted his decision to withhold from publication the ethnographic details of one such marriage, writing that, "no purpose would have been served, and much damage would have been done to the two individuals, whose private lives were at stake, by the publication of the details of my research. If any professional body had then informed me that by doing this I was *unprofessionally* engaging in clandestine research of a confidential nature and keeping the results secret, I would have told them to mind their own business" (Belshaw 1976:284). But Belshaw's argument falsely assumed researchers are ethically obligated to share all findings. Past and present versions of the AAA's PPR clarify that decisions to not report findings anchored in a desire to not harm research participants are in accordance with good ethical practice. Additionally, the processes of cherry-picking which results are to be shared or withheld, even when undertaken to protect research participants in ways normally understood to fall within the standards of ethical obligations, raises other ethical concerns linked to the ways that limited data can skew research results.

Compartmented Research

The new PPR's most significant addition was the inclusion of language articulating the inherent dangers of compartmented research. This addition argues that "compartmented research by design will not allow the anthropologist to know the full scope or purpose of a project; it is therefore ethically problematic, since by definition the anthropologists cannot communicate transparently with participants, nor ensure fully informed consent."[2] This new language cautions anthropologists against working on projects in which they do not clearly understand what, in the present and foreseeable future contexts, will be done with the data they collect, and stresses that because voluntary informed consent cannot be given for unspecified uses of data, anthropologists should disengage from research projects increasing such potential vulnerabilities. Just as research participants need to be aware of what will be done with the results of research, anthropologists need to understand what will become of the fruits of their research.

Obviously anthropologists cannot be expected to know all possible applications or uses of the data they gather, but this language clarifies the responsibility of all researchers to inquire of sponsors and others with oversight responsibilities about "the full scope or purpose of a project" before beginning work on a project. Compartmented research raises issues of concern for researchers (who may have only limited knowledge of to what uses their work will be put), sponsors (who may have knowledge of research applications not available to researchers), and research subjects (who may have limited understanding of the scope of a research project), and it highlights the importance for anthropologists of making sponsors aware of the ethical guidelines under which their research will be conducted.

Recognizing the potential dangers of compartmented research magnifies the importance of maintaining control over research data. While it is obvious that people cannot give consent for unarticulated uses of data collected about them, it is less clear what ethical guidelines limit the later use of data. Some re-uses of data appear to clearly be problematic; examples include instances where populations were told data would be collected for one specific use, but it was later used by these researchers for other purposes (e.g., the Havasupai case as described by Marks 2010). But what are the ethical limitations for scholars who, at some future date, for new previously unforeseen ends, repurpose published or archived data that were gathered by other anthropologists engaging in proper disclosure and achieving voluntary informed consent? There are largely unexamined ethical questions for consumers purchasing services, whose data may have been procured with an unclear provenance of disclosure—questions that are raised by a host of new commercial DNA mapping services drawing on biological samples collected from peoples around the world who were never notified of any possible subsequent uses.[3]

Historically, there have been several notable instances in which anthropological research was commissioned by sponsors, in intentionally compartmentalized ways that hid the eventual uses of this work from the unwitting anthropologists working on these projects. In these instances these anthropologists would not have approved of the uses to which their work was later put. The most egregious of these examples might be the intelligence racket exposed by anthropologist Delmos Jones in Thailand in the late 1960s, where anthropologists and other social scientists were funded to come and do village studies in northern Thailand on subjects of their individual choosing, while unbeknownst to them a military-intelligence research consortium read and used their reports to develop insurgency and counterinsurgency operations in the region (see Jones 1971, 1976; Price 2011). Other instances include anthropological research funded by the Human Ecology Fund, which unbeknownst to them was a CIA funding front, run out of Cornell Medical School. The Human Ecology Fund sponsored social scientists working on a range of projects looking at things like the cultural mitigation of stress or physical anthropologists developing typologies for reading body language, projects that were later revealed to be articulated (in ways unknown to the individual participants) with research leading to the production of the CIA's 1963 *Kubark Counterintelligence Interrogation manual*. Yet in these examples it was impossible or extremely difficult for these researchers to know who was actually funding their work or to what uses their work would be put (Price 2007).

While the PPR's new language cautioning anthropologists about their involvement in. compartmented research projects in which they do not know the full scope or use of their contributions is an important recognition of the dangers of such relationships, it seems unlikely that most anthropologists would be aware of the sort of nefarious projects described in the preceding paragraph, and in the more common settings in which anthropologists gather data on populations, few contract anthropologists have enough agency to meaningfully understand to what uses this data might later be put by their employers. The PPR's new language on compartmentalized research recognizes the necessity of understanding the possible future applications of our research if we are to obtain meaningful voluntary informed consent, yet anthropologists working on large projects designed by others do not always have the opportunity to realize this basic requisite condition of ethical research.

Other Approaches to Disclosure, Secrecy, Deception, and Power

The PPR does not address the possibility of differing forms of disclosure on the basis of power relations, though such shifting standards are advocated or practiced by some anthropologists. Laura Nader argues that many ethnographers come to understand there is something like "a sliding scale of openness" adopted by anthropologists committed to not betraying the confidences shared by those with little power. Nader asks,

> [W]hat anthropologist is going to "write all" in an ambiance of exploitation, one in which they would be viewed as hired guns? My own field notes, work supported by a Mexican government grant, are replete with information on indigenous knowledge that is exploitable. I never published this material, and have destroyed data that might give leads to exploitation by multinational pharmaceuticals." (Nader 1999)[4]

As PPR Principle 4 states, anthropologists engage in relationships that "create conflicting, competing or crosscutting ethical obligations" that are themselves marked by "asymmetries of power implicit in a range of relationships," and while the PPR provides an ethical framework for considering these issues, it does not divine solutions for the *political* issues raised by these situations.

Because anthropologists traditionally first used protective forms of secrecy, such as pseudonyms, to shield the relatively poor and powerless peoples they studied, some anthropologists have questioned whether these same forms of protective secrecy should be used to protect rich and powerful individuals or organizations studied by anthropologists. While the AAA's 2012 PPR approaches issues of clandestine research and pseudonyms from a uniform perspective that does not differentiate on the basis of positions of power, counter arguments for other approaches remain active in the discipline.

Some scholars, like Nancy Scheper-Hughes (2004), advocate some forms of secret and covert research. Scheper-Hughes' research into organ trafficking relied on covert ethnographic methods and used elements of deception. She argued that "all the normal rules of fieldwork practice and ethics seemed inadequate" as she traveled "incognito" gathering information on illegal activities in the international trafficking of human organs (2004:41).[5] Richard Mitchell argued that claims of instances of harm from secret *ethnographic* research are greatly exaggerated, in part by conflating the horrible occurrences in medical research, such as the Tuskegee syphilis experiment, and laboratory-based social psychological experiments, with naturalistic field research. Mitchell maintained that conducting observational fieldwork in a non-contrived setting does not raise the same ethical concerns, nor does it necessarily require voluntary informed consent (Mitchell 1993:24-28). Mitchell argued that *power relations* should mitigate prohibitions against covert research and other forms of secrecy in research. Mitchell wrote that,

> Anatole France observed that the law, in all its neutral majesty, prevents both the rich and poor alike from sleeping under bridges at night. And we are reminded...that codes serve similarly to protect the powerful and the weak from being studied without their explicit permission. There are radical, or "strong," and nominal, or "weak,"readings of this position." (Mitchell 1993:29)

While Mitchell and Scheper-Hughes make strong arguments for secret or covert research, such activities remain highly problematized in the PPR.

Some anthropologists argue that the power relations between anthropologists, the institutions and sponsors for whom they work, and the peoples and nations studied, impact the ethical framework used to evaluate the appropriate uses of anthropological knowledge. Many anthropologists follow Laura Nader's position holding that when anthropologists consider issues of power and transparency, the "weaker parties must have the upper hand" (see Nader 1999), though such a position is not itself embedded within the PPR or other codes. Thirty years ago, sociologist John Galliher proposed that the American Sociological Association code be revised to withhold some of the expectations of privacy or anonymity from U.S. governmental employees, stipulating that "when actors become involved in government and business or other organizations where they are accountable to the public, no right of privacy applies to conduct in such roles" and to clarify that "the revelation of wrongdoing in positions of public trust shall not be deemed 'confidential information' within the meaning of this rule" (Galliher 1982:162). While this approach has attractions for individuals working within their own culture, where public officials do not have the same standards of privacy, and studying their public statements or deeds does not require voluntary informed consent, when crossing cultural boundaries, as anthropologists often do, such calls for relativistic considerations of ethics depending on one's position of power raise many difficulties.

While the PPR acknowledges that "anthropologists must be sensitive to the power differentials" of all relationships, it also specifies that "while moral, political, legal and regulatory issues are often important to anthropological practice and the discipline, they are not specifically considered here. These principles address ethical concerns." The PPR does not argue that moral, political, legal, and regulatory issues are not important, or that they need not be addressed by anthropologists—only that these issues are of another dimension than those addressed by the PPR. There may be instances where the sort of power differentials identified by Nader and others influence anthropologists' decisions on how to interpret the PPR.

Clandestine or Secretive Research

Despite the clear ethical problems associated with covert ethnographic research, the attractions of clandestine or secretive research are obvious: naturalistic observations of human behaviors and interactions often appear to have greater value than those mitigated by awareness of observation. There are several recent instances of both applied and university-based academic anthropologists undertaking research projects in which they did not adequately disclose their identities as researchers to all with whom they came into contact.

One of the more public examples of this is documented in Cathy Small's (published under the penname Rebekah Nathan) 2005 book, *My Freshman Year: What a Professor Learned by Becoming a Student*. In critiquing Small's use of a pseudonym to protect her own identity, anthropologist Robert Lawless argued that "anthropologists often try to protect the privacy of their informants by granting anonymity to them and their location. The use of such secrecy for anthropologists themselves is much, much less frequent, and the use of deceit in interactions with informants is greatly frowned upon within the discipline" (Lawless 2005). A similar recent inversion of the use of pseudonyms to protect researchers rather than protecting studied populations (populations unable to provide voluntary consent) was the insistence of Human Terrain Team "social scientists" appearing in international news stories that they be identified only by pseudonyms. One of these pseudonymized ethnographers, a West Point trained anthropologist identified in news reports only as "Tracy," described herself as a "high-risk ethnographer"—without clarifying to whom this "high risk" applies: herself or those she studies (see Gezari 2013).

The rise of consumer anthropological research brings shifting standards with marketers measuring public and private behaviors, and increasing pressures to observe naturalistic consumer behaviors that can weaken standards of ethical practice (see Wood 2013). Because many of those working in market research come from disciplines outside of anthropology, the industry has different normative standards of disclosure, standards that can at times come into conflict with professional ethical statements like the AAA's PPR, or the Society for Applied Anthropology's Statement of Ethics and Professional Responsibilities. But the PPR and other documents expressing anthropology's ethical research standards can be used to empower anthropologists seeking to improve the disclosure and openness standards of the projects on which they work. Anthropologists who work on projects with research protocols that ignore principles of openness and honesty can use the PPR to initiate discussions with employers, explaining the importance of maintaining professional standards of ethical practice, and to negotiate ethically appropriate ways of carrying out the needed research while meeting the basic ethical standards of the discipline (see Chapter 8).

The power relations influencing relationships between researchers, sponsors, and research participants must be clearly identified and considered before the ethically appropriate uses of secrecy can be properly understood. While the demands of sponsors and employers can impact the lives and attitudes of researchers, they should not shape anthropologists' ethical decision-making processes.

Even with strong arguments against secrecy and duplicity, the desires to conduct secret and covert research remain strong in the social sciences for reasons methodological, political, and of convenience. Nevertheless, we hope that, even with such temptations, the principles expressed in the PPR and the personal engagements of anthropologists interacting with research participants can help cement commitments to engage in open and honest research in ways that do not privilege knowledge gathering over human relations.

As one of the AAA's most vocal mid-twentieth century advocates for conducting open and honest research, Gerald Berreman argued that,

> There is no scholarly activity any of us can do better in secret than in public. There is none we can pursue as well, in fact, because of the implicit but inevitable restraints secrecy places on scholarship. To do research in secret, or to report it in secret, is to invite suspicion, and legitimately so because secrecy is the hallmark of intrigue, not scholarship." (Berreman 1982:66)

NOTES

1. Special thanks to Alec Barker, Monica Heller, and Jonathan Marks for sharing their views on how this principle applies to biological and linguistic anthropology and archaeology.

2. Perhaps the most significant removal from the code was the previous PPR and Code of Ethics' declaration that "anthropological researchers have primary ethical obligations to the people, species, and materials they study and to the people with whom they work" (1998 AAA CoE).
3. Personal communication, Jonathan Marks to author, January 15, 2014.
4. Yet, the destruction of data can raise other issues. For example, the destruction of such notes could eliminate records that might, at some future date, support claims by local groups in intellectual property lawsuits. Nader's argument is that such protections should not be afforded to the powerful, thus extending the following argument: "On the other hand, if I want data on the location of toxic dumps in the United States and on disease clusters based on information gathered through tax moneys, I expect to get it. It is a sliding scale of openness. Weaker parties must have the upper hand as in the transnational genetic diversity studies amongst indigenous peoples" (Nader 1999).
5. Nancy Scheper-Hughes received clearance from her university for this research after she by-passed the University of California's Human Subject Protection Committee and instead cast this work as that of a "human rights investigative reporter" and gained the clearance of colleagues in the School of Journalism (2004:44-45). While such forms of "IRB-shopping" can solve institutional problems of gaining research clearance, they do not resolve the fundamental ethical problems associated with covert research.

REFERENCES

Barnes, Brooks
2009   Disney Expert Uses Science to Draw Boy Viewers. New York Times, April 14: A1, 10.

Belshaw, Cyril S.
1976   The Sorcerer's Apprentice: An Anthropology of Public Policy. New York: Pergamon.

Berreman, Gerald
1982   The Politics of Truth: Essays in Critical Anthropology. Atlantic Highlands, NJ: Humanities Press.

Galliher, John F.
1981[1973] The Protection of Human Subjects: A Re-examination of the Professional Code of Ethics. *In* Social Research Ethics: An Examination of the Merits of Covert Participant Observation. Martin Bulmer ed. Pp. 152-165. New York: Holmes & Meier.

Gezari, Vanessa
2013 When the Eggheads Went to War. Newsweek, August 16. http://mag.newsweek.com/2013/08/16/the-human-terrain-system-sought-to-transform-the-army-from-within.html, accessed February 14, 2014.

Glenn, David
2007 Anthropologists Vote to Clamp Down on Secret Scholarship. Chronicle of Higher Education (News Blog), December 1. http://chronicle.com/news/article/3532/anthropologists-vote-to-clamp-down-on-secret-scholarship, accessed February 14, 2014.

Harmon, Amy
2006 DNA Gatherers Hit Snag: Tribes Don't Trust Them. New York Times, December 10.

Jones, Delmos
1976 Applied Anthropology and the Application of Human Knowledge. Human Organization 35:221-229.
1971 Social Responsibility and the Belief in Basic Research: An Example from Thailand. Current Anthropology 12 (3):347-350.

Lawless, Robert
2005 Book Review of Rebekah Nathan's My Freshman Year: What a Professor Learned by Becoming a Student. Anthropology Review Database, December 19. http://wings.buffalo.edu/ARD/cgi/showme.cgi?keycode=2810, accessed January 13, 2014.

Marks, Jonathan
2010 Science, Samples and People. Anthropology Today 26(3):3-4.

Mitchell, Richard G., Jr.
1993 Secrecy and Fieldwork. Qualitative Research Methods, vol 29. Newbury Park: Sage.

Nader, Laura, ed.
1999 Secrecy in Science: Exploring University, Industry and Government Relationships. Paper delivered the AAAS Conference on Secrecy in Science: Exploring University, Industry and Government Relationships, Cambridge, MA. March 29. www.aaas.org/spp/secrecy/Presents/nader.htm, accessed September 15, 2013.
1996 Naked Science: Anthropological Inquiry into Boundaries, Power and Knowledge. New York: Routledge.

Nathan, Rebekah
2013 Anthropology Inc. The Atlantic, March, 2013. www.theatlantic.com/magazine/archive/2013/03/anthropology-inc/309218, accessed May 22, 2013.
2005 My Freshman Year: What a Professor Learned by Becoming a Student. New York: Penguin.

Price, David
2011 Counterinsurgency, Vietnam, Thailand, and the Political Uses of Militarized Anthropology. *In* Dangerous Liaisons: Anthropologists and the National Security State. Laura A. McNamara and Robert Rubinstein, eds. Pp. 51-76. Santa Fe: School for Advanced Research Press.
2007 Buying a Piece of Anthropology, Parts One and Two. Anthropology Today 23(3):8-13; 23(5):17-22.

Redden, Elizabeth
2007 Secrecy and Anthropology. Inside Higher Ed, December 3. www.insidehighered.com/news/2007/12/03/anthro, accessed September 15, 2013.

Scheper-Hughes, Nancy
2004 Parts Unknown: Undercover Ethnography of the Organs-trafficking Underworld. Ethnography 5(1):29-73.

Skloot, Rebecca
2010 The Immortal Life of Henrietta Lacks. New York: Broadway Books.

Wood, Graeme
2013 Anthropology Inc. The Atlantic, March. www.theatlantic.com/magazine/archive/2013/03/anthropology-inc/309218, accessed May 22, 2013.

CHAPTER SIX

Make Your Results Accessible

Alex W. Barker

Results of anthropological research should be disseminated in a timely fashion. It is important to bear in mind that these results may not be clear cut, and may be subject to multiple interpretations, as well as susceptible to differing and unintended uses. In some situations, limitations on dissemination may be appropriate where such restrictions will protect participants or their cultural heritage and/or tangible or intangible cultural or intellectual property. In some cases, dissemination may pose significant risks because once information is disseminated, even in a limited sphere, there is great likelihood that it will become widely available. Thus, preventing dissemination may sometimes be the most ethical decision. Dissemination and sharing of research data should not be at the expense of protecting confidentiality.

Anthropologists should not withhold research results from research participants, especially when those results are shared with others. However, restrictions on disclosure may be appropriate and ethical, such as where study participants have been fully informed and have freely agreed to limited dissemination, or where restrictions have been placed on dissemination to protect the safety, dignity, or privacy of research participants or to minimize risk to researchers. Proprietary, classified or other research with limited distribution raises ethical questions which must be resolved using these ethical principles.

As a general rule the results of anthropological research or projects should be disseminated in a timely fashion, and should not be withheld from research participants if they are shared with other communities of interest. Most of us would agree that anthropological work should have a purpose beyond dilettantism or the satisfaction of individual curiosity, and this implies that our results should be shared in one or another appropriate format to increase knowledge or to achieve some impact. The nature of the research, results, and desired impact will influence appropriate formats or venues for dissemination.

Despite this general expectation, however, there are some contexts in which limited or restricted access seems appropriate. Disclosing the precise location of archaeological or paleontological sites is generally viewed as unethical because it places these sites at increased risk from looting, for example. Similar concerns can be raised regarding the locations or movements of rare or endangered species or biological communities, or the identities of individuals who might be at risk based on such disclosure. Some changes to AAA's ethical codes proposed in the period leading up to the current revision forbade any research resulting in data or results that could not be freely shared; examples like the restriction of archaeological site location were acknowledged but viewed as special cases that could be tacitly understood as exceptions.

Issues of dissemination and access thus played a key role in the current revision of the AAA Principles of Professional Practice. In 2007 anthropologist Terry Turner introduced a motion at the AAA Business Meeting to restore parts of the older 1971 version of the AAA code of ethics (see also Chapters 3 and 5). These passages included a requirement that all research be made available to the public, and where practicable to research participants or subjects. To some this represented a strongly worded requirement privileging the rights of research participants over all, and, in fairness, some on the Task Force shared this view. While it is possible to assume that was the intent of the wording, I feel this interpretation requires some special pleading or exegetical gymnastics. The plain language requires sharing results with "the public," and with research participants in those cases where such sharing is practicable. And from the context it seems unlikely that sharing with "the public" can be understood as requiring that anthropologists present their results in the popular media in easily understandable or intellectually accessible forms. Instead, "the public" refers to not-private, providing a negative definition rather than designating a specific audience. Indeed, it seems by implication and practice that publication in scholarly journals or communication through scholarly venues entirely satisfies the requirement. As a result, the new Principles make an important switch. Instead of requiring that data be shared with one's colleagues and, if practical, with the individuals and communities being studied—as was mandated in earlier statements and was the standard to which AAA was urged, in 2008, to return—the new Principles place a greater obligation on sharing results with research participants.

Does this mean that results must always be shared with research participants? Not necessarily or inevitably. If participants fully understand the project, its sponsors and purposes, and freely consent to participate despite restrictions on distribution of results, then those restrictions may not necessarily violate applicable principles (but see Chapter 7).

And therein lies the rub. One of the more contentious issues in anthropological ethics in the opening decades of the twenty-first century has been the appropriateness and ethical status of research with results that are classified, confidential, proprietary, privileged, restricted, or otherwise limited in distribution. On the one hand questions regarding research with restricted results reflect concern over weaponization of anthropological scholarship by the military and intelligence communities (e.g., Berreman 1991), and on the other arise from the use of anthropological research to advance capitalist, industrial or commercial ventures.

In part, these debates mark deeply buried fault lines within the discipline. Broad prohibitions of research leading to restricted data—whose distribution would itself be unethical within parts of the discipline because such disclosure might place irreplaceable sites or vulnerable populations at risk—were viewed by some as appropriate or even necessary, and allowable because the few recognized exceptions are trivial or lie outside the "real" focus of both anthropological inquiry and its principles of professional practice. The ethics code is, from this perspective, concerned primarily with the proper practice of cultural anthropology in its traditional academic forms, and "special cases" from other parts of the discipline or applying to anthropologists in other contexts of professional practice are simply understood to lie outside its bounds. One can, I think, fairly question the value of a statement of professional responsibility identifying uniform standards that are tacitly understood to not apply in certain contexts, or in the cases of entire subdisciplines. More generally, in a world in which communities are increasingly asserting their rights to intellectual property and intangible cultural heritage it is not clear that those circumstances where it may be appropriate to allow restrictions on dissemination of research results are either "special cases" or necessarily restricted to subdisciplines viewed as peripheral or marginal to anthropology *sensu stricto*.

The issue is contentious for multiple reasons, since it refers to an outcome that may have a range of possible causes. In some instances restricted research reflects strategic or tactical uses of anthropological knowledge by the military, a weaponization of scholarly inquiry that is objectionable to many on both moral (ought we be doing this?) and ethical (does it satisfy expectations of informed consent, beneficence, or other ethical considerations?) grounds. From an ethical standpoint, at least, whether the work is done for military or intelligence services ought not be the issue. Anthropological inquiry studying topics of interest to, or even conducted through the sponsorship of, military/intelligence agencies is not inherently unethical, as long as it fully and fairly satisfies other ethical requirements (avoidance of harm, transparency and openness, fully informed and freely given consent, etc.). Most of us can readily imagine examples where such projects pose no inherent ethical concerns—an anthropologist conducting an archaeological survey on a military base to minimize damage to archaeological sites associated with a new building is not necessarily violating any ethical precepts, for instance, in undertaking the project or accepting restriction on the dissemination of the results.

The key word, of course, is "necessarily," as there may well be other ethical issues that should give pause (e.g., Albro 2007; Goldstein 2010; Lucas 2009; Price 2011; Rubinstein et al. 2012). Unlike prescriptive codes offering easy (albeit rarely adequate) cookbook solutions to ethical quandaries, educative codes like that of the American Anthropological Association focus on questions or issues an individual should consider in assessing what constitutes ethical practice in any given situation. Educative codes are therefore more useful in tackling new or rapidly changing circumstances, since they offer frameworks for considering the ethical implications of action, while prescriptive codes are generally reactive responses to previously encountered problems—like lightning bugs, prescriptive codes carry their illumination behind them. Educative codes place greater responsibility on the shoulders of individual anthropologists, since instead of checking a code to be sure their actions aren't specifically disallowed, they must continually weigh their own actions in terms of a range of ethical core concerns and professional responsibilities.

Returning to our hypothetical anthropologist conducting an archaeological survey on a military base, s/he would need to further consider whether all of the principles of professional responsibility, as they apply in this instance, are adequately satisfied. I've chosen the example with some care, as it's generally acknowledged that archaeologists need not (and indeed ought not to) reveal the precise locations of archaeological sites, as this would place those sites at greater risk of looting and pillage. But this doesn't mean that all restrictions are equally appropriate; while restrictions regarding the precise locations of sites may be appropriate, restrictions on subsequent publications of cultural-historical results, or particularly control over the content of the interpretations based on those results, are problematic and would need to be weighed carefully in deciding whether the project was appropriate.

But while there may be circumstances where restrictions on dissemination are appropriate, the new principles do not allow clandestine or compartmented research. Clandestine research cannot satisfy these principles because by its nature the participants would not be able to fully understand its scope, purpose and sponsors, or to give free and fully informed consent. In the case of compartmented research it is unlikely an anthropologist *could* fully disclose the purposes, sponsors or potential consequences to participation in such projects, since they may be unknown by or misrepresented to the anthropologist, and the anthropologist would have no reasonable way of knowing whether they possessed full knowledge, nor could participants freely offer informed—or anything approximating informed—consent.

But what about the narrower case where the results of a project are limited by contract? Wouldn't such projects, which might, for example, be undertaken by applied anthropologists working for external clients (Malefyt 2009; Sunderland and Denny 2007), be equally problematic and unethical? Once again, whether such limitations on distribution satisfy applicable ethical expectations depends largely on whether the research participants fully understood and freely consented to these restrictions from the start. In the case of research on living human communities this would include the individuals or communities being studied, while in other cases it might include those responsible for approving or issuing permits for the project. As long as the anthropologists and the research participants are fully informed and freely consent to the level of restriction or dissemination from the outset, the project does not necessarily violate expectations for ethical practice (but see Chapter 5).

For the most part these concerns regarding applied anthropology are raised by anthropologists in academia looking askance at colleagues in private practice whose results might be governed by work-for-hire rules or contractual arrangements with commercial entities; Peter Pels has observed that this is part of a larger process in which the presumptive authority of anthropology to represent or intervene is being replaced with a need to negotiate—with funders and policymakers, with businesses and clients, and with the people being studied (1999:112)—and that this is a positive development rather than a breach of ethical standards.[1] This is not a wholly comfortable process, as it challenges the privileged position of anthropology as presumed interlocutor for the analytical Other.

A more substantive issue may be determining whether an anthropologist in a given context has appropriate authority to disseminate knowledge, particularly traditional indigenous knowledge, and whether anthropologists collecting such knowledge can assume, assign, or transfer rights to traditional knowledge or practice upon which their research results are based (e.g., Geismar 2013; Janke and Iacovino 2012; Brown and Nicholas 2012; even business ethicists have begun to address the issue of indigenous knowledge, e.g., Orozco and Poonamallee 2014. Rights of indigenous groups to control tangible and intangible heritage are integral to the United Nations' Declaration on the Rights of Indigenous Peoples). Consider, for example, the case of the Glenbow Museum and its 1988 *The Spirit Sings: Artistic Traditions of Canada's First Peoples* exhibition. Designed to showcase Native artistic traditions during the 1988 Olympics in Calgary, the exhibit may have been intended as an attempt to engage a broader public with issues in anthropological aesthetics and non-western art and thereby disseminate the work of museum anthropologists, but the Lubicon Lake Cree protested the exhibition because 1) Native artifacts had been borrowed or were being exhibited without explicit permission; 2) the Museum employed non-Native persons as curators of the exhibition; 3) the exhibition did not necessarily reflect Cree concerns or interests; and 4) the Museum had accepted sponsorship funds from Shell Oil, with whom the Lubicon Lake Cree were engaged in a protracted legal battle. As controversy over the exhibit grew, anthropologists found themselves in unexpected positions, torn between the conflicting interests of different stakeholders. Michael Ames, one of the most influential critics of traditional museum practice, found himself defending the use of corporate sponsors. "I'd love clean money," he said, "but there isn't clean money anymore" (Halpin 1988:91; Harrison et al. 1988; see also the excellent discussion of such tensions within museum anthropology in Gonzalez et al. 2001). In this instance disseminating anthropological results was perceived as improperly representing and co-opting Native knowledge and expression. Ames' remarks highlight the complex negotiations between interested parties that characterize anthropological practice in situations like these.

Earlier in this chapter I questioned the value of an ethical standard tacitly understood to not apply in many cases, and after enumerating instances where dissemination may not be appropriate a critical reader may well feel dissemination has the same flaws—"anthropologists are expected to disseminate their results, except when they're not." There is, however, a distinction that is important for understanding the rather different character of the new principles. Past codes generally represented normative rules of behavior, prescribing or proscribing specific actions. Implicit was a privileging of certain areas of practice as the more common or dominant form or context of anthropological inquiry, and it was understood that some aspects of these rules might therefore not apply in other contexts of practice or sub-disciplinary settings. The new principles instead identify a series of core concerns that any anthropologist in any context should consider in determining an appropriate course of action. No, a paleoanthropologist need not obtain informed consent from the hominid ancestor s/he is studying, but appropriate permissions, permits, and approvals must be obtained, representing equivalent concerns and with the same expectations of disclosure applying. Similarly, in the case of making one's results accessible, anthropologists should understand that there is an expectation of timely dissemination but that this expectation may take different forms in different contexts and must always be balanced against other principles. The complex and changing social terrain that all anthropologists navigate—whether in terms of ethnographic informants, descendant communities, permitting agencies, policymakers, interest groups, funders, obligations to students, or simply departmental cliques and factions—can be better traversed through simpler principles informing decision-making on a daily basis. In part this represents a shift from reactionary codes that respond to problematic actions by prohibiting them in the future to prospective and proactive standards that can be used in assessing new circumstances and challenges, and in part a shift away from codes that define unethical conduct, with the implicit presumption that all else is ethical, and toward a set of separate principles that must be balanced on an ongoing basis.

So for most anthropologists, in most contexts, timely dissemination is an expectation of ethical practice. But what constitutes dissemination? For many previous generations of anthropologists, most of whom practiced exclusively or largely within academia, making one's results accessible meant publishing in scholarly journals, through scholarly presses or by discussing one's results through presentations at professional meetings.

But while these venues made results generally accessible to scholars within the discipline, or at least scholars within the developed world and with adequate personal means ("the public," within the rubric of the 1971 principles), they could not reasonably be said to make results freely accessible. Journal subscription rates have never been low relative to other costs, academic volumes have always commanded hefty prices in keeping with their weighty topics and limited print runs, and professional meetings have traditionally been in equal parts exclusive, expensive, and esoteric. "Accessible" in such settings had a specific and restrictive meaning. There also exists an extensive gray literature of technical reports, policy briefings, white papers, and expert opinions that are disseminated, albeit narrowly distributed. For some subdisciplines such as archaeology these probably outnumber academic reports and publications by a substantial margin. Within the United States, for example, the National Archaeological Database (NADB) comprises more than 350,000 limited distribution reports, and does not capture all such documents. In England and Scotland the Archaeological Data Service (ADS) has collected more than 12,600 unpublished reports, and the number continues to increase (see Moore and Evans 2013; Ford 2010; Seymour 2009, 2010).

Within the past decade the term "accessible" has come to have other commonly accepted meanings, including making results accessible and distributable without charge (Kelty et al. 2008). While a full discussion of the ethical implications of open access lies well beyond the scope of this chapter, it does not lie beyond the horizon for the discipline. At least at this stage, however, open access does not yet represent the unalloyed good or moral imperative we might wish. Just as issues like ownership and copyright refer to a bundle of complex rights that may not fully transfer, open access refers to a range of access and rights that may be more or less open and more or less accessible (Laakso et al. 2011; Harnad et al. 2004).[2] The most familiar of these distinctions is between gold and green open access. Currently (2015) the American Anthropological Association employs a green open access/hybrid gold open access model; authors may post their works to their own websites or to a repository, and alternatively the author or their home institution may pay a fee to make their contributions gold open access at time of publication.

Most gold open access is based on an author-pays model; this is workable in many of the physical and life sciences where grants pay for both research and its dissemination. In disciplines like anthropology, where relatively less research is fully funded by grants, and funding agencies can fund dissemination costs only at the expense of other projects, this model is more problematic. Gold open access makes results more accessible to those in less privileged positions, but in making the results accessible to more, it allows publication to fewer, denying those in less privileged positions the ability to publish and themselves contribute to academic discourse. Instead of paying to consume they must pay to contribute—hardly an improvement. This is not a reason to eschew open access, of course, but a challenge that we must overcome to make scholarship broadly accessible without constraining the ability of subaltern or less advantaged groups to contribute to scholarly discourse and the increase of knowledge.

As in most of the other principles in the new Principles of Professional Responsibility, "Make Your Results Accessible" is neither a simple cookbook solution nor a one-time check-box, but requires deliberate discussion and ongoing communication by all involved or affected by the unfolding research process. In some senses results are almost always disseminated in abbreviated or partial form. Presentation of results is by its nature reductive and a distillation of larger datasets or experiences into key elements. Linguistic anthropologists may report their results on an analysis of specific speech events, for example, without necessarily disseminating every utterance. As a result, at the trivial level what constitutes adequate dissemination will vary on a case-by-case basis, depending on what needs to be communicated to allow a reader or viewer to assess the robustness of the conclusions being drawn. In some cases results may be made accessible by making them available to students, colleagues, or others who can employ them appropriately in their own research. More substantively, perhaps, whether there are valid reasons to limit dissemination becomes less a yes-or-no question and instead a more nuanced issue of what kind, form, and degree of dissemination may be most appropriate given other valid ethical concerns.

NOTES

1. Pels also argues that the development of professional standards or codes like that being discussed here is not necessary, and may hinder the teaching of anthropological ethics. While I disagree, such concerns have influenced the development of the current Principles of Professional Responsibility, which emphasize that anthropological work inherently involves negotiated relationships that are complex and fluid, and frames principles that may conflict with one another in real-world cases and be

continuously weighed and balanced—which is to say negotiated—by individual anthropologists in their individual contexts of practice.
2. See also http://bit.ly/oa-overview.

REFERENCES

Albro, Robert
2007 Anthropology's Terms of Engagement with Security. Anthropology News 48(1):20-21.

Berreman, Gerald D.
1991 Ethics vs. 'Realism' in Anthropology. *In* Ethics and the Profession of Anthropology: Dialogue for a New Era. Carolyn Fluehr-Lobban, ed. Pp. 38-71. Philadelphia: University of Pennsylvania Press.

Brown, Deirdre, and George Nicholas
2012 Protecting Indigenous Cultural Property in the Age of Digital Democracy: Institutional and Communal Responses to Canadian First Nations and Maori Heritage Concerns. Journal of Material Culture 17(3):307-324.

Ford, Matt
2010 Hidden Treasure. Nature 464:826-827.

Geismar, Haidy
2013 Treasured Possessions: Indigenous Interventions into Cultural and Intellectual Property. Durham: Duke University Press.

Goldstein, Daniel M.
2010 Towards a Critical Anthropology of Security. Current Anthropology 51(4):487-517.

Gonzalez, Roberto J., Laura Nader, and C. Jay Ou
2001 Towards an Ethnography of Museums: Science, Technology and Us. *In* Academic Anthropology and the Museum: Back to the Future. Mary Bouquet, ed. Pp. 106-116. New York: Berghahn Books.

Halpin, Marjorie
1988 Museum Review: "The Spirit Sings: Artistic Creations of Canada's First Peoples." Culture 8(1):89-93.

Harnad, Stevan, Tim Brody, François Vallières, Les Carr, Steve Hitchcock, Yves Gingras, Charles Oppenheim, Heinrich Stamerjohanns, and Eberhard R. Hilf
2004 The Access/Impact Problem and the Green and Gold Roads to Open Access. Serials Review 30:301-314.

Harrison, James D., Bruce G. Trigger, and Michael Ames
1988 Point/Counterpoint: "The Spirit Sings" and the Lubicon Boycott. Museum 6(3):12-25.

Janke, Terri and Livia Iacovino
2012 Keeping Cultures Alive: Archives and Indigenous Cultural and Intellectual Property Rights. Archival Science 12:151-171.

Kelty, Christopher M., Michael M.J. Fisher, Alex Golub, Jason Baird Jackson, Kimberly Christen, Michael F. Brown, and Tom Boellstorff
2008 Anthropology Of/In Circulation: The Future of Open Access and Scholarly Societies. Cultural Anthropology 23(3):559-588.

Laakso, Mikael, Patrik Welling, Helena Bukvova, Linus Nyman, Bo-Christer Bjork, and Turid Hedlund
2011 The Development of Open Access Journal Publishing from 1993-2009. PLoS ONE 6(6): e20961. doi:10.1371/journal.pone.0020961

Lucas, George R.
2009 Anthropologists in Arms: The Ethics of Military Anthropology. Walnut Creek: Altamira Press.

Malefyt, Timothy de Waal
2009 Understanding the Rise of Consumer Ethnography: Branding Technomethodologies in the New Economy. American Anthropologist 111(2):201-210.

Moore, Ray, and Tim Evans
2013 Preserving the Grey Literature Explosion: PDF/A and the Digital Archive. Information Standards Quarterly 25(3):20-27.

Orozco, David, and Latha Poonamallee
2014 The Role of Ethics in the Commercialization of Indigenous Knowledge. Journal of Business Ethics 119:275-286.

Pels, Peter
1999 Professions of Duplexity: A Prehistory of Ethical Codes in Anthropology. Current Anthropology 40(2):101-136.

Price, David
2011 Weaponizing Anthropology: Social Science in Service of the Militarized State. Oakland: Counterpunch Books.
2003 Anthropology Sub Rosa: The CIA, AAA and the Ethical Problems Inherent in Secret Research. *In* Ethics and the Profession of Anthropology: Dialogue for Ethically Conscious Practice. Carolyn Fluehr-Lobban, ed. Pp. 29-49. Walnut Creek: Altamira Press.

Rubinstein, Robert A., Kerry B. Fosher, and Clementine K. Fujimura, eds.
2012 Practicing Military Anthropology: Beyond Expectation and Traditional Boundaries. Boulder CO: Lynne Rienner Publishers.

Seymour, Deni J.
2010 In the Trenches Around the Ivory Tower: Introduction to Black-and-White Issues About the Grey Literature. Archaeologies 6(2):226-232.

Seymour, Deni J., ed.
2009   International Perspectives on the Archaeological Grey Literature. The Grey Journal 5(2):63-110.

Sunderland, Patricia L., and Rita M. Denny
2007   Doing Anthropology in Consumer Research. Walnut Creek: Left Coast Press, Inc.

CHAPTER SEVEN

Obtain Informed Consent and Necessary Permissions

Robert Albro and Dena Plemmons

Anthropological researchers working with living human communities must obtain the voluntary and informed consent of research participants. Ordinarily such consent is given prior to the research, but it may also be obtained retroactively if so warranted by the research context, process, and relations. The consent process should be a part of project design and continue through implementation as an ongoing dialogue and negotiation with research participants. Normally, the observation of activities and events in fully public spaces is not subject to prior consent.

Minimally, informed consent includes sharing with potential participants the research goals, methods, funding sources or sponsors, expected outcomes, anticipated impacts of the research, and the rights and responsibilities of research participants. It must also include establishing expectations regarding anonymity and credit. Researchers must present to research participants the possible impacts of participation, and make clear that despite their best efforts, confidentiality may be compromised or outcomes may differ from those anticipated. These expectations apply to all field data, regardless of medium. Visual media in particular, because of their nature, must be carefully used, referenced, and contextualized.

Anthropological Ethics in Context: An Ongoing Dialogue, pp. 119-144. © 2016 Left Coast Press, Inc. All rights reserved.

Anthropologists have an obligation to ensure that research participants have freely granted consent, and must avoid conducting research in circumstances in which consent may not be truly voluntary or informed. In the event that the research changes in ways that will directly affect the participants, anthropologists must revisit and renegotiate consent. The informed consent process is necessarily dynamic, continuous and reflexive. Informed consent does not necessarily imply or require a particular written or signed form. It is the quality of the consent, not its format, which is relevant.

Anthropologists working with biological communities or cultural resources have an obligation to ensure that they have secured appropriate permissions or permits prior to the conduct of research. Consultation with groups or communities affected by this or any other type of research should be an important element of the design of such projects and should continue as work progresses or circumstances change. It is explicitly understood that defining what constitutes an affected community is a dynamic and necessary process.

The American Anthropological Association's 2012 statement on ethics continues a trend of recent decades of the discipline's increased attention to the obligations and responsibilities of professional anthropologists to their research counterparts, where it is largely taken for granted—though no longer explicitly stated—that an anthropologist's primary ethical responsibility is to the people s/he studies. Nevertheless, as has been noted, it was not until the late 1990s that the doctrine of informed consent was embraced in the discipline as one fundamental way of meeting that obligation (e.g. Schrag 2010), with specific language about informed consent incorporated into the Association's official statement on ethics in 1998. And despite evident variations of the meaning of informed consent across disciplines (see Lederman 2007), if recent volumes updating the hows and whys of anthropological ethics (Fluehr-Lobban 2013; LeCompte and Schensul 2015; Whiteford and Trotter 2008) are any indication, attention to ethics vis-à-vis one's counterparts in the field has become a notably larger proportion of the disciplinary ethical conversation than previously.

"Informed consent" has also become an umbrella under which an increasing variety of considerations, linked by questions of power and concerns for asymmetries and risks in research relationships, have been grouped. Though about many things, arguably the most significant disciplinary controversies of the past two decades—the Darkness in El

Dorado scandal and the most recent active debate over anthropology and the military (see Lamphere 2003; Price 2011 respectively)—were also significantly about the absence, impossibility, or inadequacy of informed consent. Among anthropologists, the concept of informed consent, in other words, has evolved relatively rapidly from a largely absent or marginal question of disciplinary conduct to a major anthropological principle and subject of regular and sometimes heated discussion about our effects upon the agency of counterparts in our work.

Yet we believe there remain significant challenges in how the discipline of anthropology conducts its discussions of informed consent. In what follows we examine some of the implications of the disconnect between what we describe as largely presentist debates about professional anthropological ethics and a notably historicizing turn in the anthropology of morality and ethics, with attention to what this might mean for informed consent as a taken-for-granted doctrine. Beginning with the experience of the 2009 Task Force for Comprehensive Ethics Review (hereafter referred to as the Task Force) as a case study, we go on to consider how disciplinary approaches to informed consent too often tacitly rely on ahistorical and holistic accounts both of "the field" and of the relationships of ethnographers to their counterparts "in the field." Even if we often recognize the field as a dynamically changing research environment, when it comes to discussions of informed consent, we continue to refer to a normative status quo of social arrangements in the field, treated as a bounded and self-contained place. But this normative account does not square with current anthropological conceptions of the field as a much more open-ended, and less place-based, set of local and global social arrangements. This disconnect has led to mischief in the ways informed consent has been brought into anthropology's ethical discussions.

The Task Force and Informed Consent/Secrecy

When the AAA's Task Force began meeting to discuss the elements of a Code of Ethics (CoE) for the profession and potential directions for revision, members were still keenly aware of the small but significant revisions that had been voted in by the membership in early 2009. The discussions by the ad hoc committee formed to review the suggested changes resulted in the submission of a majority and a minority report to the AAA's Executive Board for consideration. Though the primary focus of these changes concerned the availability and dissemination of research results to research participants, also implicated in both the discussion and subsequent changes were various ideas relating to informed consent, which had been problematized—we think appropriately—throughout the revision process.

The Turner resolution, brought to the floor during the business meeting of the 2007 annual AAA meeting, initiated a year-long process leading up to the 2009 revision (see Chapter 3). And the Turner resolution referenced a particular paragraph of the 2007 final report of the Commission for the Engagement of Anthropology with the Security and Intelligence Communities (CEAUSSIC), which reads in full:

> Anthropological ethics may be compromised by national security mandates that *conflict with standards of full informed consent* of participants in research. Pre-1986 versions of the CoE offered more clarity on such interactions with the proviso that, "classified, or limited dissemination restrictions that necessarily and perhaps understandably are placed upon researchers *do conflict with openness, disclosure, and the intent and spirit of informed consent* in research and practice. *Adherence to acknowledged standards of informed consent* that conflict with conditions for engagement with national security agencies may result in a decision not to undertake or to discontinue a research project" (CoE 1971-1986). As discussed in the "Recommendations" section, the AAA Ethics Committee may wish to examine the possibility of reincorporating such language into the current CoE. (italics added)[1]

This paragraph calls our attention to full and informed consent as it relates specifically to additional concerns about control over and availability of data, dissemination of results, and transparency in research. The animating context of the debate then being had hinged on the question of clandestine research and secrecy as related to working in national security settings (see Price 2007).

In CEAUSSIC's presentation of these issues, not surprisingly given its mandate to say something about working with national security agencies, we also encounter the presumption that the spirit of informed consent is fundamentally altered by a lack of openness and limits upon disclosure. Not coincidentally, the question of informed consent, as it was made a part of this broader discussion, foregrounded an account that emphasized the internal relationship between informed consent generally and openness specifically in ways suggesting that these concepts are inevitably mutually entailed. But consent, and openness or disclosure, are not synonymous concepts. Of course they do often engage each another, typically, around how much information one responsibly should provide in order to insure consent. But in this case, we might say that the question of consent had, for the purposes of CEAUSSIC's mandate and discussion, been connected to a set of concerns that related to possibilities of abuse or harm represented by powerful state security agencies and were understood to involve secrecy, coercion, and potentially problematic limits upon dissemination.

In an attempt, therefore, to better articulate the particular relationship between informed consent and openness or dissemination, the majority report that the 2008-2009 ad hoc committee submitted to the Executive Board suggested language for Section VI, "Dissemination of Results," stating that "If the results of studies will not be made available to the persons or communities being studied, this should be clearly disclosed at the outset to all concerned." But this sentence was stricken from consideration by the authors of the minority report, and did not make it into the version voted on and approved by the membership. During the 2008-2009 discussions relating to this change, one member wanted to know why we couldn't satisfy our commitment to our informants through prior and full disclosure: "Is it okay to withhold results if you disclose to research participants that they will not get to see the results of the research?" Another member responded that to do so would violate Turner's intent. Again, as in the recommendation by CEAUSSIC, the connection between informed consent and restricted dissemination was foregrounded and prioritized. The implication seemed to be that informed consent allowed only one interpretation of the concept (except of course when it doesn't, a scenario we explore further in the remainder of this discussion).

This account of informed consent, as a self-evident doctrine, relies upon a corresponding belief that transparency, or openness, and secrecy are 1) *sui generis*, 2) irreducibly opposed categories, and 3) understood only in contrast to one another. In other words, any research situation that inhibits openness or allows secrecy as a possible and viable limiting condition would, with this conception, be unacceptable and informed consent impossible. It seems evident that employing these absolutes would not only impact work with the security sector, but also in non-academic practices of anthropology—in other words, in any situation where the researcher herself does not enjoy complete autonomy in the field to enact these imperatives. Indeed, the conversations that CEAUSSIC undertook in part aspired to clarify different circumstances of secrecy, non-disclosure, and limited dissemination, while taking into consideration not just security work, but any practice of anthropology conducted in situations where the likelihood of full disclosure is absent.

As this debate suggests, informed consent presents itself in specific contexts in different ways. This was apparent throughout the many conversations had by CEAUSSIC, the 2008-2009 ad hoc committee, and the Task Force about informed consent. The conceptualization of, and expectations for, informed consent change significantly, depending on the subject of debate, where other key issues—harm, transparency, dissemination, ownership—are understood to be critical. We should recognize the extent to which the shifting semantic properties of informed consent are a recurrent characteristic of the discussion: informed consent, like anthropology itself, is contingent, historical, and constantly re-created in relation to current and encompassing realities, both within and outside the discipline. The contexts of such debates are constitutive of how informed consent is dealt with, and can only ever capture a partial presentation of the issues. Key ethical terms are not self-evident. We might even suggest that these terms are essentially empty until filled with various content derived from the contours of a particular debate or discussion about them, and as argumentatively connected with or positioned against other key meanings. Indeed, Hoeyer, and Hogle (2014:348) have concluded precisely that about "informed consent," which they insist often functions as an "empty signifier" upon which people "project very different hopes, concerns, and intentions."

An Ethical History of the State/Informed Consent

Anthropology's ethical turn and greater preoccupation with the circumstances of informed consent is hardly parochial. The discipline's internal debates are simultaneous with and engage a prevailing public ethical turn, including a relatively recent "globalization of ethics" (Ignatieff 2012), where the ethical language of responsibility and transparency has come to be viewed as an unassailable public good to which governments should be more responsive (Plemmons and Albro 2012:179-180), and to which scientists of all sorts should be more accountable.[2] Ongoing since 2011, the U.S. government has been reviewing—in order to reform—its regulations for federally-funded research with human subjects. Likewise, one of the first projects of the Presidential Commission for the Study of Bioethical Issues was to assess federal research standards, in light of the support by the U.S. Public Health Service of unethical research in the late 1940s exposing thousands of Guatemalans to sexually-transmitted diseases without their knowledge or consent.[3]

The Obama Administration's attention to the ethical lapses of the U.S. government, together with anthropology's internal discussion of what the discipline's relationship should be to powerful security agencies, reminds us that a major impetus for the development of mechanisms of ethical oversight in research professions has been the unethical behavior of nation-states, in the biomedical fields and elsewhere. In contrast to an earlier era, anthropology's current enthusiasm for ethics and its increased ethical focus on counterparts in the field have coincided with a post-colonial disciplinary historical moment—which we are arguably still in—of both theory and ethnography dedicated to exposing the negative effects of state power on marginal research subjects (see Aretxaga 2003; Nagengast 1994). And anthropology's ambivalence about the behavior of nation-states, as an important historical source of thinking about informed consent, has had ethnographic consequences.

In contemporary U.S. anthropology, the field and fieldwork are now imagined as shot through with the visible or invisible effects of the state, as a privileged locus of power, with counterparts routinely thickly contextualized as state subjects (e.g., Das 2008). In this way, the nation-state has become an important constituent feature of a prevailing objectification of the field as an open-ended context and problem-space of interconnected agencies and structures of the nation-state, with local and global expressions. This is an account of the field taken from a moment in anthropology's own evolving professional self-understanding, in this case largely informed by a post-WWII set of engagements with global colonial legacies—becoming much more pronounced since the Vietnam era—and playing in the background of disciplinary ethical debate today.

Disciplinary ethical accounts of the ways that marginal research subjects are assumed to be potentially vulnerable to the negative consequences of state power represent a particular "ethical genealogy" of informed consent doctrine for the discipline (see Albro 2015).[4] If such an observation is consistent with attention to how ethical accounts are assembled as part of an emerging and comparative anthropology of morality (see Fassin and Lézé 2013), this has not been how professional anthropological ethics have been debated. As several commentators have observed (see Hoeyer and Hogle 2014; Lederman 2013), professional anthropologists have tended not to apply the insights from their own scholarship to the "practices and values" of anthropology itself, including its characteristic activities, research decisions, methods, modes of analysis, and ethical conduct. This represents a missed opportunity to understand how the disciplinary approach to the problem of the nation-state, for example, has helped to shape the ethical priorities of ethnographers in the field at particular moments.

But this also brings us to a certain challenge with the ways in which anthropology has undertaken to discuss the ethics of informed consent. We might note the regular emphasis upon the "particularistic and historicizing" qualities of the ethnographic domain (Keane 2014:6) as a source of ethical insight. And this view is consistent with the ways that attention to ethnography, culture, and power, as parts of the anthropological enterprise, has increasingly taken a historicizing turn, where what is understood to be meaningful is considered to be so in historically grounded ways (see Comaroff and Comaroff 1992). The burgeoning anthropology of morality and ethics, in comparable fashion, also frames such a project historically, for example, in ways frequently inspired by Foucault's particular historical method (see Faubion 2011; Laidlaw 2014; Zigon 2008). This has meant that when discussing professional ethics we have not, again in Lederman's (2013) words, tended to treat particular disciplinary cultures like anthropology's as "historically-contingent moral orders" in their own right.

Instead, we might point to a disconnect with the ways that ethical questions are discussed among anthropologists. Even if ethnographers are rarely aware in any detail of the parameters of informed consent prior to undertaking research, as an ethical doctrine informed consent is still often discussed in terms of relative legal or prescriptive clarity, as if it is a self-evident and transhistorical principle, despite criticism of this tendency (e.g., Bell 2014). Even if we know that relations with our counterparts rarely unfold in transactionally standard ways (e.g., Wedel 2009:18), informed consent is treated as if a largely one-off and one-size-fits all technical matter or as an up front and transparent dialogue with relatively less powerful counterparts in the field in order to negotiate mutually well-defined obligations and expectations, and in the process ideally to achieve full disclosure (Plemmons and Albro 2012:181, 187). Put another way, Hoeyer and Hogle (2014:349) have recently referred to the "fantasy of informed consent" as a morally appealing political space that is "remarkably resistant to concrete experiences." Informed consent, as a normative and prescriptive professional principle, is relentlessly dehistoricising.

This problem has to do with the ways anthropologists have conducted their self-reflexive conversation to date about what anthropology is and what anthropologists do, or should do. As Lederman (2013) puts it, this is most often done in reference to "present-oriented involvements," that is, a disciplinary ethical crisis in the present tense (e.g. anthropologists' engagement with challenges related to the U.S. military's occupations of Afghanistan and Iraq). Historical precedents are, of course, noted as part of these debates, but typically mobilized in ways aligned with present concerns to further reinforce an urgent account of the ethics of now: the 1960s-era project Camelot is retrospectively used to illustrate the same problem for informed consent as anthropologists' involvement with the U.S. military today, a basic lack of transparency and the dangerous instrumentalization of anthropology by powerful state agencies (e.g., González 2009, Price 2011). We can compare our presentist ethical habits to the broadly critiqued and disempowering fallacy of ethnographic presentism (see Fabian 2014; Hastrup 1990), but the lessons have not been carried over. This disconnect helps to keep our ethical conversation at a distance from our professional practice, but also from the agency of our counterparts.

Margins of the Field and the Ethnographer's Magic

Addressing this disjunction is a task that awaits. Doing so involves wedding more closely the discipline's professional discourse about ethics, as instantiated in its statements on ethics and regular debates about ethical conduct in the field, with the emerging anthropology of morality and ethics. This task includes historically informed accounts of anthropology's own practices, as these shape moments of ethical encounter and debate among each other and with counterparts. While disciplinary ethical debates regularly incorporate historical precedents, these precedents are typically specific cases of questionable or infamous conduct by particular anthropologists, and are usually offered against a taken-for-granted background of disciplinary identity, theory and method. However, it is exactly this taken-for-granted reference to "the field," "culture," and "counterparts," often used as a short hand in ethical discussions of informed consent, that needs more unpacking and where ethical work on the anthropological self is largely yet to be done. This means accounting for how anthropology has evolved over time as a knowledge-producing project. For example, we continue to carry forward a largely presentist and dehistoricized conception of "the field" in our ethics talk—an artifact of our own disciplinary history now thoroughly obsolete, but which nevertheless shapes professional expectations for informed consent in sometimes problematic ways.

In Stocking's playful terms (1992:70), as the primary "ritual of the tribe," ethnographic fieldwork has been subject to "considerable mythic elaboration." And the aura of "the field" has been a primary basis of anthropological authority. Even if we are still unable to point to any "single agreed upon definition for what constitutes participant observation" (Dewalt and Dewalt 2000:259), particularly early on and as part of the effort to identify ethnography as a rigorous and legitimate social scientific methodology, ethnographers viewed the field as a spatially contained place, territory, culture, society or neighborhood (Gupta and Ferguson 1997), as a setting for the demonstration of anthropological holism through the ethnographic reproduction of the "fiction of the whole" (Marcus 1998:33). This conception of the field, of course, fits well with Boasian historical particularism and its project of the comparison of bounded and discrete cultures (see Bunzl 2008). Likewise, the ethnographic subjects that populated this ethnographic canon—most often, native peoples—were typically collective, anonymous, and represented as largely without the agency to actively shape the terms of their engagements with ethnographers, let alone the world at large.

Potentially contaminating and boundary-transgressing contexts were separated out from ethnographic accounts of largely self-contained social and cultural worlds. Even if significantly fictitious, Malinowski's weighty ethnographies of everyday imponderabilia were kept separate from his controversial field diary, and there was little hint of the colonial circumstances enabling Evans-Pritchard's description of feuding Nuer. Instead, "the field" was a privileged source for authoritative representations of complex cultural wholes, patterns, configurations, symbolic or social systems, models or structures (see Fischer 2007). In contrast and from the historical distance afforded by current sensibilities, rather than the authoritative reports "from the field" they were treated as at the time, we might suggest that these accounts more accurately represented native subjects as "spatially incarcerated," to use Appadurai's (1988) apt phrase. As a means of maintaining the integrity of the field as a definable place, these ethnographic choices were also a good example of "disciplinary boundary-work within anthropology" (Lederman 2007:309).

A key feature of this representational conceit is a still prevalent conception of the experience of field work, as like Van Gennep's rite of passage. Spatially and socially the field has historically been conceived in terms of a set of margins that compose a typically remote location that fieldworkers journey to, enter, engage with, leave, and return from. The experience of fieldwork, in other words, has been and often continues to be conceived as a series of "phases" that the fieldworker passes through, phases insofar as the fieldworker is understood to navigate in orderly fashion a set of margins or thresholds. In this mode, ethnographers are frequently understood to undertake a stepwise process through the field, moving from "social limbo" to "achieving rapport" (Crane and Angrosino 1992:13), then to "acquiring status" and perhaps even a "claim to membership" (Anderson 1990:47), to a more stable and legible "identity."

Participant-observation is also often treated as "highly individualistic" (Dewalt and Dewalt 2000:261), foregrounding the agency of the anthropologist-cum-ethnographer. And here again we often encounter a conception of fieldwork in phases (see Anderson 1990; Wengle 1988; Jackson 1990). The stepwise phases of fieldwork have been understood, in Stocking's phrase (1992:109), as the process of acquisition of the anthropologist's "divinatory powers." Geertz's (1973) now classic description of his flight from a police raid on an illegal cock fight, together with Balinese, is offered up as a breakthrough in rapport, and is among the best known examples of the fieldwork-as-phases convention.

Intersections of anthropological method with theory have depended upon this conception, whether in the movement from open-ended to more structured interviews, from experience-far to experience-near ethnography, or from thin to thick description (Geertz 1973, 1983; for other kinds of examples of the movement from observation to participation, see Stoller 1989 and Attinasi and Friedrich 1995). These various examples all embrace an idea of fieldwork as a stepwise process, where successive thresholds in the field provide the phenomenal opportunities to fashion an authoritative ethnographic encounter.

Informed Consent as a Phase

Conventional descriptions of ethnography in terms of phases are easy to find (e.g., Dewalt and Dewalt 2010), even though descriptions of the specific number, order and duration of the phases vary. And a conception of ethnography as a process of identifiable steps underwrites associated conceptions of ethics in fieldwork, where the ethical process is understood as presenting a sequential series of ethical questions, from initial research design, through funding and research, to eventual publication (see Fluehr-Lobban 1998:180), that are resolved in that order along the way. More recently, LeCompte and Schensul (2015) similarly describe the progress of ethical decision-making in ethnographic research as a process that begins with the IRB, moves through the role of learner and identity creation in the field, to the responsibilities of longer-term relationships, and then to negotiating an exit from the field. The freedom to enter and leave the field, and to progress through it in a stepwise fashion, is one notable way in which the boundaries of the field are reconstituted, and these margins also continue to underwrite our relationships, ethical and otherwise, with people we encounter "in the field."

Discussions of the question of "informed consent," in other words, often tend to articulate the need to pursue and successfully obtain informed consent, firstly, against the taken-for-granted background of a well known normative framework, typically summarized by reference to the set of obligations required by IRBs, in turn, derived from concepts articulated in *The Belmont Report*, encoded in U.S. government's Common Rule, and largely carried over from extensive discussion of the risks to human subjects posed by biomedical research. This inherited and encompassing set of normative assumptions, of course, has been extensively critiqued among anthropologists in multiple ways. Notable critiques include that they are incompatible with ethnography and that even when informed consent is assumed to be "dynamic, continuous and reflexive," it takes for granted transactions among autonomous rational individuals in ways not accounting for alternative cultural and historically specific ideas of personhood and competing moral claims, and other forms of social accountability (see Bell 2014:513; Hoeyer and Hogle 2014:355).

Yet, the account of informed consent told by professional anthropology today nevertheless begins with the negotiation of this set of normative concepts (e.g., Fluehr-Lobban 2013:56-57; Bell 2014:512-513), including their disciplinary critique and the "deceptions" required of ethnographers to pass successfully through the IRB stage prior to beginning fieldwork (see Plemmons and Albro 2012:183-185). Entering the field, in other words, begins with the IRB process. And disciplinary common sense assumes that the acquisition of informed consent is a particular identifiable social transaction and one part of the wider set of social relationships composing our connections with the field—a methodological step we typically incorporate into our research design as an initial stage of fieldwork, and that we variously associate with the negotiation of "rapport" as a relatively early stage in the overall field experience.

But, furthermore, this normative set of ideas about informed consent—even as critiqued and contested—is also underwritten by a disciplinary conception of the field as a bounded social space or definable geographic place researchers can enter and leave and pass through in systematic fashion. Although in different ways, the goal of informed consent is contingent upon rapport as something achievable against a stable background of ethnography as a known and knowable enterprise. This is what Kirsten Bell (2014:515) also points to when discussing the fallacy of the dichotomy between "fully" informed consent versus not at all. Even if a continuous process, we proceed as if informed consent is a transaction we can complete, just as the field is a place we can leave. In our self-reflexive disciplinary conversation about the ethics of informed consent, this conversation remains meaningfully connected to a particular disciplinary history and conception of the field as a place defined by traversable margins. Contemporary anthropology continues to tell a story that relies upon a particular set of social arrangements "in the field" consistent with the bounded field concept in order to make its argument of ethical responsibilities to counterparts. But this is an objectification of the field with normative implications, in the words of Webb Keane (2014:7), an outdated "ethical affordance" smuggled into the present from anthropology's methodological past.

Empowering Counterparts and the Open-ended Field

At present we do not tend to conceive of the field as bounded or contained. In contrast to a Boasian legacy of the comparative description of cultural difference, in recent decades much more often the field has become a site and context for describing encompassing relations of power and structures of inequality. As a site of research efforts dedicated to revealing the workings of power and to correcting the ethnographic marginalization of contexts of power, the field has in the process come to be significantly less describable as a place and much more deterritorialized. Fieldwork has become more multi-sited and focused on diverse trans-boundary relationships and problems. If Laura Nader's (1974) call to "study up" and comparable attention to colonizers and powerbrokers set this in motion, today ethnographers—and diverse global anthropologies—

engage a wide array of global projects and actors. A short list of these might include varied global flows; local-global disjunctions, interfaces and relationships; transnational networks; nation-states; a myriad of global civil society actors; the activities and effects of transnational capital, media and publics, including overlapping virtual and non-virtual worlds (see Inda and Rosaldo 2007), among many other identifiably trans-local contexts, structures, and agents.

In efforts to ethnographically describe often trans-local agencies and structures of power and inequality, we now find ourselves at a moment when anthropology's historical focus on complex wholes, patterns, configurations, and symbolic systems has often given way to incommensurable discourses of biopower and to talk of rhizomes, scapes, networks, and assemblages (e.g., Collier and Ong 2005).[5] This shift has been problematic for the replicable experience of the field, now with much less locatable margins and no longer a privileged place that ethnographers can authoritatively enter and leave. Put more plainly, if the field has lost its characteristic shape and is now, at one time, both "here" and "there," fieldwork as a stepwise set of phases is an obsolete conception. However, we lack a corresponding professional vocabulary to describe this ethnographic experience and associated ethical obligations to others.

The greater anthropological focus upon power and inequality at present in comparison with the past, along with the transformation of the field into an experience with increasingly less definable margins, has directly influenced the purposes of ethnography and notably reshaped the relationship between ethnographers and their counterparts in the field. In a recent statement signed by over 1,000 members of the profession and supporting a AAA boycott of Israel, given its recent treatment of Palestinians, the discipline was described as a "community of scholars who study problems of power, oppression, and cultural hegemony," as engaged in the promotion and protection of human rights, and as "committed to supporting social change efforts"[6] arising from interactions between anthropologists and communities. Such a description carries forward an account of anthropology, emergent since at least the 1960s and one we often assume we still operate within, that is committed to the transformation of the relations of power at the heart of ethnographic relationships.

We can only briefly refer here to some of the ways this turn has been expressed in disciplinary terms in recent decades. One way it has been expressed is through a shift in the representational politics of ethnography. The ethnographic subject is "exotic no more" (MacClancy 2002), and the ethnographic spirit of the times routinely combines scholarly research with advocacy in ways intended to promote the agency of our counterparts. This has taken many forms, including the redeeming of voices otherwise silenced by the canon; sophisticated representations of cultural virtuosi; more fully acknowledging the contributions of informants to the construction of ethnographic texts; privileging modes of knowledge and experience of ethnographic subjects; and subjects who actively obstruct, subvert, and recruit the anthropologists to their own projects, in particular, diverse practices of self-making and world-making (see Battaglia 1995; Tedlock and Mannheim 1995), among other shifts in the representational work of anthropology and in the ways that ethnographic projects are now framed.

Another way this turn has been expressed is illustrated by the account of anthropology's recent history offered by a former AAA president. She describes a politically engaged discipline for which "the study of power is central," and which characteristically generates its knowledge and theory through "forms of engagement, collaboration, advocacy and activism" on behalf of research counterparts (Mullings 2015:10). She is clear that anthropology should be—and increasingly is—about supporting diverse sites of activism, resistance, and sources of "alternative knowledge production" that advance the agendas and "ongoing collective actions" of our counterparts (Mullings 2015:7), now only uncomfortably identified as research subjects.

It is increasingly a given across the discipline, if in different ways, that the task of anthropology is not that of comparatively theorizing about the cultures or societies of research subjects. Rather, it should more directly express, and be shaped by the marginalized "peripheral perspectives" of our counterparts themselves (see Shore and Trnka 2013), in support of their contests with state planners and corporate incursions (see Kirsch 2006) or their demands for rights.

And this evident shift in the power relation between anthropologists and their counterparts is not true only for sociocultural anthropology. Expectations around control over and access to genetic materials and tangible or intangible cultural heritage, to take two examples, have changed dramatically in recent decades. Human rights, and other domestic and international frameworks, now increasingly promote legal regimes identifying these resources as "property" individually or collectively owned by counterparts with whom biological anthropologists or archaeologists routinely work (see Brown 2003),[7] a relatively recent development that now shapes the possibilities for research across all anthropological sub-disciplines. But how flexible is our professional ethical language for accommodating these new alignments in the field, given, in particular, the ways that our understanding of the negotiation of ethical relationships with counterparts still assumes an outdated conception of the field as a definite place of navigable margins?

The Task Force and Informed Consent/Risk and/or Harm

When, in 2009, the Task Force began its work on the review and revision of the recently updated 2009 CoE, specifically with regard to its discussion of informed consent, it hoped to keep the complexity associated with this concept in the forefront. As with the previous discussion of secrecy, transparency, and dissemination, but while also taking up the concept of "harm," the Task Force aspired to draw attention to some of the ways the informed consent concept can become an inextricable part of other key principles and practices. But in the course of its work, the Task Force found itself hampered both by the discipline's particular history of informed consent and by a tendency toward the reification—or perhaps even fetishization—of the doctrine of informed consent, as prescribed in the regulations that govern federally-funded research with human subjects in the U.S., called 45 CFR 46 and typically referred to as the Common Rule. We suggest this difficulty was, at least in part, a result of the embedding of such a prevailing normative account as part of the fieldwork-as-phases story of ethnography we continue to tell ourselves when orienting our ethical relationships to counterparts, even as we typically imagine the field in very different terms today.

Task Force members had several conversations about keeping the discussions of informed consent clear of the federal framework and its particular structuring of "informed consent," in order to better pursue a disciplinary-appropriate ethical account of this concept. During the course of the Task Force's three years of work, members had the opportunity to meet with various constituencies regarding the review and anticipated revisions, and they were somewhat surprised by the number of conversations that articulated the concerns of the Code of Ethics in ways consistent with the concerns of university IRBs, with the expectation that the Task Force would formulate a code that would align with and support 45 CFR 46. While the Task Force did have some parallel discussions about how the Association might better provide resources that would be helpful for anthropologists in navigating their own IRBs, the Task Force was clear that what it wanted the code to do was to lay out broad principles first, and then to proceed to help illuminate the messiness of those principles in practice.

When the Task Force posted the principle entitled "Obtain informed consent and necessary permissions" to the blog site for review and comment, the scarcity of comments received – nine – was surprising. Less surprising, though frustrating, was that almost every comment tied what we might describe as a practice or process of crafting and negotiating relationships in the field to the requirements of "informed consent" found in federal regulations and interpreted by IRBs, as illustrated by the following responses:

> *The IRB would probably say that informed consent should also address the risks and benefits of participating in research. Perhaps this is what is meant by the phrase "possible impacts of participation" although that phrase is somewhat ambiguous. Explicitly referring to risks and benefits would improve this principle.*
>
> ....
>
> *I agree with the comment on the need for acknowledging the idea of risks and benefits. Additionally, I would suggest that the principle also acknowledge the fact that informed consent is a "process" not a form. The principle is to provide people with sufficient information to allow them to make an informed decision about participation in a project. That principle can be achieved verbally, graphically, in writing, using video, etc. etc. etc. This addition to the principle would be very beneficial in negotiating different processes for informed consent with IRBs, for anthropologists who are working with people for whom signing a written consent form is not the best way of accomplishing the goal/principle in various cross cultural settings.*
>
> ....
>
> *I have served on two IRBs and indeed both would want us to explain risks and benefits. In principal I agree with this. However, I think it is important to note explicitly that IRB protocols in the US and elsewhere developed largely with regard to experimental sciences. This is important because by definition an experiment involves a much greater degree of control than participant-observation fieldwork. And this is important because those who design experiments, and thus exercise or aim to exercise control, are also in*

a privileged position to anticipate risks and benefits. Many of us are not. I think we need some kind of standard that we consider and communicate costs and benefits as much as possible, but we also need to acknowledge that established ethnographic methods can limit our ability to do this. In my experience IRBs are responsive to learning this, and understand that sometimes the most they can do is hold a research proposal accountable to the researchers' own professional standards. So a code of ethics that makes this explicit will help not only graduate students and other PIs, but also members of IRBs who are trained in the experimental sciences.

....

That informed consent is a process should be upfront in the beginning of an anthropological ethics statement. This is the opposite of the usual IRB expectation, where everything to be done is spelled out in advance and premises a literate Western subject. The essence of anthropological research is that the researcher hopes to learn from the "subjects," i.e., hosts. An ethics principle for anthropology should state this, and that learning from and working with the site hosts is a process that cannot be foretold.

....

I like the addition that informed consent does not need to [be accomplished] via a written form. I find such a form very off-putting and worrying for many local peoples outside of the European cultural milieu—they worry about what they are signing and moreover they often worry about remaining anonymous. Hopefully adding this part will help influence IRBs to realize that written consent forms are often not the best way to obtain consent in many fieldwork contexts.

....

In these comments, rather than responding to the content actually posted for review, readers appeared to enter directly into a conversation with the regulations, primarily as institutional artifacts of IRBs. This was the case, despite the fact of our familiarity with the unpredictability of anthropological work on the ground and with the ways that practice can be disruptive to, can spill beyond, and is even contradictory to, the boundaries that these normative pronouncements are meant to create and to contain, including disciplinary ethics codes themselves. In these responses, the calls to conceive of consenting as a *process* appear to be a direct reaction to the requirements of the federal regulations, which envision "informed consent" as something rather more specific, stable, and discrete than we know to be the case, a state-of-affairs that has been subject to considerable scrutiny and critique among anthropologists (see Corrigan et al. 2009). And yet, responses were nevertheless pitched at the regulatory level, and as such, carried over its generalizable normative justifications.

Additionally, responses notably framed the conversation in terms of "risk," and the language of risk is regularly used across disciplines with respect to human subjects. This is likely the result of experiences with university IRBs, and based on 45 CFR 46. The language of risk can, therefore, exert an influence on ethnographers' expectations and practices. However, anthropologists historically have not described their ethical preoccupations primarily in terms of risk so much as "harm," which is where the discipline's primary ethical conversation has been located (see Fluehr-Lobban 1994). As part of an email exchange with DP regarding the code revision, one commenter—a scholar and professor in international politics—wrote:

> [T]he vibe I am getting is that the AAA focuses on the no harm principle (with a vocal minority being really concerned about secrecy) and that informed consent gets less air time. So, presumably, a AAA member should not conduct a piece of research that has the full and informed consent from its subjects if there is any risk that they might be harmed in some way in the process. That is, the research subjects' say is actually severely constrained and potentially significant research could be ruled out on the basis of the risk of some minor harm. (personal communication 2011)

We might say that the commenter here was raising the specter of the "risk of harm," in this case to the human subject of research, quite correctly linking the assessment of risk to the awareness of risk, both on the part of researchers and of human subjects of research. The primacy of the concept of harm with respect to informed consent appears to depend, in this account, on a differential awareness of risk between researcher and research subject, where the potentially broader scope of possible risk entertained by the researcher could qualify the autonomy of the research subject to consent.

In conversations with the AAA's membership during the crafting of this particular principle, it was notable how many colleagues conceived of "harm" not as deriving from the specific circumstances of research and associated methodologies, but from the *potential* uses or consequences of the *results* of the research (e.g., as associated with possibilities like the objectification of the Other in disciplinary writing; the creation of a successful marketing campaign for tobacco products; or the potential military uses of cultural data collected in a conflict zone for the purposes of control). In its immediate absence, "harm" was nevertheless invoked as a real if theoretical possibility deserving of ethical attention, and as a critical feature of anthropology's own normative account or moral discourse around risks of violence, marginality, and vulnerability,[8] if in ways that tended to divert attention away from the various specific contexts and landscapes within which anthropologists operate.[9] In these exchanges, the "particularistic and historicizing" implications of ethnography are disregarded while the normative is foregrounded. In other words, the ways we conduct our professional ethical conversations continue to be divorced from the ways we theoretically and ethnographically engage with ethics.

Informed Consent at Present

The tendency to engage in ethical discussion in normative but ethnographically empty ways highlights recognition of the (geographic, social, and contextual) distance we are compelled to travel in the effort to articulate the relevance and application of disciplinary standards such as informed consent for the vagaries of field work "on the ground," where there is no perfect fit between stated ethical injunctions and the unpredictably socially contaminated daily realities of fieldwork. The necessity of negotiating this distance between standards (or ideals or values) and practices (or the field or the ground) is itself in fact a part of how we continue to imagine the unitariness of anthropological practice, particularly in the field. We continue to assume that it is a relatively routine process to re-connect practice with prevailing ethical standards. One of the preconditions for doing so, however, continues to be to treat informed consent as if a question negotiated at a particular stage of fieldwork, and against a background of the field as a knowable micro-world with identifiable margins.

We are at an odd juncture where ethnographers at once promote the agency of research counterparts while emphasizing their vulnerability as increasingly central to our relationship with them. Bell (2014:517) observes that current research ethical guidelines frame research with human subjects as an "intrinsically risky enterprise," where the interests of researchers and of research participants are assumed to be fundamentally opposed, and so research subjects must be "protected" from researchers. This is given a particular spin in the mode of ethnographic research, where, as Fluehr-Lobban (2013:68, 75) explains, "The list of at-risk populations that anthropologists study is a lengthy one," including "all manner of relatively powerless and disadvantaged people" who are subject to "extreme vulnerability." The present emphasis on the vulnerability of research counterparts coincides with the relatively more recent ethnographic turn to understanding the problems of power and its accompanying dedication to the promotion of the goals and projects of counterparts.

As we have explored throughout this chapter, "free and informed" is often internally linked with a problematic conception of "autonomy and consent." If routinely normatively asserted, such a conception assumes a well-defined and typically collective cultural subject that, at least in contemporary ethnographic terms, is static and ahistorical. If consistent with projects of rights and recognition in which indigenous peoples worldwide are engaged, often with support from activist anthropologists, this is an autonomy underwritten by an atavistic conception of the field as a place of definable margins, divested of trans-local state structures or global flows. It is not at all clear whether our ethical lexicon is up to the task of sorting through these several and competing historical accounts of the field, with their different implications for the relationships we maintain with counterparts in the field.

NOTES

1. Final report of the AAA's Commission on the Engagement of Anthropology with the U.S. Security and Intelligence Communities (2007:16).
2. See the recent AAAS report on scientist's own working understandings of their "social responsibilities": /www.aaas.org/report/social-responsibility-preliminary-inquiry-perspectives-scientists-engineers-and-health.
3. Details about this 2011 report, "Moral Science: Protecting Participants in Human Subjects Research," can be found at http://bioethics.gov/node/558. Interestingly this incident involved the same Public Health Service physician involved in the infamous Tuskegee syphilis experiment, the project that resulted in *The Belmont Report*, in turn, leading to the creation of our current ethics regulations for federally-funded research.
4. For the purposes of ethical discussion, the anthropological preoccupa-

tion with the state as a critical context for ethnographic projects of diverse sorts illustrates what Webb Keane (2014: 16) has called the "the historicity of ethics."

5. The effort to re-describe "the field" in the present has, as this list suggests, set off an active search for apt descriptors that too often serve a more metaphorical purpose to substitute for the disappearance of finding the field in definable places.

6. The full statement of "Anthropologists for the Boycott of Israeli Academic Institutions" can be found at https://anthroboycott.wordpress.com/.

7. See, for example, article 31 of the 2007 UN Declaration on the Rights of Indigenous Peoples, which asserts the right of control of indigenous peoples over their genetic resources and their cultural heritage, and which describes both as "property."

8. Such responses appear to register concern about supralocal and encompassing structures of power, encompassing structures that are rarely knowable in their entirety and, at least in fieldwork, are often left "to different degrees off-stage" (Marcus 1998:43) in the form of ethnographically hard-to-contain but not straightforwardly locatable sources of power and harm.

9. See Briody and Pester (2014) for a discussion of the lack of fit of the AAA's current CoE with the activities of practicing anthropologists, with particular attention to the differences between "do no harm" and "do some good."

REFERENCES

Albro, Robert
2015 Ethics of Anthropological Research. *In* International Encyclopedia of the Social and Behavioral Sciences, vol 1. 2nd edition. Neil J. Smelser and Paul B. Baltes, eds. Pp. 734-739. London: Elsevier, Ltd.

Anderson, Barbara Gallatin
1990 First Fieldwork: The Misadventures of an Anthropologist. Long Grove, IL: Waveland Press.

Appadurai, Arjun
1988 Putting Hierarchy in its Place. Cultural Anthropology 3(1):36-49.

Aretxaga, Begoña
2003 Maddening States. Annual Review of Anthropology 32:393-410.

Attinasi, John, and Paul Friedrich
1995 Dialogic Breakthrough: Catalysis and Synthesis in Life-changing Dialogue. In The Dialogic Emergence of Culture. B. Mannheim and D. Tedlock, eds. Pp. 33-53. Urbana: University of Illinois Press.

Battaglia, Debbora, ed.
1995 Rhetorics of Self-Making. Berkeley: University of California Press.

Bell, Kirsten
2014 Resisting Commensurability: Against Informed Consent as an Anthropological Virtue. American Anthropologist 116(3):511-522.

Briody, Elizabeth, and Tracy Meerwarth Pester
2014 The Coming of Age of Anthropological Practice and Ethics. Journal of Business Anthropology. Special Issue 1:11-37.

Brown, Michael
2003 Who Owns Native Culture? Cambridge, MA: Harvard University Press.

Bunzl, Matti
2008 The Quest for Anthropological Relevance: Borgesian Maps and Epistemological Pitfalls. American Anthropologist 110(1):53-60.

Collier, Stephen J., and Aihwa Ong
2005 Global Assemblages, Anthropological Problems. *In* Global Assemblages: Technology, Politics, and Ethics as Anthropological Problems. S. Collier and A. Ong, eds. Pp. 3-21. London: Wiley-Blackwell.

Comaroff, John L., and Jean Comaroff
1992 Ethnography and the Historical Imagination. Boulder, CO: Westview Press.

Commission on the Engagement of Anthropology with the US Security and Intelligence Communities (CEAUSSIC)
2007 Final Report. Arlington, VA: American Anthropological Association.

Corrigan, Oonagh, John McMillan, Kathleen Liddell, Martin Richards, and Charles Weijer
2009 The Limits of Consent: A Socio-Ethical Approach to Human Subject Research in Medicine. Oxford: Oxford University Press.

Crane, Julia G., and Michael V. Angrosino
1992 Field Projects in Anthropology: A Student Handbook. Long Grove, IL: Waveland Press.

Das, Veena
2008 Violence, Gender, and Subjectivity. Annual Review of Anthropology 37:283-299.

Dewalt, Kathleen M., and Billie R. Dewalt
2010 Participant Observation: A Guide for Fieldworkers. Walnut Creek: AltaMira Press.
2000. Participant Observation. *In* Handbook of Methods in Cultural Anthropology. R. Bernard, ed. Pp. 259-300. Walnut Creek: AltaMira Press.

Fabian, Johannes
2014 [1983] Time and the Other: How Anthropology Makes its Object. New York: Columbia University Press.

Fassin, Didier, and Samuel Lézé
2013   Moral Anthropology. London: Routledge.

Faubion, James D.
2011   An Anthropology of Ethics. Cambridge, UK: Cambridge University Press.

Fischer, Michael
2007   Culture and Cultural Analysis as Experimental Systems. Cultural Anthropology 22(1):1-65.

Fluehr-Lobban, Carolyn
2013   Ethics and Anthropology: Ideas and Practice. Walnut Creek: AltaMira Press.
1998   Ethics. *In* Handbook of Methods in Cultural Anthropology. H. Russell Bernard, ed. Pp. 173-202. Walnut Creek: AltaMira Press.
1994   Informed Consent in Anthropological Research: We are Not Exempt. Human Organization 53(1):1-10.

Geertz, Clifford
1983   Local Knowledge: Further Essays in Interpretive Anthropology. New York: Basic Books.
1973   The Interpretation of Cultures: Selected Essays. New York: Basic Books.

González, Roberto
2009   American Counterinsurgency: Human Science and the Human Terrain. Chicago: Prickly Paradigm Press.

Gupta, Akhil, and James Ferguson, eds.
1997   Anthropological Locations: Boundaries and Grounds of a Field Science. Berkeley: University of California Press.

Hastrup, Kirsten
1990   The Ethnographic Present: A Reinvention. Cultural Anthropology 5(1):45-61.

Hoeyer, Klaus, and Linda F. Hogle
2014   Informed Consent: The Politics of Intent and Practice in Medical Research Ethics. Annual Review of Anthropology 43:347-362.

Ignatieff, Michael
2012   Reimagining a Global Ethic. Ethics & International Affairs 26(1):7-19.

Inda, Jonathan Xavier, and Renato Rosaldo, eds.
2007   The Anthropology of Globalization: A Reader. Oxford: Blackwell Readers in Anthropology.

Jackson, Jean E.
1990   I am a Fieldnote: Fieldnotes as a Symbol of Professional Identity. *In* Fieldnotes: The Makings of Anthropology. R. Sanjek, ed. Pp. 3-33. New York: Cornell University Press.

Keane, Webb
2014 Affordances and Reflexivity in Ethical Life: An Ethnographic Stance. Anthropological Theory 14(1):3-26.

Kirsch, Stuart
2006 Reverse Anthropology: Indigenous Analysis of Social and Environmental Relations in New Guinea. Palo Alto: Stanford University Press.

Laidlaw, James
2014 The Subject of Virtue: An Anthropology of Ethics and Freedom. Cambridge: Cambridge University Press.

Lamphere, Louise
2003 The Perils and Prospects for an Engaged Anthropology. A View from the United States. Social Anthropology 11(2):153-168.

LeCompte, Margaret D., and Jean J. Schensul
2015 Ethics in Ethnography: A Mixed Methods Approach. Walnut Creek: AltaMira Press.

Lederman, Rena
2013 Ethics: Practices, Principles, and Comparative Perspectives. In The Handbook of Sociocultural Anthropology. James G. Carrier and Deborah B. Gewertz, eds. Pp. 588-611. New York: Bloomsbury Academic.
2007 Comparative Research: A Modest Proposal Concerning the Object of Ethics Regulation. PoLAR: Political and Legal Anthropology Review 30(2):305-327.

MacClancy, Jeremy, ed.
2002 Exotic No More: Anthropology on the Front Lines. Chicago: University of Chicago Press.

Marcus, George E.
1998 Ethnography through Thick and Thin. Princeton: Princeton University Press.

Mullings, Leith
2015 Anthropology Matters. American Anthropologist 117(1):4-16.

Nader, Laura
1974 Up the Anthropologist: Perspectives Gained from Studying Up. In Reinventing Anthropology. Dell Hymes, ed. Pp. 284-311. New York: Vintage Books.

Nagengast, Carole
1994 Violence, terror, and the crisis of the state. Annual Review of Anthropology 23:109-136.

Plemmons, Dena, and Robert Albro
2012 Practicing Ethics and Ethical Practice: The Case of Anthropologists and Military Humanitarians. Humanity: An International Journal of Human Rights, Humanitarianism, and Development 3(2):179-197.

Presidential Commission for the Study of Bioethical Issues
2011   Moral Science: Protecting Participants in Human Subjects Research. Washington DC.

Price, David H.
2011   Weaponizing Anthropology: Social Science in Service of the Militarized State. Petrolia, California: CounterPunch.
2007   Anthropology and the Wages of Secrecy. Anthropology News 48(3):6-7.

Schrag, Zachary M.
2010   Ethical Imperialism: Institutional Review Boards and the Social Sciences, 1965–2009. Baltimore: Johns Hopkins University Press.

Shore, Cris, and Susanna Trnka, eds.
2013   Up Close and Personal: On Peripheral Perspectives and the Production of Anthropological Knowledge. Methodology and History in Anthropology, vol. 25. NewYork: Berghahn Books.

Stocking, George W.
1992   The Ethnographer's Magic and Other Essays in the History of Anthropology. Madison: University of Wisconsin Press.

Stoller, Paul
1989   The Taste of Ethnographic Things: The Senses in Anthropology. Philadelphia: University of Pennsylvania Press.

Tedlock, Dennis, and Bruce Mannheim, eds.
1995   The Dialogic Emergence of Culture. Champaign: University of Illinois Press.

Wedel, Janine
2009   Ethical Research Across Power Divides. Anthropology News 50(6):18.

Wengle, John L.
1988   Ethnographers in the Field: The Psychology of Research. Tuscaloosa, AL: University of Alabama Press.

Whiteford, Linda M., and Robert T. Trotter II
2008   Ethics for Anthropological Research and Practice. Long Grove, IL: Waveland Press.

Wyndham, Jessica, Robert Albro, J. Ettinger, K. Smith, M. Sabatello, and M. S. Frankel
2015   Social Responsibilities: A Preliminary Inquiry into the Perspectives of Scientists, Engineers and Health Professionals. Report prepared under the auspices of the AAAS Science and Human Rights Coalition and AAAS Scientific Responsibility, Human Rights and Law Program, March 2015. doi: 10.1126/srhrl.aaa9798.

Zigon, Jarrett
2008   Morality: An Anthropological Perspective. New York: Bloomsbury Academic.

CHAPTER EIGHT

Weigh Competing Ethical Obligations to Collaborators and Affected Parties

Nathaniel Tashima and Cathleen Crain

Anthropologists must weigh competing ethical obligations to research participants, students, professional colleagues, employers and funders, among others, while recognizing that obligations to research participants are usually primary. In doing so, obligations to vulnerable populations are particularly important. These varying relationships may create conflicting, competing or crosscutting ethical obligations, reflecting both the relative vulnerabilities of different individuals, communities or populations, asymmetries of power implicit in a range of relationships, and the differing ethical frameworks of collaborators representing other disciplines or areas of practice.

Anthropologists have an obligation to distinguish the different kinds of interdependencies and collaborations their work involves, and to consider the real and potential ethical dimensions of these diverse and sometimes contradictory relationships, which may be different in character and may change over time. When conflicts between ethical standards or expectations arise, anthropologists need to make explicit their ethical obligations, and develop an ethical approach in consultation with those concerned.

Anthropologists must often make difficult decisions among competing ethical obligations while recognizing their obligation to do no harm. Anthropologists must not agree to conditions which inappropriately change the purpose, focus, or intended outcomes of their research. Anthropologists remain individually responsible for making ethical decisions.

Anthropological Ethics in Context: An Ongoing Dialogue, pp. 145-166. © 2016 Left Coast Press, Inc. All rights reserved.

Collaborations may be defined and understood quite differently by the various participants. The scope of collaboration, rights and responsibilities of the various parties, and issues of data access and representation, credit, and acknowledgment should be openly and fairly established at the outset.

Living on the High Wire: Balancing Competing Obligations

There is nothing simple about being a good anthropologist. We are the professional strangers (Agar 1980) who largely work in others' places and cultures; we are the comets that orbit in and out of others' systems and when we follow the rules of our disciplinary physics, expect that we will do no harm, and if the stars align, that we will do some good. As anthropologists we live in continuous ambiguity working and often living in the liminal spaces between and around others' cultures.

One of the greatest complexities for anthropologists is in understanding and balancing the competing duties we have to our many stakeholders, including research participants, students, staff, professional colleagues, employers, and funders. In this chapter we will explore some of the competing obligations we may encounter, the ethical standards and practical planning that can help us to anticipate and address, if not always to resolve, the dilemmas we encounter. As appropriate, we will discuss differences in obligations experienced by anthropologists working across the major divisions of the discipline including academic anthropologists, that is, those whose major work is conducted from the platform of a university; applied anthropologists, those who are embedded in a university or other academic institution but who conduct research or other activities focused outside of academic research; and professional or practicing anthropologists, those whose usual work is fully independent of an academic institution and whose livelihood is derived from using the discipline of anthropology in a government, non-profit, for-profit, or other setting. It should be noted that this final category includes those who are acting as professional anthropologists, that is whose job description and institutional position recognize their disciplinary membership, as well as those who practice independently or within an anthropologically based or informed organization. Whatever our position, it is important to remember that we are all subject to

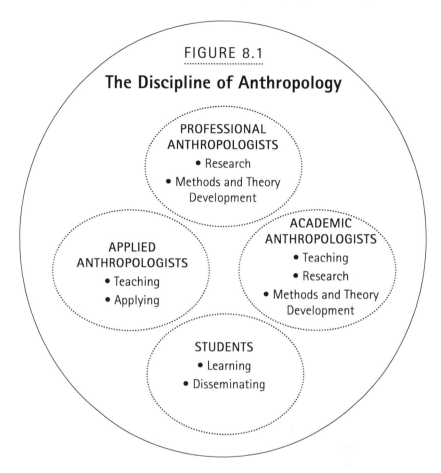

FIGURE 8.1
The Discipline of Anthropology

the same standards and challenged by the complexity of the sometimes competing obligations to our stakeholders. While we may assume different roles, we reflect the diversity and contribute to the wholeness of our discipline, as illustrated in Figure 8.1. Note that we see students as an integral part of the circle, as they move into the discipline, and, in the best scenario, graduate to being active anthropologists in one of the spheres, contributing to the development of the discipline. They also stand at the nexus of understanding of the other, as their training, ideally, fully prepares them to successfully function in one or more spheres of the discipline and to navigate the competing obligations.

Particularly for professional anthropologists, their training must fully prepare them as they face away from the everyday academic core of the discipline. The importance of understanding the obligations that they have to others and the competing ethical obligations is critical.

The Heart of Complexity

A fundamental part of the discussion of anthropological ethics lies in the twin themes of complexity and engagement. We, as anthropologists, work in complex systems (cultures), dealing with issues that are often of significant importance to human populations. And, frequently, we work to understand process and change at the intersection of multiple systems and cultures. Whether we are concerned with the past through the archaeological enterprise, engaging as cultural anthropologists with the cultures of communities and how the shape and functioning of those cultures affect their current welfare, or looking, as medical anthropologists, at a disease process in a population context, ours is a discipline that is fraught with complexity. The tasks that we undertake hold the potential for great benefit if conducted well and, in many cases, significant harm if conducted poorly. We also work in an atmosphere of ambiguity as we learn and continue to learn through our research and understand what is not understood. And, for many professional anthropologists, the work is frequently conducted in relative or complete isolation from other anthropologists. This isolation can be challenging for the individual in accounting for and being able to act to address and balance competing obligations.

We also spiral out from specific individuals and communities who work with us as partners in our project activities to audiences who are disconnected from the immediate cultural contexts and participants. Our work becomes part of policy discussions and informs and forms the decisions that affect funding, program design and evaluation, and ultimately the wellbeing of people in communities around the world. And, finally, we are subject to and engage in a variety of legal obligations such as grants, contracts, and partnerships that create additional or extended and sometimes competing responsibilities. In the remainder of this chapter we will discuss the nature of our obligations to our stakeholders and provide some guidance for prioritizing and managing the inevitable competing obligations.

Understanding and Accounting for the Others

> *Anthropologists have an obligation to distinguish the different kinds of interdependencies and collaborations their work involves, and to consider the real and potential ethical dimensions of these diverse and sometimes contradictory relationships, which may be different in character and may*

change over time. When conflicts between ethical standards or expectations arise, anthropologists need to make explicit their ethical obligations, and develop an ethical approach in consultation with those concerned.

(AAA 2012)

As we consider our research and the ethics of its design and conduct, an essential analysis is that of the structural relationships that will affect the interactions between and among the stakeholders. In this section, we will explore some of the key relationships and how they may affect the ethical conduct of research.

Individual Respondents

Respondents, whether individuals or groups, are generally at the heart of our research and as such critical to its construction, conduct, and success. This means that without their active participation we cannot succeed; this creates a particular pressure on the anthropologist to gain and sustain their willing involvement. Respondents are also often at a structural disadvantage in relationship to the anthropologist—less educated, less privileged, and with access to fewer resources. And, it is the intersection of our need and their disadvantage that, if not addressed early, may result in ethical challenges. In designing a project, it is the responsibility of the anthropologist to carefully consider the nature of the respondents' participation and the potential for creating conflicts among and between the project's goals and the respondents' values and role within a family, community, and other social networks.

The AAA ethics statement is clear that we have a particular obligation to protect the interests of our respondents. There are times when a project's goals and objectives and associated "data" to be developed may place an individual respondent in a position of choosing to continue participation or to withdraw. It may not be clear to a respondent at the beginning of a project that a conflict may arise in the future and it is the responsibility of the anthropologist to ensure that if a respondent desires to withdraw from participation there is a way out for the respondent as well as a means for the anthropologist to continue the work. If an accommodation cannot be constructed within the framework of the respondent's values and the needs of the project, the anthropologist should attempt to create alternative questions or research processes that may achieve the same outcomes. Table 8.1 presents some of the issues

TABLE 8.1 Example Issues and Concerns Regarding Competing Obligations

Issue	Examples of Concerns
Confidentiality and Safety	• Can the anthropologist completely shield the respondent from identification if needed? If needed is that a part of the structure of the research from design through completion (including archiving of data)? • Can the anthropologist ensure that the identity of the respondent will not be discernable in reporting? • Can the anthropologist ensure that the research will not put the respondent in physical or psychological danger? Or that the respondent is in a position to determine the potential for danger versus the importance of their participation and make an informed decision?
Transparency	• Is the purpose of the research made clear to each potential participant? • Is the use and benefit of the collected information made clear?
Benefits of Research	• Is there a clear and understood benefit to the respondents or her/his community/culture? • Are the results of the research available and accessible to the respondent and her/his community for their use?
Incentives	• Are the incentives for participation appropriate [the incentives are not so excessive as to convince someone to engage in the research against their better judgment]?

we need to address as we design and prepare to carry out research, in order to be particularly vigilant about the concerns of our respondents and protecting them from competing obligations, whether to ourselves or other stakeholders.

Communities/Group Respondents

Communities and groups of respondents present the anthropologist with particular challenges as they may have requirements, needs, and desires that reflect the centrality of their position but may conflict with other obligations. For example, a community sponsor may want to attend interviews where individuals are promised confidentiality. Groups may want to review and edit documents prior to their becoming public, potentially endangering the independence of the research. And, communities and groups may desire to utilize the products of the research for their own purposes, potentially creating conflict with donors. An essential understanding for the anthropologist is that entering into and engaging communities and groups is rarely neutral; their requirements, needs, and desires must be understood early, their needs addressed, and issues that create ethical conflicts resolved. Ensuring that other obligations are managed so that the desires of communities and groups for access to and the benefit of the research products are guaranteed is vital, as well.

Funders

Funders are a particularly potent stakeholder. Often they have set terms of engagement before a request for proposal (RFP) or a request for application (RFA) or other vehicle is distributed. They may have regulatory requirements and authority regarding the research design and conduct and the ownership of data and products. And, they are often powerful organizations with future opportunities, professional cachet, and employment not only for the anthropologist but for others, as a part of a successful engagement. In each of these areas, there is the potential for the funder to request or require the anthropologist to act in ways that may engender competing obligations.

Those institutions that fund anthropological research range from the National Science Foundation to the Department of Health and Human Services; from the Robert Wood Johnson Foundation to the John Templeton Foundation; and, from Motorola to General Motors. Each institution has a purpose for the research that advances its own interests and each has conditions for eligibility and conduct that must be agreed to in order to receive support. And, in a very real way, each directs the research through its RFA/RFP process and funding decisions.

There is a vast array of funding sources for anthropological work and under which anthropologists work. For individual employment, almost any industry has need for an anthropological perspective. From General Motors to State Farm Insurance, from Google to IBM, anthropologists have found rewarding and useful employment. Government agencies, foundations and international non-governmental agencies all have need of anthropologists. The military, law enforcement, pharmaceutical companies, and advertising all employ individual anthropologists. Many of these organizations also work through grants and contracts. Regardless of what funding mechanism is employed, anthropologists must consider the basis of their funding and make a basic ethical decision as to whether or not they believe the derivation of the funding for their project or employment meets the individual anthropologist's understanding of ethical behavior. The obligation to investigate the roots of support must be universal across anthropology; both professionals and academics must know where funding comes from and that our work is not supporting, directly or indirectly, unethical activities. Individuals working within an organization must consider examining the sources of overhead funding for their university or organization as they may be supported by funds from sources that may challenge their ethical values.

Anthropologists, academic, applied, and professional, sometimes fail to understand the requirements and/or they fail to credit the seriousness of the assumed legal obligations. Because we agree to the purpose and the conditions determined by the funder does not make the endeavor inherently more or less ethical. However, if we are unaware or indifferent to the implications, our work and our ethics can be jeopardized and we may fail in our obligations to other stakeholders. This lack of understanding has sometimes led to confrontations between anthropologists and funders after work is underway or products are being finalized. These confrontations may include the anthropologist citing a higher authority for their lack of willingness to comply with a particular requirement. The time for such discussions is prior to accepting the grant or the contract, not once an agreement has been made (see Chapter 10). Such confrontations are largely unnecessary and are detrimental to relationships as well as to the view of anthropologists as responsible social scientists. An essential shield against this kind of problem is the preparation of all anthropologists to directly address the legalities of accepting funding from any source and the ethical implications. This is also an area in which the AAA could play an important role in continuing to hone the skills of anthropologists beyond the university setting and in providing education and advocacy support in negotiations. This is also where the AAA could offer on-going educational opportunities for developing research proposals and for understanding how the process articulates with protections for participants, responsiveness to and transparency with participants and funders, and data ownership and publication rights and responsibilities, and for understanding how these issues relate to the AAA Statement on Ethics. With this type of preparation and support, all anthropologists should be better positioned to determine the appropriateness of funding opportunities and to advocate for terms that present the fewest opportunities for competing responsibilities with other stakeholders.

Employers

Employers, whether a university, a consulting firm, a governmental agency, or a non-profit organization, may exert significant control over the shape and conduct of anthropological research, and may determine for their own purposes, or in response to sponsors or funders, the use and ownership of data. And, as with funders, they have the power of employment, reputation, and future opportunities and, importantly, they are owed a variety of responsibilities by the anthropologist.

With employers, anthropologists must be students of both the general and the particular. That is, we must first understand the specific standing policies of the organization, often published in the organization's personnel manual or other available documents. For all organizations there is a more general legal and regulatory environment that will affect the ways in which the organization functions. Without becoming a legal scholar, it is incumbent on the anthropologist to research and understand the environment in which they and their organization function. For particular projects, as appropriate to the anthropologist's position in the organization, reading and understanding the research proposal and work plan is essential. And, as possible, engaging in the design phases allows the anthropologist to begin to affect the shape of the research and to possibly identify and address areas of potential competing obligations. Anthropologists must also be as active participants as possible in discussions of the research endeavor if our concerns are to be understood and acted upon. Early identification of issues may allow for preemptive actions; late identification may unravel ongoing research, alienate partners, and jeopardize funding. And, not inconsequentially, may endanger our team, our employers' funding and reputation, and potentially the anthropologists' future employment. These are not reasons to avoid identification of issues but rather should be motivation to be thoughtful and proactive.

While the stakeholders discussed here are those most often encountered by anthropologists, they are not the entire range of those to whom we have responsibility. The anthropologist must carefully assess and account for the field of potential stakeholders in any research endeavor.

Practical Precursors

As good anthropologists, there are a variety of activities that we can undertake that will help to ensure that our work responds to our PPR and that will help us to identify and address competing obligations. In this section we will discuss some practical precursors to address before undertaking any anthropological endeavor. Figure 8.2 illustrates frequently found stakeholders in anthropological research; particular research may involve other stakeholders. And, we have offered them in what we see as the general order of priority: beginning with the individual respondents and their families (if

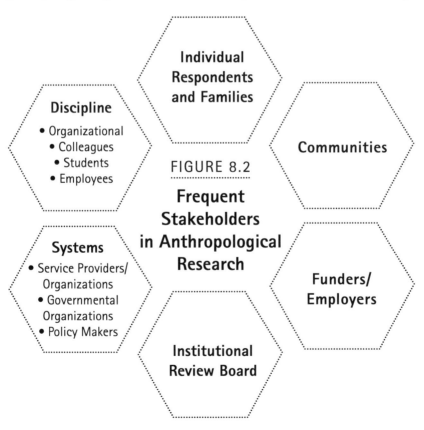

FIGURE 8.2
Frequent Stakeholders in Anthropological Research

this is the kind of research undertaken) and moving through the community and then to other involved or engaged parties. In the next section, we will discuss some of the particular challenges in balancing competing obligations with some of the other classes of stakeholders.

Know your Ethics

A fundamental responsibility for all anthropologists is to read and fully explore the meaning of the PPR. While this may seem an obvious step, it is one too frequently overlooked. The statement on ethics is clear and has direction that will guide the individual in considering research. In addition, it is important to explore other fundamental documents such as *The Belmont Report* (1979). And, for those anthropologists who work in other fields, referencing professional guidance for those areas is essential. For example, when engaged in evaluation activities, knowing and accounting for the American Evaluation Association's principles of 2004 as a source of specific guidance is important. If you are conducting research under Federal funding knowing and understanding the guidance provided by the Office for Human Research Protections (OHRP) is an important part of preparing to conduct responsible and ethical research in concert with AAA's PPR. All anthropologists should have training in ethical research practices beginning in the university setting. For example, the Collaborative Institutional Training Initiative at the University of Miami (CITI Program) offers an online series of modules on human subjects protection and related ethical issues. The CITI Program (www.citiprogram.org) certification provides researchers with a standard assessment of knowledge about human subjects protection and highlights concerns for researchers engaging with a variety of human subjects issues as well as administrative and other types of research protections.

Ethics training, the review of the suggested documents, and active engagement with other disciplines may also require mediating conflicts of obligations among the provided guidance. But, being knowledgeable and recognizing the need to account for the potential for competing obligations from the beginning of planning through implementation and closing out research will help to reduce the opportunity for harm to stakeholders and disruption of research.

Enumerate Your Stakeholders and Your Promises

In designing research and lookig for funding and other supports, we have both explicit and assumed responsibilities to others. A practical

156 Anthropological Ethics in Context

TABLE 8.2. **Examples of Areas of Potential Conflict Involving Competing Ethical Obligations**

Source(s) of Funding	Purpose of Research	Research Design
Confidentiality in data collection and after	Protections for Different Kinds/Classes of Respondents	Transparency of research activities
Amount of Honoraria for Participating	Access to/Ownership of Data	Rights in Publication

step is to create a table or other graphic that helps you to visualize who your stakeholders are and what you plan to or have agreed to do/not do/provide to/for them. Important aspects of this exercise are to look for conflicts between/among stakeholders and to determine what is expected of you by the PPR and legally. This exercise will help you to determine where the points of conflict occur and potential options for resolution. Table 8.2 presents examples of areas in which conflict may occur and the anthropologist will need to weigh competing ethical obligations.

This is a brief list and the topics are provided at a high level. Each anthropologist will need to clearly enumerate all of the particular issues in her/his research planning and determine how to anticipate and best address or resolve the issue.

Are Data Ownership and Access Issues Clearly Specified in all Contracts and Agreements?

Once the scope of work and budget have been formalized in a contract or grant, part of the responsibility of the anthropologist is to read the fine print before signing, because that is the last time you will have the opportunity to negotiate these issues. The contract or grant terms and conditions will govern conduct of the research, ownership of data, on-going access to the data, rights to access and dissemination of products of the work, as well as publication rights. These aspects of implementation of the research, as well as ownership and access to data, must be clearly defined. And when the anthropologist signs the contract or grant award, they must be clear that they are agreeing to all of the terms and conditions included in the document. After-the-fact recognition that the contract or grant agreement requires collaborative planning or restricts ownership of data or rights of publication without consent of the funder does not put the anthropologist in a legal position to re-negotiate the terms and conditions of award because "they did not understand what they had signed" or "they had never seen a clause like this" or "they should be able to do as they wish with the information." Reading the fine print in the award will prevent ethical as well as practical problems after the fact. While not an issue unique to anthropology, this undertaking is a proactive responsibility of an anthropologist when signing an award agreement. It is the responsibility of the individual anthropologist to carefully review the document and ensure that the ethical concerns that are raised by the AAA Statement on Ethics are appropriately represented in any agreement. And it is the individual anthropologist's responsibility to work with the funder or employer if there are any areas where the requirements of the work are likely to engender competing obligations.

Protection of Participants

Most grants and contracts will include language about obligations to inform and protect respondents; these obligations must be carefully reviewed to ensure that they provide sufficient protection to respondents. It is the obligation of the anthropologist to ensure that the activities that provide protection to participants are clear and accessible to all who are engaged in the project. Consent forms in the participant's language and leveled for the appropriate educational experience should be developed, as well as methods for obtaining consent and for documenting such consent. For communities where written documents are not practicable and consent to participate may not follow western cultural values, or where danger may be created through written documents, it is critical to be proactive in developing appropriate methods of obtaining consent to participate.

Consent for an individual may not always be an independent activity. In some cultures it may be important and expected that there will be others in addition to the respondent who may need to understand the research and be consulted prior to agreeing to participate. And, while anthropologists need to be sensitive to issues of consenting in different cultures they must be clear about undue influence by others, particularly on those who are vulnerable in the population. In many cultures these vulnerable populations include but are not limited to women, children, and ethnic and sexual minorities. Discerning and assessing influence and its cultural appropriateness requires significant insider knowledge of a culture. Determining from whom such knowledge may be reliably acquired is an early challenge in fieldwork.

As noted earlier, protection of the participant may extend to ensuring that those around the respondent including other individuals and leaders in the community do not have special, unplanned access to data. Engaging in recognized training that ensures that you are fully conversant with participant protection issues and actions is essential.

Inventory your Desires and Benefits from the Research

Being clear about why the research is important to you and what benefits you anticipate deriving from the research is a part of being clear and focused in analysis and decision-making around competing priorities. These benefits are in contrast to the estimated benefits to participants and host communities. With this analysis clearly articulated, you will be better able to recognize and account for instances when your desires and benefits compete with those of other stakeholders and to weigh your decisions about competing obligations.

Engage your Colleagues

As noted earlier, the anthropological endeavor is frequently very complex and engages a range of stakeholders. In undertaking the ethical analysis, it is important to bring trusted others into the analysis. These others should include people who are senior and experienced in anthropological fieldwork and who have demonstrated concern for understanding and addressing ethical standards in research, in particular people who have the analytical skills needed to identify and deal with competing obligations while supporting the design of the research.

Avoid Isolation

Many anthropologists work outside of their discipline. For example, medical anthropologists may work in health care or policy settings. Cultural anthropologists may be found anywhere where an understanding of human behavior and interactions is needed, including non-profit organizations, governmental organizations, and private sector organizations. This is one of the fundamental differences between academic/applied and professional/practicing anthropologists. The former have a disciplinary home to which they return and a cohort of other anthropologists. Too often the latter is the only anthropologist in an organization.

Examples of the situations that challenge isolated anthropologists include: where others are in control of the terms of engagement for research; where the anthropologist is in a vulnerable position in relationship to those responsible; and where competing ethical guidelines may cause the anthropologist to experience conflicts that are difficult to navigate. For the isolated anthropologist it is important to establish a disciplinary reference group. This may mean joining and engaging with a local or national anthropology organization. Utilizing other professionals to support analysis and decision-making regarding the design and conduct of research and in analyzing and addressing competing obligations is essential. Additionally, working in an isolated context will mean being clear about your ethical obligations when involved with any research controlled by others. It is often easier to gain understanding before designs and relationships are set, and so offering to brief others on the PPR as the research planning begins may help others to account for issues in the planning.

Engage with an Institutional Review Board (IRB)

If you are an organizational principal undertaking human research, engaging with an IRB is an important aspect of ensuring that your research is ethical and free of foreseeable conflicts. Identifying an IRB that is sensitive to and knowledgeable about anthropology will be beneficial in making them an asset in your research planning and conduct.

Obtain Federalwide Assurances

If you are a principal in a research organization conducting research for the federal government, then applying for and committing to the requirements of a Federalwide Assurance (FWA) is essential. The FWA is the only type of assurance currently accepted and approved by OHRP. Through the FWA, an institution commits to the Department of Health and Human Services (HHS) that it will comply with the requirements in the HHS Protection of Human Subjects regulations at 45 CFR part 46 (OHRP).

The essence of these steps is being knowledgeable and proactive. Appropriate steps should be undertaken prior to accepting a grant, signing a contract or other agreement, or making verbal promises to stakeholders to ensure that the anthropologist is clearly aware of the commitments that are being agreed to as well as the consequences for the proposed study, project, or activity.

The Anthropological Challenge of Balancing Context, Necessary Judgments, and Competing Obligations

We walk a high wire on which we must balance ethical perspectives that can shift over time or among various members who are engaged in the work. It is not possible to anticipate all the potential paths that may carry our work forward or who will seize on a portion of the work and incorporate it into their perspective without the full context of our approach, data, and analysis. However, from the moment a project is undertaken we can begin realistically assessing the potential positive and negative outcomes and weighing the relationship between them. If at that point we believe that we should move forward, then, being transparent with the participants so that they can make an informed decision about whether they wish to participate in our work should be the next step.

Once the values of a project have been considered, stakeholders must be identified. There are no simple relationships free of ties to other individuals, families, and/or communities. Individuals exist within a web of social networks, and the anthropologist enters into these webs of interconnection and interdependence. The ethnocentric view of an independent, self-reliant individual able to make decisions for themselves works in a fairly limited context. For much of the human world, individuals are embedded within a social network that involves family, friends, and community. The definitions of each of these groups depend on the cultural context within which they live and the organizing values. This cultural context must be a foundation of ethical decision-making for the anthropologist. This understanding of local values may shift over time as an anthropologist gains greater understanding of the community and people of interest to the project. As this knowledge is developed, it is important to revisit ethical understandings of the project's activities so that this new, grounded knowledge can be used to guide decisions about project activities. At the same time, the requirements of the AAA Statement on Ethics should serve as the overarching perspective within which the anthropologist judges the ethical appropriateness of actions, work, and analysis.

In the following sections we discuss a few more issues that are important for the anthropologist to actively consider when designing ethically informed research.

Can You Keep Your Promises?

In our world, the pressure is to do more with less and to do it quickly. And, while this is not a peculiarly anthropological issue (nor one that affects all anthropologists), it is one that may affect our ability to do quality work and to honor the commitments that we make. The temptation is to agree to produce an outcome that fits the funder's timeframe within the budget that is available. If, however, the desired outcomes either cannot be developed within the requested timeframe or within the funding that is available or if obligations to stakeholders may not be able to be honored, it is essential to address that before signing a grant or a contract. Being clear about where reductions in scope of work and anticipated outcomes will occur in order to fit the work within the available time and funds allows both parties to make informed decisions. It is not appropriate to say to the funder near the end of the project that it will take another X number of months to complete or that additional funds are necessary in order to complete the work. Once agreed to, a grant document or contract delimits what can be expected and the compensation; renegotiating based on understood changes can then occur. If the timeframe or funds preclude appropriately engaging with respondents and communities, that issue must be addressed before the grant or contract is signed. Although this does not sound like an ethical dilemma, it can be the root of misunderstandings and promises about outcomes that are unrealistic from the beginning.

Are Obligations for Privacy and Secrecy Clearly Understood?

Contracts and other agreements may contain clauses that limit the ability of the anthropologist to discuss, control, or publish the results of the research they undertake. This is not a bar to ethical behavior in the conduct of the research if the information is sensitive or proprietary. However, the anthropologist must be certain before signing an agreement that complying with the terms of the agreement does not create an ethical dilemma. And, it is essential in designing research that all stakeholders are clearly informed of the limitations prior to engaging in the research.

Are the Concerns of all Stakeholders Understood and Accounted for in Project Planning and Development?

An important design concern that has ethical implications, as discussed earlier, is that all of the stakeholders need to be identified. This begins with an inclusive scan of individual participants, community members, community leaders, and people and systems/services that may not be geographically local, but may be involved in decision-making or whose consent or notification may be considered by the primary participants as necessary in order to legitimatize their participation. This can become a complex web of social networks, and a Western identification of individuals and relationships may result in too linear or limited a perspective. As research proceeds information about people, social networks, relationships, values, and the functioning of those values is gathered. This knowledge will ultimately figure into the reports, briefings, and policy papers that may result from the project. The anthropologist may be faced with having gained knowledge that will bring harm to participants or to communities and may therefore be obligated not to use that information. Ethical considerations for anthropologists must be an active process that accounts for perspectives gained during the research and does not end with IRB approval.

Are Field Workers Properly Trained and Supervised for Ethical Behavior and to Work to Disciplinary Standards?

Projects for which an anthropologist is responsible and which engage individuals other than fully trained anthropologists must be designed with particular care and analyzed for ethical challenges and competing obligations. The concerns begin with who the others are and how they relate to the research community/respondents. For example, the use of graduate students in research is common, and all must be trained and supervised to ensure that their work meets both the ethical and professional standards of our discipline. Engaging non-professional individuals from a country, region, or community requires special attention to who they are and how they relate to the people and topics of the research. It also requires special attention to training and oversight to ensure appropriate attention to methods and ethical behavior. The complexities of ethnicity, language, socio-economic status, and gender must be carefully accounted for in the recruitment, training, and oversight of workers. And, the complex relationship among the values of the researcher/project implementer, the field staff, the participating communities, and individuals must be carefully considered and cautiously managed as the project progresses. Anthropologists must consider the obligation to provide training and research experience for local project staff and the design requirements to develop accurate and complete data for the research.

Are Data Handled in a Respectful and Ethical Manner?

Anthropological data can be developed in a variety of forms from direct observations, videos, one-on-one interviews, focus groups, discussions with a number of participants, and casual conversations. In some cases, survey work or questionnaires can also be employed, as well as online electronic surveys. All these data gathering methods require that records be kept. It is the anthropologist's obligation to ensure that each kind of record is treated with respect and that the appropriate level of security is ensured. They must ensure that data are properly stored and destroyed, as determined by the final research plan. Anthropologists must be trained, beginning in their undergraduate work, to manage data appropriately and to respect the importance of the obligation undertaken with the collection. While we may have an obligation to train our students, we must ensure that the principle of preserving both the physical safety and the confidentiality of records is clearly observed.

The anthropologist should carefully consider the importance of being able to retain data for long periods of time. Contracts and grants will specify a period of time the researcher must retain files, but once that period expires it is up to the anthropologist to decide whether to maintain or destroy files. If files are then retained, has adequate protection been developed? If there is any belief by the anthropologist during the development of a project that data will be maintained for an extended period of time, is there a responsibility to inform a respondent? Can the confidentiality and safety of data be maintained? Is there a locked, fireproof facility or computer storage method that assures the integrity of the promise made by the anthropologist?

Anthropologists have an obligation to keep and preserve research records, and in some cases this obligation is a requirement of a grant or contract. The obligation to preserve the records of our research must be balanced against potential harms that could come to our research participants in particular.

Is Data Analysis Free of Bias and Consistent with Best Disciplinary Practices and Standards?

Planning for analysis of data that ensures that the conclusions represent the best use of the data is an obligation that all anthropologists must undertake. It is critical that the anthropologist continually examine assumptions and conclusions to ensure that they truly are based on the data. Participants have taken precious time from their daily lives to work with the anthropologist and expose their lives to a stranger, and have only a general idea of what this could mean when the information is analyzed and synthesized as part of the construction of the report that is often the outcome of the work. This obligation also goes to the importance of the anthropological discipline in informing other social scientists, in informing the development of services, and in the making of policy.

Are Reports and Presentations Available and Accessible?

Where our results are intended to inform diverse audiences, it is essential that we plan for means by which those audiences can have access to appropriately leveled and formatted information in accessible language. We must design our projects to ensure that those to whom the results will be delivered have appropriate access; this may mean that there may be multiple versions of the same results—differently leveled, in different languages, in different media. In most cases it is not enough to believe that publishing reports, articles, or in books suffices to make results available to diverse stakeholders. With the advent of social media and web resources, creative opportunities exist for anthropologists to make their work broadly available. Video conferences provide opportunities for anthropologists to engage in presentations with local stakeholders and be a virtual presence in some communities. Not all communities have electronic access, but greater numbers of communities can participate to some extent in these virtual relationships so that the outcomes of anthropological research can become accessible to a wider network of participants and stakeholders. This desire to make research outcomes available to participants extends the anthropological endeavor from one that is shared with colleagues in universities to one that is shared with a variety of stakeholders in mostly real time. The importance of sharing outcomes in real time is also a consideration that should be part of the planning, so that research is not held hostage to dissemination at a time in some other future. The immediacy of electronic availability provides the anthropologist with an ideal process for sharing outcomes and engaging in an on-going conversation with participants.

This critical obligation is pushing the anthropological endeavor to greater levels of transparency. As part of the project design, anthropologists must account for the opportunities to return information to participants and stakeholders in forms and forums that do not focus on the academic process of university lectures, published journal articles, and books. These traditional forms of communication retain their importance, but alternative methods and processes must be incorporated into thinking about transparency and accountability. This means that accessibility of the information also must be thought of in terms of social media and other opportunities for sharing the outcomes with participants.

As noted in the AAA "Principles of Professional Responsibility, 5. Make Your Results Accessible," one must consider the diverse stakeholders that have been involved in the work, from funders through individual respondents. During the course of the work stakeholders should be informed of the nature and potential outcomes of the research. This begins with the funding proposal and continues to conversations with potential respondents and securing appropriate informed consent to participate in the research.

Clearly, this list is not exhaustive, but begins to outline the wide variety of places and spaces in our work where we must be vigilant about practicing our ethics. We must be prepared to understand and account for the views and needs of others, while being attentive to preserving our disciplinary quality. We must be prepared to walk away when we cannot find a path that satisfies our personal and professional ethics. Even the best preparation before starting work with a community cannot possibly anticipate all of the potential situations that may arise. The best plans may not always provide guidance for the immediate experience. However, what is critical is that the anthropologist has explored a variety of scenarios prior to engaging in fieldwork. These exercises of "what if…?" start a process of assessment before the reality of time, pressure, people, and place begin to enter into the equation. And, the creation and maintenance of a community in which the anthropologist can find support for working through ethical issues is clearly important.

Competing Obligations

In working with those from other disciplines, in highly complex and fast-moving situations, and away from a core of colleagues, there will always be the need to address competing obligations. Funders, including but not limited to government agencies, foundations, community-based organizations, and for-profit organizations, all engage anthropologists to conduct work. In the ideal project, all of the relevant stakeholders would share a common ethical framework that aligns with the American Anthropological Association's "Statement on Ethics: Principles of

Professional Responsibility." However, when this does not occur, the anthropologist must find a means to anticipate competing obligations and develop an ethical path that acknowledges the competing values and perspectives while honoring our disciplinary responsibilities.

Entering into the process of the anthropological endeavor places an individual within a variety of cultures. In order to act ethically, the anthropologist will be required to be aware of the potential ethical systems in which he or she is working and be proactive in assessing the ethical demands of those systems. The balancing of perspectives that is required of an anthropologist is an on-going process and requires vigilance in order to be effective.

Anthropologists, no matter what their positional relationship to the discipline, work in continuous complexity and ambiguity. It is this complexity and ambiguity that results in rich and nuanced research outcomes that fully reflect the experiences, needs, and perspectives of stakeholders. We must as a discipline embrace the complexity even as we work to ensure the ethical quality of our research.

REFERENCES

Agar, Michael
1990 The Professional Stranger: An Informal Introduction to Ethnography. New York: Academic Press.

American Anthropology Association
2012 Code of Ethics, Section 4: Weighing Competing Ethical Obligations Due Collaborators and Affected Parties. American Anthropology Association, November 1, 2012. http://ethics.aaanet.org/ethics-statement-4-weigh-competing-ethical-obligations-due-collaborators-and-affected-parties/

The Belmont Report
1979 The Belmont Report: Ethical Principles and Guidelines for the Protection of Human Subjects of Research. http://hhs.gov/ohrp/humansubjects/guidance/belmont.html, accessed March 29, 2015.

Office of Human Research Protections
N.d. Federalwide Assurances (FWAs). www.hhs.gov/ohrp/assurances/assurances/index.html, accessed March 29, 2015.

CHAPTER 9

Protect and Preserve Your Records

Alex W. Barker

Anthropologists have an ethical responsibility for ensuring the integrity, preservation, and protection of their work. This obligation applies both to individual and collaborative or team research. An anthropologist's ability to protect and use the materials collected may be contingent upon complex issues of ownership and stewardship. In situations of disagreement, contestation, or conflict over ownership, the primary assumption that the researcher owns her or his work product applies, unless otherwise established. Other factors (source of funding, employment agreements, negotiated agreements with collaborators, legal claims, among others) may impact ownership of records. Anthropologists should determine record ownership relating to each project and make appropriate arrangements accordingly as a standard part of ethical practice. This may include establishing by whom and how records will be stored, preserved, or disposed of in the long term.

Further, priority must be given to the protection of research participants, as well as the preservation and protection of research records. Researchers have an ethical responsibility to take precautions that raw data and collected materials will not be used for unauthorized ends. To the extent possible at the time of data collection, the researcher is responsible for considering and communicating likely or foreseeable uses of collected data and materials as part of the process of informed

Anthropological Ethics in Context: An Ongoing Dialogue, pp. 167-181. © 2016 Left Coast Press, Inc. All rights reserved.

consent or obtaining permission. Researchers are also responsible for consulting with research participants regarding their views of generation, use and preservation of research records. This includes informing research participants whether data and materials might be transferred to or accessed by other parties; how they might be transformed or used to identify participants; and how they will be stored and how long they will be preserved.

Researchers have a responsibility to use appropriate methods to ensure the confidentiality and security of field notes, recordings, samples or other primary data and the identities of participants. The use of digitalization and of digital media for data storage and preservation is of particular concern given the relative ease of duplication and circulation. Ethical decisions regarding the preservation of research materials must balance obligations to maintain data integrity with responsibilities to protect research participants and their communities against future harmful impacts. Given that anthropological research has multiple constituencies and new uses such as by heritage communities, the interests of preservation ordinarily outweigh the potential benefits of destroying materials for the preservation of confidentiality. Researchers generating object collections have a responsibility to ensure the preservation and accessibility of the resulting materials and/or results of analyzed samples, including associated documentation.

Anthropology has aptly been described as the most scientific of the humanities and humanistic of the sciences. The broader discipline represents a "big tent" encompassing everyone from hard scientists studying the biological evolution of specific enzymes to humanistic scholars studying ethnopoesis or writing autoethnographic essays. The kinds of records produced by such diverse scholars may differ fundamentally, but any perspective responsibly requires an emphasis on documentation of observations and accessibility of texts, grounding one's work and allowing others to meaningfully assess its merit.

Given the fluid nature of social settings, the effects of observation and environmental change on biological communities, and the impact on archaeological sites of post-depositional processes or excavations themselves, it is rare for the conditions documented by many anthropologists to be precisely replicated. The information on which inferences are based, and the contexts in which they were observed, must be recorded and those data preserved. Humanistic approaches, while perhaps less preoccupied with the replicability of observations, focus on engagement with objects, constructs or texts and interrogating them in meaningful ways. Without reference to an external, accessible text such discourse is endlessly recursive. Regardless of approach, the recording and preserving of the analytic or intellectual bases by which arguments are warranted and conclusions justified is of central importance to the discipline.

Many anthropologists remain extraordinarily possessive of "their" notes and data, and are reluctant to cede control over them by arranging for their longer-term curation and preservation. In some instances this is from fear that they will expose their own failures, inconsistencies, or mistakes, or simply because their field notes are such intensely personal documents (Jackson 1990). Caplan (2010:17) notes another reason—archiving one's records may suggest that one is no longer working on them, and unlike cognate disciplines that focus on proximate "findings" or "results" with presumed beginnings and ends, many anthropologists in all subdisciplines return to their records regularly throughout their career.

Preservation of records requires more than retention, however, and may also imply permanent curation and archiving beyond the professional life of the anthropologist generating the research results and the material on which these results are based. It has long been argued that archives and museums are ultimately attempts to belie mortality (Derrida [1995], citing a Freudian fear of death, is perhaps the most celebrated example), and in the need for making plans for the preservation of anthropological records that is precisely (albeit rather naively) the case. In an increasingly digital age, preservation of records may also require more than acid-free folders and stable ambient environments, creating new challenges for the discipline and its practitioners. The ease of duplication and circulation of digital records poses significant risks to the privacy of research participants, while at the same time requiring greater activity (periodic refreshing of media, etc.) to ensure long-term data integrity.

For many anthropologists the new principle's requirement to responsibly preserve one's records may be satisfied by naming an appropriate literary executor to ensure that literary property, intellectual products, and anthropological records are properly managed after that anthropologist's death (see, for example, http://copar.org/bulletin 6.htm). Depending on the nature of the records or objects, it may be more appropriate to formally arrange for their acceptance in an archive, repository or museum. University archives may be one venue, and national archives such as the Royal Anthropological Institute Archives in

England (www.therai.org.uk/archives-and-manuscripts), the Australian Institute of Aboriginal and Torres Strait Islander Studies archive (www.aiatsis.gov.au) or the U.S. National Anthropological Archives (www.nmnh.si.edu/naa/faq.htm) are another.

Holding records or objects in an institution is not, however, always sufficient to ensure proper care and access. Universities and other entities frequently "inherit" collections from retired, deceased, or otherwise departed scholars. Sometimes these collections do not include all the necessary information to be meaningful, often because the necessary information departed with the anthropologist who created the collection in the first place. The paucity of accompanying data is often not the result of carelessness or irresponsibility—the scholar working with these records on a daily basis likely understood the significance and sources of the records (as well as areas where they might be problematic) implicitly, and failed to make these qualities explicit precisely because they were so familiar.[1] Dealing with these orphaned collections, whether of papers, digital records, objects, or all three, is a growing problem in anthropology, and it is the ethical responsibility of practicing anthropologists to make appropriate provisions for the maintenance and accessibility of their records now so they don't exacerbate this problem later.

These concerns apply not only to records but to objects as well. In many areas of anthropological practice, objects, samples, or other physical materials are collected and play an integral role in anthropological discourse. Consider the single example of archaeology, chosen less as a special case than because it's the example with which I am most familiar. Many, albeit not all, archaeological projects generate objects or collections. A range of repositories, museums and other entities exist that can maintain those collections as an accessible research archive.[2] These may include freestanding or university-based museums, governmental or other repositories, departmental collections or other institutional homes, with the best choice dependent largely on the specific characteristics of the collection and its likely uses over time. It is a generally accepted principle that the records accompanying, documenting or describing those collections are as valuable as the collections themselves, and are curated as part of the larger collection.

A range of studies have shown the continuing value of older collections and their associated collections records for current research; examples include reanalysis of Franz Boas' Native American anthropometric data in biological anthropology (e.g., Gravlee et al. 2003; Relethford 2004; Sparks and Jantz 2002, 2003; Szathmáry 1995; more generally, see Herring and Swedlund 2003) or a range of restudies of archaeological materials recovered from specific archaeological sites like Spiro Mounds in eastern Oklahoma (e.g., Barker et al. 2002; Brown and Rogers 1989; Brown 1996; Hamilton et al. 1974; Phillips and Brown 1978; Sievert et al. 2011; see also Barker 2004).[3] Similar arguments could be advanced using examples from all subdisciplines (e.g., Cantwell et al. 1981), and it is difficult to imagine the growth of meaningful anthropological scholarship in any area if the published record were the only archive or touchstone for understanding past professionals, practices, or projects.

In some instances the data are born digital or have a significant digital component, which may be beyond the expertise or means of a departmental archive or physical museum to maintain. Permanent digital repositories are available through many universities, as well as through freestanding entities like tDAR (the Digital Archaeological Record; www.tdar.org/). These tend to be passive repositories focused on providing permanent curation and maintenance of data; other venues focus on publication of digital data to increase access or foster creation of shared datasets using similar metadata and quality standards. Open Context (http://opencontext.org/), for example, reviews, edits, and publishes archaeological data (as opposed to reports or articles), increasing the accessibility of anthropological datasets and records. Many of the unique concerns relating to digital archives are addressed by the Digital Curation Centre (www.dcc.ac.uk/) or the CASPAR project (www.caspar-preserves.eu/).

A directory of ethnographic archives is maintained by the Council for the Preservation of Anthropological Records (CoPAR; copar.org/links.htm), and a range of open access repositories are available internationally (a list is maintained at www.opendoar.org/countrylist.php). Linguistic records present special challenges both because of the technical challenges of preserving records and recordings in varying media (e.g., Turin 2011; see also http://copar.org/bulletin8.htm), and because many theorists have noted that archived recordings of performances or interviews differ in significant ways from the initial act of performance (e.g., Phelan 1993).

Ownership and control of records may be complicated and contentious, due to claims for the results of work for hire by sponsoring entities, claims by research collaborators or participants, claims by state entities or agencies, or intellectual property issues, including tangible and intangible cultural heritage. The validity and priority of different claims may lead to contradictory expectations regarding preservation, retention, title to, and control over the records, results, and objects generated by anthropological inquiry. The ownership, scope, period of retention or restriction of records, and their ultimate disposition, if applicable, should be an integral part of project planning and the process of obtaining permits, permissions, funding, or informed consent.

Preservation of records is thus not a simple ethical imperative that can be applied universally or uncritically. Concern for the privacy or anonymity of informants, the confidentiality of site locations, or the protection of endangered populations (among other concerns) mitigate against fully open access. A range of restrictions and retention in "dark" archives is possible, and may be appropriate in certain cases. Determining appropriate levels and kinds of restrictions will usually involve consultation with all parties involved and careful consideration of both the sources and gravity of the risks that inappropriate access may pose. Rights and restrictions should be understood both by research participants and by any literary executors, archives, or repositories, as well as any funders or permitting agencies, to help ensure that commitments are understood by all concerned.[4]

Issues of record retention and preservation as mandated by the PPR lie at the intersection of several complex and sometimes contradictory ethical and intellectual trends. Zeitlyn (2012) provides a useful overview of the ethical tensions that archives, as both concept and discrete institutions, must balance. Theorists have noted that archives are not simply passive repositories (Dirks 2002) but, taken as a whole, are also instruments of control through which both colonialist control is exercised (e.g., Richards 1993) or marginal groups further marginalized (Trouillot 1995), thus simultaneously serving as instruments of subversion precisely because they record and document those acts of control (Burton 2003; Foucault 1980; Stoler 2009). At the more immediate level, theorists have also explored the role of individual archivists (or, by extension, curators) in shaping knowledge through daily decisions made regarding what to keep and what to cull or reject (e.g., Schwartz and Cook 2002; Harris 2002).[5] Zeitlyn (2012) identifies more immediate tensions involving privacy and anonymity, consent, and possessiveness regarding data as ethical issues for which extant ethical codes provide scant or ambiguous guidance. The new PPR recognizes these tensions, but offers no cookbook solutions—there are none.

Privacy concerns generally presume that data should be anonymized to protect the dignity and privacy of individual research participants,[6] but the process of anonymization may decrease the long-term research value of the records, compromise their subsequent usefulness to the communities being studied, deprive individuals from claiming authorship (or ownership) of their words or work, and perpetuate power relationships privileging the anthropologist at the expense of those the anthropologist studies. Fowler, for example, cites Hopi anthropologist Hartman Lomawaima as arguing that anonymity "perpetuates a 'we-they' attitude, implying that only anthropologists can make sense of traditional data" (Fowler 1995:67). The anonymization of data to protect informants' privacy may also have the unintended effect of making the anthropologist rather than the informant the authority for the information being communicated.

Another difficult question involves consent. Research participants may give consent to a study based on the purposes and potential utility of the research proposed, but the preserved or archived records documenting that research may later be useful for a range of future projects that neither the researcher nor the individual giving consent might reasonably have foreseen (e.g., Parry and Mauthner 2004:147). Certainly, data may be subsequently used by others for other purposes, and concerns about unintended future use are warranted and should be considered in research designs and record management plans. These concerns are intrinsic to any form of research, however, and, while equally applicable to publications or public pronouncements, rarely are considered reasons for scholars to not address contentious or sensitive issues. Except in extraordinary cases the value of preservation outweighs concerns regarding unknown, and in some respects uncontrollable, future use (see, for example, the discussion of counterbalancing concerns in Caplan 2010).

Arguing for preservation of objects and records is not, however, an argument for their uncritical use. Perhaps the most widely discussed example of ethically-problematic reuse of stored records or collections involves blood samples collected from the Havasupai Tribe of Arizona. The Havasupai have a remarkably high incidence of diabetes (55% for adult women and 38% for adult men, as of the time the project began), and a genetic project was undertaken, with tribal permission, to better understand why these rates of incidence were so high. Tribal members apparently signed consent forms agreeing to provide blood samples for genetic studies on behavioral and medical disorders (Dalton 2004:501), but opinions differ regarding what was disclosed to participants and the documentary record is incomplete. The initial project did not find genetic markers believed associated with Type II diabetes, but genetic information was also used in research on inbreeding in small communities (Markow and Martin 1993), which was objectionable to tribal members, and the participants allege that the researchers used the samples without consent to study mental illness and advance theories regarding the tribe's origins that disagreed with the tribe's traditional knowledge. In the end Arizona State University, the institutional sponsor of the research, paid tribal members $700,000, returned the remaining original samples, and provided other kinds of assistance to the Havasupai Tribe.

The case highlights both the need for informed consent and the complexities of obtaining fully informed and freely given consent in specific instances (but see Chapter 7), as well as ethical questions surrounding the prospective value of records, objects, and samples for future projects unimagined when the initial research was undertaken. For medical samples the issues seem clearer than when applying those same standards to information gained from participant observation. Consider, for example, whether it would be ethical for linguistic data collected as part of a project to preserve a tribe's language to be used for lexicostatistical analyses of the similarity of that language to other languages, which might suggest relationships and histories at odds with tribal oral histories. If a researcher used recorded, documentary or object-based data with tribal permission to advance a particular theory or argument, would it be unethical for another researcher who had not received the same permission from the tribe to subsequently re-examine the evidence or dispute those findings?

These questions become increasingly problematic as the locus of research shifts. Activist anthropologists often justify an absence of informed consent or misrepresentation of their role, identity or intentions as serving a larger social justice purpose—Nancy Scheper-Hughes, for example, discusses the ethical dimensions of undercover ethnography and what she describes as "transgressive uses of anthropology" (Scheper-Hughes 2004:41). While many would argue for a moral difference between using data without consent from organ-traffickers to uncover their exploitation of others versus using information collected previously but without new consent as techniques improve and new questions arise, the difference seems to lie in the degree to which we sympathize with the research participants—treacherous ethical ground by any measure.

Anthropologists are enjoined by the PPR not only to preserve but to protect their records. Protection involves not only maintaining the physical integrity of records but also their security as well. In some cases harmful or deleterious future uses are so apparent or reasonably foreseeable, or the risks to research participants so great, that the danger these records pose outweighs the expectation that records should be preserved. In these cases destruction of records is appropriate and warranted. Such instances should be considered carefully, however, both because it is rare that records of research place participants at grave and immediate risk in ways that conducting the research itself does not, and because the authority and veracity of research results cannot be assessed without repetition, which would presumably pose new sets of risks to participants.

A separate set of concerns regarding retention of records involves anthropological work done in "non-traditional" settings, particularly on a contractual or for-hire basis. An increasing number of anthropologists work in private practice, and the records and results of this work are often the property of the sponsoring entity. The Society for Applied Anthropology's code of ethics allows for this, and argues that "while respecting the needs, responsibilities, and legitimate proprietary interests of our sponsors we should not impede the flow of information about research outcomes and professional practice techniques" (www.sfaa.net/about/ethics/, accessed May 15, 2014). Legally, whether notes and records are the property of the researcher or the sponsor depends on the specifics of the agreement. As in all anthropological research, details regarding the use, preservation, and access to data after the completion of the project should be explicitly considered as part of the initial agreement and research design. In the absence of specific language in the agreement, however, anthropologists should assume they are responsible for the preservation and protection of their records, and specific repositories and resources have been created to assist anthropologists in practicing contexts to preserve and protect their records. Most notable are the Canadian Applied Anthropology Project (CAAP), sponsored by the Society for Applied Anthropology in Canada, and the Applied Anthropology Documentation Project at the University of Kentucky (van Willigen 1995).

These are complex and contentious issues. Because information gained through applied research may be considered proprietary by the client or sponsor, some anthropologists have asserted that all such research is inherently unethical and inappropriate. During debates leading up to the AAA decision to revisit its ethical code in its entirety, one senior anthropologist (working at an academic institution) repeatedly asserted that anthropology done in commercial contexts should be prohibited, and specifically called for a return to language in earlier AAA ethics statements that results must be made available to the public and to research participants when practical.[7]

A growing body of law and practice surrounds the protection of and control over intangible cultural property (e.g., Francioni 2011; Jaarsma 2002; Lixiniski 2013; Torsen and Anderson 2010), but there remains limited agreement over best practices or the assessment of competing claims. This is hardly surprising, as these claims may reflect competing or contradictory constructions of property, originality, authorship, or identity, and the past itself, making any choice problematic at best. While it is relatively commonplace for anthropologists to champion the rights of the communities they study to "their" intangible cultural heritage and to control over constructions of "their" past, such rights and constructions usually impinge on other communities inhabiting the same cultural or physical landscape in complex and potentially troubling ways.

Just as ethical principles are grounded in (and in some senses constrained by) current practice, questions regarding control over information are ongoing matters of process rather than one-time determinations, and both assertions of rights and levels of community interest or engagement may change markedly over time (e.g., Dobrin and Holton 2013). Moreover, records rarely comprise a distinct set of materials to which clear, unambiguous, and consistent rights can be assigned. Rights to the words being recorded or transcribed may be held by the person uttering the words, but rights to that recording or transcription may reside with the interviewer or recorder (e.g., Parry and Mauthner 2004:142); art museums have long struggled with parallel constraints, where a museum may own a painting but the copyright to that painting—and hence all rights regarding use of images—may nevertheless reside with the artist. Records may therefore contain a remarkable number of actual or potential rights-holders under copyright rules alone, even before issues of tangible or intangible cultural heritage arise.

It would be far simpler, of course, if the new principles could just offer a recitation of the dos and don'ts of record retention, preservation, and access, or a simple checklist that, if dutifully ticked, would ensure that all ethical concerns had been satisfied. Neither the new principles nor real-world anthropological situations allow for such easy answers, however. The ethical questions involved are complex, precisely because records and objects are so fundamental both to anthropological discourse and to the identity and interests of the communities we study. As anthropologists we owe to both a thoughtful and deliberate consideration of the ethical issues raised, recognizing that they can and do differ in differing circumstances.

NOTES

1. For archaeological collections, for example, limited resources are available for dealing with "orphaned" collections (e.g., http://scahome.org/sca-grants/orphaned-archaeological-collection-grant-available/).
2. As this book was being compiled, the U.S. Office of Science and Technology Policy directed all federal agencies that support research or amass collections through the research they conduct or support to develop clearer guidelines for the management, preservation, and care of collections (see John P. Holdren, "Improving the Management of and Access to Scientific Collections," Memorandum for the Heads of Executive Departments and Agencies, 20 March 2014; https://www.whitehouse.gov/sites/default/files/microsites/ostp/ostp_memo_scientific_collections_march_2014.pdf).
3. In biological anthropology and archaeology the preservation of records assumes special significance, as original collections including human remains and artifacts may no longer be accessible from different areas of the world due to repatriation or disposition to descendant communities or other claimants.
4. Anthropologists in practicing contexts, for example, may have limited or no rights to their work products or control over their use, unless those rights and restrictions are clearly outlined in the original agreement (see Chapter 8).
5. More generally museums and archives play a crucial role in the initial definition and subsequent maintenance of disciplinary boundaries (e.g., Whitehead 2009).
6. In some areas this is codified under applicable law, as in the UK Data Protection Act.
7. It is ironic that this language actually privileges the rights of academics over those of the research participants.

REFERENCES

Barker, Alex W.
2004 Stewardship, Collections Integrity and Long-Term Research Value. *In* Our Collective Responsibility: The Ethics and Practice of Archaeological Collections Stewardship. S. Terry Childs, ed. Pp. 25-42. Washington, DC: Society for American Archaeology.

Barker, Alex W., Craig E. Skinner, M. Steven Shackley, Michael D. Glascock, and J. Daniel Rogers
2002 Mesoamerican Origin for an Obsidian Scraper from the Precolumbian Southeastern United States. American Antiquity 67(1):103-108.

Brown, James A.
1996 The Spiro Ceremonial Center: The Archaeology of Arkansas Valley Caddoan Culture in Eastern Oklahoma. Memoirs of the Museum of Anthropology 29. 2 volumes. Ann Arbor: University of Michigan Museum of Anthropology.

Brown, James A., and J. Daniel Rogers
1989 Linking Spiro's Artistic Styles: The Copper Connection. Southeastern Archaeology 8(1): 1-8.

Burton, Antoinette
2003 Dwelling in the Archive: Women Writing House, Home and History in Late Colonial India. New York: Oxford University Press.

Cantwell, Anne-Marie, James B. Griffin, and Nan Rothschild, eds.
1981 The Research Potential of Anthropological Museum Collections. Annals of the New York Academy of Sciences 376.

Caplan, Pat
2010 Something for Posterity or Hostage to Fortune? Archiving Anthropological Field Material. Anthropology Today 26(4):13-17.

Dalton, Rex
2004 When Two Tribes Go to War. Nature 430:500-552.

Derrida, Jacques
1995 Archive Fever. A Freudian Impression. Diacritics 25:9-63.

Dirks, Nicholas
2002 Annals of the Archive: Ethnographic Notes on the Sources of History. In From the Margins: Historical Anthropology and its Futures. B. K. Axel, ed. Pp. 47-65. Durham: Duke University Press.

Dobrin, Lise M., and Gary Holton
2013 The Documentation Lives a Life of its Own: The Temporal Transformation of Two Endangered Language Archive Projects. Museum Anthropology Review 7(1-2):140-154.

Foucault, Michel
1980 Power/Knowledge: Selected Interviews and Other Writings, 1972–1977. Brighton, UK: Harvester.

Fowler, Catherine
1995 Ethical Considerations. In Preserving the Anthropological Record. 2nd edition. Sydel Silverman and Nancy Parezo, eds. Pp. 63-72. New York: Wenner-Gren Foundation for Anthropological Research.

Francioni, Francesco
2011 The Human Dimension of International Cultural Heritage Law: An Introduction. EJIL 22(1):9-16.

Gravlee. Clarence C., H. Russell Bernard, and William R. Leonard
2003 Heredity, Environment and Cranial Form: A Reanalysis of Boas' Immigrant Data. American Anthropologist 105(1):125-138.

Hamilton, Henry W., Jean Tyree Hamilton, and Eleanor F. Chapman
1974 Spiro Mound Copper. Columbia, MI: Missouri Archaeological Society Memoir 11.

Harris, Verne
2002 The Archival Sliver: Power, Memory and Archives in South Africa. Archival Science 2:63-86.

Herring, D. Ann, and Alan C. Swedlund, eds.
2003 Human Biologists in the Archives: Demography, Health, Nutrition and Genetics in Historical Populations. *In* Cambridge Studies in Biological and Evolutionary Anthropology 35. Cambridge: Cambridge University Press.

Jaarsma, Sjoerd R., ed.
2002 Handle with Care: Ownership and Control of Ethnographic Materials. Association for Social Anthropology in Oceania Monograph Series. Pittsburgh: University of Pittsburgh Press.

Jackson, Jean E.
1990 I am a Fieldnote: Fieldnotes as a Symbol of Professional Identity. *In* Fieldnotes: The Making of Anthropology. R. Sanjek, ed. Pp. 3-33. Ithaca, NY: Cornell University Press.

Lixinski, Lucas
2013 Intangible Cultural Heritage in International Law. New York: Oxford University Press.

Markow, T.A. and J. F. Martin
1993 Inbreeding and Developmental Stability in a Small Human Population. Annals of Human Biology 20(4):389-394.

Parry, Odette, and Natasha S. Mauthner
2004 Whose Data Are They Anyway? Practical, Legal and Ethical Issues in Archiving Qualitative Data. Sociology 38(1):139-152.

Phelan, Peggy
1993 The Ontology of Performance: Representation without Reproduction. *In* Unmarked: The Politics of Performance. P. Phelan, ed. Pp. 146-166. London: Routledge.

Phillips, Philip, and James A. Brown
1978 Pre-Columbian Shell Engravings from the Craig Mound at Spiro, Oklahoma. Peabody Museum of Archaeology and Ethnology. Cambridge: Harvard University.

Relethford, John H.
2004 Boas and Beyond: Migration and Craniometric Variation. American Journal of Human Biology 16:379-386.

Richards, Thomas
1993 The Imperial Archive: Knowledge and the Fantasy of Empire. London: Verso.

Scheper-Hughes, Nancy
2004 Parts Unknown: Undercover Ethnography of the Organs-Trafficking Underworld. Ethnography 5(1):29-73.

Schwartz, Joan M., and Terry Cook
2002 Archives, Records and Power: The Making of Modern Memory. Archival Science 2:1-19.

Sievert, April K., J. Daniel Rogers, and Javier Urcid
2011 Artifacts from the Craig Mound at Spiro, Oklahoma. Smithsonian Contributions to Anthropology 49. Washington, DC: Smithsonian Institution.

Sparks, Corey S., and Richard L. Jantz
2003 Changing Times, Changing Faces: Franz Boas's Immigrant Study in Modern Perspective. American Anthropologist 105(2):333-337.
2002 A Reassessment of Human Cranial Plasticity: Boas Revisited. Proceedings of the National Academy of Sciences 99:14636-14639.

Stoler, Ann L.
2009 Along the Archival Grain: Epistemic Anxieties and Colonial Common Sense. Princeton: Princeton University Press.

Szathmáry, Em ke J. E.
1995 Overview of the Boas Anthropometric Collection and its Utility in Understanding the Biology of Native North Americans. Human Biology 67(3):337-344.

Torsen, Molly, and Jane Anderson
2010 Intellectual Property and the Safeguarding of Traditional Cultures: Legal Issues and Practical Options for Museums, Libraries and Archives. Geneva: World Intellectual Property Organization.

Trouillot, Michel-Rolph
1995 Silencing the Past: Power and the Production of History. Boston: Beacon Press.

Turin, Mark
2011 Born Archival: The Ebb and Flow of Digital Documents from the Field. History and Anthropology 22(4):445-460.

Van Willigen, John
1995   The Records of Applied Anthropology. In Preserving the Anthropological Record. 2nd edition. Sydel Silverman and Nancy J. Parezo, eds. Electronic document, http://copar.org/par/par12_van_willigen.pdf, accessed May 15, 2014.

Whitehead, Christopher
2009   Museums and the Construction of Disciplines: Art and Archaeology in Nineteenth Century Britain. London: Duckworth.

Zeitlyn, David
2012   Anthropology in and of the Archives: Possible Futures and Contingent Pasts. Archives as Anthropological Surrogates. Annual Reviews in Anthropology 41:461-480.

CHAPTER TEN

Maintain Respectful and Ethical Professional Relationships

Dena Plemmons

There is an ethical dimension to all professional relationships. Whether working in academic or applied settings, anthropologists have a responsibility to maintain respectful relationships with others. In mentoring students, interacting with colleagues, working with clients, acting as a reviewer or evaluator, or supervising staff, anthropologists should comport themselves in ways that promote an equitable, supportive and sustainable workplace environment. They should at all times work to ensure that no exclusionary practices be perpetrated on the basis of any nonacademic attributes.

Anthropologists may gain personally from their work, but they must not exploit individuals, groups, animals, or cultural or biological materials. Further, when they see evidence of research misconduct, they are obligated to report it to the appropriate authorities.

Anthropologists must not obstruct the scholarly efforts of others when such efforts are carried out responsibly. In their role as teachers and mentors, anthropologists are obligated to provide instruction on the ethical responsibilities associated with every aspect of anthropological work. They should facilitate, and encourage their students and research staff to engage in dialogue on ethical issues, and discourage their participation in ethically questionable projects. Anthropologists should appropriately acknowledge all contributions to their research, writing, and other related activities, and compensate contributors justly for any assistance they provide. They are obligated to give students and employees appropriate credit for the authorship of their ideas, and encourage the publication of worthy student and employee work.

In A Beginning

In 1987, James N. Hill, past President of the Association, wrote a chapter in the *Handbook on Ethical Issues in Anthropology*, giving a brief overview of the contexts in which the Association first established, in 1970, its Committee on Ethics. The first Committee on Ethics drafted the 1971 Principles of Professional Responsibility (PPR), and also contributed to the 1973 creation of a grievance process. All of these came about almost exclusively as a result of broad ethical concerns about the use of anthropological methods for intelligence and defense work, some of which were immediately evident given the context of the very unpopular Vietnam War then going on and some of which were lingering concerns about the "alleged perversion of professional research goals" in earlier situations (government sponsored foreign area research). The Committee on Ethics, then, was established as a body to address such grave and far reaching concerns, and the grievance function was developed to ensure due process for both complainants and accused in the investigation of future claims of unethical anthropology brought to the Association through the Committee.

This is not, however, the way the grievance process came to be used in the ensuing years. Writing about the charge of the Committee on Ethics (COE) vis-à-vis its grievance function in particular, Hill noted:

> The entire issue of secret and clandestine research, passed (temporarily?) into history by 1972, essentially with the ending of the Vietnam War. Since that time, the cases and inquiries presented to the COE have been quite different and varied. The Committee receives roughly three to six cases per year, the most common of which involve grievances concerning collegial relationships. The most frequent of these have concerned plagiarism, followed distantly by a variety of cases involving faculty-student relations (including faculty exploitation of graduate students). These kinds of grievances, between and among individuals, are increasingly the most common ones lodged with the COE. (Hill 1987)

Seven years later, in 1994, Janet Levy, then the immediate Past Chair of the AAA Committee on Ethics, wrote a similar kind of article in the *Anthropology Newsletter* entitled "Anthropological Ethics, the PPR & the COE: Thoughts from the Front Line." While the article addressed different aspects of the relationship between the code of ethics and anthropological practice, it included a significant focus on the Association's grievance procedures and processes. Levy drew attention to Section I of the prevailing PPR (the 1971 PPR, which had by then been twice amended and has been referred to as the RPPR) and wrote, "…it is section I of the PPR, *Responsibilities to people whose lives and cultures anthropologists study*, that addresses the core of ethical concerns" of anthropology. Addressing issues brought to the Committee on Ethics for adjudication after 1973 and through the writing of her article, she noted

> Although Section I is the core ethical statement of the PPR, for the past many years not one grievance filed referred to Section I…. Instead, almost all complaints are about relations between anthropologists involving publications, reviews of grant proposals, or personnel practices. (Levy 1994)

In other words, and as Hill had earlier related, the focus of these complaints was not a concern about relationships that are constituted "in the field" through ethnography—those presupposed in Section 1 of the PPR, and which create and contain our idea of what "anthropology" is—but the relationships between academics/peers/colleagues in the context of a professional life, not having anything necessarily to do with anthropology specifically. She urged the AAA to reconsider the grievance process—indeed, the grievance function altogether.[1]

When the 2008 Task Force began discussions about revisions to the 1998 Code of Ethics, our questions (and subsequent conversations) were in many ways similar to those Levy shared in her 1994 article. While our Task Force discussions were about many things—whether it is possible for a Code to equally represent all of the sub-disciplines of anthropology[2], how a Code actually, practically, functions for an organization—one of our primary questions was How can (should) a Code best deal with allegations of violations of ethics, and on how broad a spectrum? Similar in our experience were the kinds of concerns/ requests that were coming to the Committee on Ethics; several of us (Barker, MacKinnon and Plemmons, and for a brief time, Levy) on the Task Force had been Chairs of the Committee on Ethics and had the same experience that Levy and Hill recounted.

The "big ticket" ethical concerns that help to shape disciplinary practice—or as Hill wrote, those "ethical problems that might damage the reputation of the Association or the profession"— weren't handled by the Committee on Ethics, but rather were taken up by other ad hoc committees/commissions/task forces (e.g., Commission to Review the Statement on Ethics; El Dorado Task Force; Commission on the Engagement of Anthropology with the US Security & Intelligence Communities). The overwhelming majority of cases that were seen by the standing Committee on Ethics implicated relationships between/among anthropologists (peers, colleagues, collaborators and students) and differing interpretations of what comprised "ethical" practice in various (non-field) contexts where the boundaries are ill (if at all) defined and ambiguous (e.g., what is a substantial enough contribution to a manuscript to warrant authorship, and who decides? In a collaborative relationship, who "owns" the data, and on what basis is ownership defined and decided? How are contracts with agencies to be managed when there are restrictions on timing or place of publication?).

Dear Committee on Ethics

During my time on the Committee on Ethics (2006-2010), the Committee, with the invaluable assistance of the ad hoc consultative body The Friends of the Committee on Ethics (the Friends), reviewed and responded to several queries from independent researchers, university faculty, practicing anthropologists, and students. The questions were almost always about whether or not some decision made by another party—an anthropologist who was an institutional colleague; some institutional body; another professional in a different discipline, perhaps at a different institution, or perhaps not in the academy at all—could be considered an ethical breach, and what, if anything, could the committee and by extension, the AAA, do to address that breach and/or to provide some definitive word about what one could do or couldn't be asked to do in a situation with competing interpretations of what would be appropriate. Again, these were not concerns of "the field," and so perhaps not seen as "anthropological" in that very circumscribed way, but rather were situated in the arena of professionalism. The queries fell along a broad spectrum and captured concerns about, for instance, data ownership and management, mentoring, publication, authorship, and the functioning of Institutional Review Boards. The following are three examples—representative of the whole—of the many queries the Committee received over those years (used with permission, slightly edited for clarity and brevity, and with most identifying information removed).

Case 1. At the 2005 AAA meeting in Washington, DC, I was part of a panel of four presenters (two other presenters and a discussant) offering papers concerning the status of theory XXX as an anthropological paradigm. My paper was founded in theory YYY, and deeply critical of theory XXX. I laid out the principles that show the inadequacy of XXX, distinguished between various forms of XXX in a new way, and offered several examples from senior anthropologists illustrating both XXX's hegemony and its deficiencies.

The organizer of the panel did a good job of getting participants to share papers prior to the meeting, and I sent the other participants an email responding to their papers from a YYY perspective. This too was a critique, offered in the hope of engaging others in a productive debate. When I asked at the panel if any of them had received it in time to give it consideration, it turned out that none of them had. So I mentioned verbally that I had sent it, and invited response.

Immediately after the session, the panel organizer broached the idea of having the three papers supporting XXX published as a unit. I asked him why not also include my paper, to which he replied, "You're not a [XXX theorist]." Since I knew there was an email from me waiting for him and the other panelists, I said nothing more. I heard nothing subsequently from anyone, until recently.

A few weeks ago, as a professional courtesy, I sent the discussant an excerpt from my recently published book, [which included] a critique of his stance on XXX as published in his introduction to another text. He did not reply to the theoretical substance of my critique, but did send a copy of the introduction he had written to the publication of the three other papers from the 2005 AAA panel. I don't subscribe to the journal in which the papers were published, and this was the first I had heard that such a publication had taken place.

I was astonished to see that my paper was not mentioned, let alone included in the published set. Nobody reading the discussant's introduction would have any reason to suspect that there were any number of papers other than the three which appeared in publication, or that a fourth had been excluded.

I wrote back to the discussant expressing my consternation. On two occasions I saw him and asked if he would discuss the matter with me, and on both he said he was too busy. When he did respond, he sent an email stating that my paper didn't fit thematically with the others, and that I had been "notified" at the conference that it would not be included. The "notification," apparently, was the panel convener's suggestion that the three XXX papers be published. Because at that time I knew that my email critique of their papers was waiting for them, and had verbally invited response to that email and my own paper, I believed the ball to be in their court. I assumed they would at least read and consider my critique. No one replied to my critique, and, of course, they didn't publish my paper.

In my judgment, it was at least unprofessional, and perhaps unethical, to omit a countervailing theoretical perspective presented in a single, formal, professional context. There was deception by omission when neither the panel discussant nor the publishers of the other papers contacted me as to their intentions to publish without including my paper. And there was misrepresentation by omission when he wrote in the introduction that, "The result [of the panel] was… the present set of articles."

My chief concern is not in how I was treated, although that was indeed poor. I am more concerned with the persistent bypassing of the principled critique of a key anthropological paradigm. To ignore my panel paper; ignore my email to the panelists about their papers; fail to communicate with me about the intended publication; fail to actually publish my paper; fail to respond to my more recent substantive remarks about the shortcomings of XXX as included in recent emails to the panel discussant; and to glibly assert that nothing can be done about the matter now are all ways of avoiding critique and debate.

Since theory cannot progress without debate, avoiding it is unprofessional. Since principled debate is our only reliable way to develop theoretical paradigms that more and more closely match the world's underlying reality, avoiding it is unethical.

Am I correct that both deception and misrepresentation by omission took place? I believe that in bringing this matter to your attention I have fully discharged my responsibility as things now stand. I'm sure you will let me know what, if anything, you believe it is your responsibility to do as chair of the AAA ethics committee.

Case 2. Over the past few months, a difficult situation has evolved with my advisor. My advisor has requested on several occasions my field diaries, notes and records. In them I have written down very sensitive information, that can potentially harm my informants and the groups I am studying. So far, I have been refusing to surrender my field notes, diaries and recordings, since I have been made aware that my adviser has taken the liberty to share the little information I have shared with her with third parties. Needless to say, I have not authorized such release of the information.

Additionally, my mentor is putting pressure on me to take my dissertation in a different theoretical direction than I have intended. My mentor requested that I present my "raw field data" in order to justify my intent to pursue this research as intended, but this presents the same problem of needing to disclose sensitive information.

I feel conflicted because I feel that my mentor is trying to lead the research in a direction I find problematic, and that the release in any way of my field information, diaries and notes can lead to potential damage of my informants.

Case 3. In April of 2010 I went to the West Bank of the Occupied Palestinian Territories as part of my employment at an organization there with a mission to promote health and literacy for women in the Middle East. I had proposed a project to the organization to conduct an evaluation of a Women's Center nearby. As part of that evaluation work, I conducted interviews with women in the center, as well as other parts of the West Bank. The project was funded by the organization. Before interviews, I told informants of their rights to decline to be interviewed, and that they could withdraw at any time. All informants agreed to be interviewed on tape with the understanding that their identities and other identifying information would not be revealed, and that I would handle all interview material with the utmost concern for their protection and privacy. As you can imagine, some of the women shared very sensitive information with me in response to the assurances I gave them regarding their confidentiality.

I am currently no longer under the employ of the organization. My former employer is requesting return of the tapes and other research materials. It is my understanding that I am bound by the American Anthropological Association Code of Ethics to not turn over any interview material or data, or produce any information that reveals informants' identities, but that I can produce and turn over reports/analyses of my findings, with identifying information removed, in relation to the organization's work.

From my understanding, the legal precedent for journalists to protect their sources also applies to anthropologists, therapists, attorneys, and those in related fields, where people could be harmed if their information gets out. I am hoping someone on the ethics committee may be able to point me to the law on this.

It is also my understanding...that the research materials and raw data belong to the investigator, but that reports generated from that data pertaining to the funding organization can be provided to that organization, once identifiers have been removed. Also, that funders of research projects, if desired, can be acknowledged for funding the work.

My former employer and her attorney are not only requesting that I turn over the tapes and materials related to this research—which to my knowledge is against the law and my professional code of ethics—but are also repeatedly contacting the transcriber on the project and requesting her to turn over the remaining tapes. She is extremely intimidated and concerned by these requests and understandably does not want to be involved.

I am hoping someone can please point me toward the law on these matters regarding protecting research subjects, ownership of research materials, and the rights and responsibilities of anthropologists conducting ethnographic and interview work.

The reactions from the Committee to each of these very distinct cases were in some ways remarkably similar, for an important reason: despite the specifics of the concern brought to the committee for review, in none of these cases did the anthropologist appear to have anticipated the likelihood of differing understandings of the roles and expectations of the relationships in which he/she was engaged, nor the possibility that thoughtful and sensible people might have a completely different interpretation of the obligations of the relationship and make different decisions about the best course(s) of action. While the person bringing the complaint legitimately thought that they were bringing violations or at the very least questionable decisions to the committee's attention, it is arguable in almost every case that the others in the relationship believed that they were acting ethically and reasonably as well. Further, it seems clear (from the admittedly limited information we had up front) that in none of these situations can it be definitively said that any of those involved set out to willfully undermine/deceive others. But it is equally clear that these concerns were not simply personal grievances: the decisions that were made in these instances had ethical implications, and ultimately illuminated broader ethical concerns begged by questions of the particular context: ownership of data in legal and moral senses, silencing of countervailing viewpoints, relationships of unequal power in the academy.

These cases, presented as concerns arising between anthropologists and counterparts in the realm of the professional, rather than as concerns specific to the relationship of anthropologist and "subject," reinforced the sense that, while we as an Association might be very good at exhaustively parsing our relationships with our interlocutors in the field—those very people articulated in Section I of the 1971 PPR in those spaces seen to be most purely "anthropological"—we have less experience (comfort/familiarity) with examining our relationships *with one another* in the many and varied contexts in which we operate. Our relationships are not confined to narrowly conceived research relationships, but include the entirety of our relationships—those that might be defined as specifically anthropological, and those that are best characterized as professional: with colleagues (both in and outside of the academy), teachers/mentors, students, and the public[3]. It remains both frustrating and fascinating that we still seem to struggle so with this much wider realm of relationships and practice. While we are keenly aware of the necessarily transactional, constructed, and contingent nature of our relationships in the field, we seem to have thought much less about the necessarily transactional, constructed, and contingent nature of our professional relationships.

The specific kind of anthropology practiced is less relevant to these concerns. Indeed, these concerns are common across *all* practices of science, as discussed later in this chapter. The common thread is that the fully realized practice of anthropology (training in theoretical orientation/research methodology; data gathering; analysis and presentation of research findings) takes place in a community of others, and takes account of *all* of the relationships we create/enter. Thus, Principle 7 was crafted to ensure that there is as much attention paid to creating, developing, negotiating, and sustaining professional relationships as we give to the relationships that are constituted through ethnography.

The 7th Principle

The inclusion of this principle was guided in part by the historical consistency of the kinds of cases coming before the Committee, which is evidence of the ambiguity inherent in many areas of professional life. Despite exhortations in our past codes of ethics or PPRs regarding responsibilities to students or to the discipline broadly, we have had very little to no explicit discussion in our discipline about the ethical dimensions/implications of our professional relationships (and I hasten to again add that this is true not just for anthropology). While it can't be said that the content of the 7th principle is completely unique to our latest revision of the PPR, (nor is the discussion in this chapter the entirety of concerns of the 7th principle) we think the principle is now a bit more purposeful and explicit in the sense that it prioritizes the task of recognizing the ethical implications of practices that arise from being a professional and a scholar, not just those that arise from being an anthropologist.

This particular inclusion was also informed by the current and broader recognition across all fields of science that trainees/students need more explicit and purposeful training and education in what is commonly called the responsible conduct of research, or RCR, but also known varyingly as scientific integrity, research integrity, or research ethics.[4] The National Institutes of Health were first in requiring training in RCR for those supported on particular NIH training grants with the first notice in 1989 (followed by updates in 1992 and again in 2009). The National Science Foundation also began requiring training in the responsible conduct of research, at first narrowly, in 2007[5], and then much more broadly—for all undergraduates, graduates, and postdoctoral fellows supported on NSF funds—in 2009.

That initial set of regulations promulgated by NIH was shaped by the 1989 Institution of Medicine (IOM) Report, *The Responsible Conduct of Research in the Health Sciences*, and reinforced by the findings of the 1995 report of the Commission on Research Integrity, *Integrity and Misconduct in Research*. The IOM report notes:

> The primary task of the committee was the development of principles and proposals to guide both national and local institutions in strengthening the professional standards of academic research.... Our concern was the...professional climate of the research environment, which influences everyday practice and sets the tone for future generations of researchers. By improving the integrity and quality of the institutional environment of research, we sought to foster professional research standards of individual researchers and to discourage future incidents of scientific misconduct.

Similarly, the Commission on Research Integrity report states:

> The Commission believes that [the] required [NIH] educational activity is essential and should be more broadly implemented to ensure that, through such training, all individuals who perform research in institutional settings are sensitized to the ethical issues inherent in

research.... Providing such training is an important step toward creating a positive research environment that stresses the achievement of research integrity more than the avoidance of research misconduct.

High profile and somewhat extreme cases of research misconduct (defined as fabrication, falsification, and plagiarism) of the '70s and '80s were a primary focus of these reports, and the impetus for the first NIH regulations. Yet, it can be argued (Kalichman 2013; Steneck and Bulger, 2007) that the requirements were in fact meant to address two different issues: the incidence of research misconduct, certainly and evidently, but also, arguably, an acknowledgment that the socialization of new scientists into the norms and expectations of practice cannot and should not be left to only mentoring and informal, ad hoc transmission of those norms and expectations; while mentoring is crucial, it's nevertheless true what we would call the responsible conduct of research must be deliberately addressed.

This prompts the question, What are those "ethical issues inherent in research" that the authors of the Commission on Research Integrity report noted, and can those issues be said to be relevant across all practices of science? There do seem to be topics, or areas of practice, that are common no matter the discipline/field: data acquisition/management/sharing/ownership; conflicts of interest/commitment; mentoring; responsible authorship and publication practices; peer review; collaborative relationships. These topics transcend disciplinary boundaries and specific concerns of practice; all scientists, researchers, and scholars engage in these activities, enter into these relationships, and have these concerns. Importantly, all of these areas of practice or concern require a foundation of respectful relationships, built on open and constant communication and transparency, which takes commitment and work and guidance.

It does not seem so great a stretch that these concerns are relevant to anthropology, and not just tangentially—the requests for guidance that have come before the Committee on Ethics for the past several years indicate their significance. It is also the case that anthropology departments across the country are now more frequently providing "RCR education" to their students, given the NIH and NSF requirements for this education, though it remains to be seen if that education is targeted toward or at least captures these concerns of professional relationships, or if it focuses primarily and not surprisingly on those questions that pertain in large degree to work with human subjects[6].

What does seem clear, despite the required training, is that this specific RCR framework has not particularly guided our broader Association-wide discussions about these issues, and the Task Force thought it might be at least a useful beginning orientation. Principle 7 was meant to help provide some structure to our discussions of these issues as part of the educational mission of the Committee on Ethics, most importantly, we think, for our students, who will benefit from purposeful discussions and mentoring about the ethical dimensions of professional relationships, but also for seasoned anthropologists. The cases that have, for decades, come before the Committee on Ethics for review are excellent vehicles for these discussions. And the review of and responses to these queries from the Committee on Ethics and the Friends provide useful illustration, as we will see, of how to think about and respond to these concerns of the professional, writ small, acknowledging the ambiguity and grey areas inherent to some of these issues. That is precisely why the RCR framework can be so powerful: we can't provide you with *the* right answer (there likely isn't one), but we can offer an array of possibilities of "rightness" because we understand that we have to work these decisions out in practice.

"Nuanced Decisions in Ambiguous Contexts"[7]

I want to turn now to the requests, relayed in the cases that came to the Committee for review and guidance.

The request from the scholar who was concerned about the silencing of dissonant voices, in Case 1, prompted similar responses from Committee members and the Friends:

> *Is this an ethical issue or a professional one? I have generally understood that editors, publishers, and the like have the right to pick and choose the articles they publish—is there a code that would require them to publish every article they receive?*

> *[T]his particular case doesn't appear to rise to the level of a scholarly ethics problem. I don't believe that the other panelists had an ethical obligation to include [the scholar's] paper in their joint publication. They were entitled to disagree with [the scholar] over whether including [his/her] paper with the others made intellectual sense; it's simply unfortunate that the exclusion was accomplished amidst an apparent communications breakdown.*

> *I agree with the previous emails that there is no ethical or practical requirement that a given perspective be represented in any given contribution. That doesn't mean we can or should suppress dissenting views, but that's not what happened here. One scholar felt [his/her] views merited an extended debate, and others didn't agree and chose not to enter that debate. [A] secondary issue involves whether or not there was a lack of courtesy or "misrepresentation by omission" in not mentioning the paper which was not included in a later publication. That's hard to determine without a close reading of the paper trail and more information from all the individuals concerned, but at the end of the day I don't believe passing mention of the eliminated paper would satisfy [the scholar's] larger concerns....*

> *[O]ne of my reactions, developed out of my past experience with [similar issues], is: being an asshole isn't unethical! Very often, what bothers the complainant is some person or persons who acted like an asshole. Of course, that is maddening and annoying and frustrating, and probably a bad thing. But, an unethical thing—at least within the terms of what I think the Code of Ethics should do—probably not.*

The Committee and the Friends saw two distinct issues in this complaint, one of which—the deliberate suppression of a different viewpoint—is a substantial ethical issue but was not found to be present in the situation, as we were made aware of it. Our interpretation was that the absence of sufficient or any communication, almost from the beginning, made this an unfortunate mess for the scholar bringing the grievance, and that this silence was construed as intentional and thus meaningful, rather than simply careless and inconsiderate.

The Committee's response, following, tried to address both that fact, and also the ethical issue suggested by this situation:

> [M]embers of the Committee on Ethics had the opportunity to review and discuss the e-mail query you recently sent.
>
> From our discussion, the collective sense was that there was no ethical breach in what you've described. The Committee concluded that legitimate decisions to publish were made in perhaps less than optimal ways; while there was no obligation to publish the papers collectively, we suspect that early, more frequent and more inclusive conversation might have helped in this situation.

Further, the Committee discussed your concerns that this episode illustrates "the persistent bypassing of principled critique" and your contention that the avoidance of debate inhibits the production and expansion of theoretical constructs. In this, we do think your case offers insight into an important larger issue that is illustrative for the Association broadly, and that would benefit from continued conversation with colleagues and others: what is the process by which paradigms shift in anthropological thinking, and how can we enter into those processes in transparent and meaningful ways? The desire to add one's new voice to an already on-going conversation can often result in moving the discipline forward, and we encourage you to continue writing from and formally presenting your viewpoint, and hope that you'll continue your engagement in conversations with those who hold other viewpoints.

Thank you for entering into this conversation with the Committee on Ethics, and with the Friends of the Committee.

While I wouldn't say that the failure to engage was unethical, I think this case makes especially clear that there are *ethical implications* to both the decisions we make and the ones we decidedly don't make; in this instance, the consequence of not engaging, for whatever reason, left a voice in silence, a voice that had been part of the conversation at one point and reasonably expected to be part of the ongoing conversation, as well. While we as a committee couldn't agree with the contention that there was "purposeful deception by omission," we were aware of the larger issues that this situation illuminated, and tried to address that in our response to the scholar, who did, in fact, later publish the critique in question.

I want to turn attention now to the student's request for guidance, included in Case 2 and the responses that the Friends and the Committee on Ethics shared with that student. Almost everyone who responded found two issues of import in the student's request for assistance: first, whether the "raw data" of the student's field-notes could legitimately and ethically be withheld from the mentor, and second, the clearly fraught relationship between the student and the mentor.

Some responses from the Friends are as follows:

Well, this sounds like a departmental or university ethics problem more than one for the AAA. While there are "anthropological" issues here—like the confidentiality of fieldnotes—other disciplines and practices like journalism also face them. But more to the point, mentoring power abuses are not specifically anthropological: they're faced by everyone (sadly). The question is: who is in the best position to advise? This is an awful situation. But unless the student's department and/or university has no grievance recourse, we are not in a good position to advise. We don't have access to adequate information from all the relevant points of view—whereas the department or at least the university should have that access....

[W]e have only one side of the story, and I can easily imagine a fair and well-intentioned advisor taking actions which could be cast in terms similar to these. The advisor could be pushing the student toward a topic which would be more appropriate and defensible for a terminal degree, for example, or seeking access to notes to confirm the validity or inferential logic for conclusions which otherwise seem anomalous or contradictory. All of us have likely had advisors or professors who tried to push our work in different directions, and there are complex issues involved in discussing the appropriateness of such actions that aren't fully addressed by the inquirer's brief description. My inclination would be to say that: 1) the student is under no general ethical obligation to turn over field notes and records unless there is some other agreement or restriction in place; but 2) [he/she] should seek counsel from an individual or entity more familiar with the particulars of [the] case to determine whether or not the specifics of [the] advisor's request, and attempt to redirect [the] research, are appropriate given the overall suite of circumstances.

The final response from the Committee, which I wrote on their behalf, was as follows:

On behalf of the Committee on Ethics, let me say how sorry we are that you are in such a difficult and painful situation, and we thank you for your patience while we took time to discuss the issues you presented.

The Committee on Ethics has an educational and advisory mandate, and is specifically prohibited from investigating or adjudicating grievances against/disputes between individuals; rather, we are here to provide advice to AAA members raising issues of practice which may have ethical dimensions. While we cannot make any definitive statement about what you can or can't do, we have shared with you various viewpoints and resources to help you in deciding on an appropriate course of action. You've received several responses from the Friends of the Committee on Ethics, as well as many links to resources in a response from [another Committee member], and an earlier, preliminary response from me with suggestions for others to contact at your institution—all responses which could be of help—and we'll reiterate that the AAA strongly supports an anthropologist's obligation to protect the participants in his/her research, a protection which could include a refusal to share one's personal fieldnotes/research diaries. The confidentiality of personal fieldnotes/diaries is assumed in most cases, and from the information you've given us, it sounds as if you have specific and written agreements with the communities in which you're working that these will remain confidential, and can be shared only with their permission.

That this has become such a troublesome situation despite what seem to be rather clear boundaries reinforces our sense that this is an issue which implicates the relationship between you and your advisor, and needs the attention of someone at your home campus; we strongly encourage you to find an ally who can work with you and your advisor to mediate this situation. Is there another faculty member on your dissertation committee, or a faculty member of another department, who might be able to help you? Or, as I asked in an earlier e-mail, is there an institutional official whose job it is to be of assistance in these kinds of situations?

Our practice takes place in a web of social relationships, and each of those relationships has varying and often competing rights and responsibilities; figuring out how to manage those competing responsibilities and rights is the challenge for all of us, and is often a very difficult undertaking, and best not done in isolation. I am hopeful that with the suggestions and resources you've received in the past several e-mail communications you have sufficient information to make an informed decision about your next steps.

In a similar way, the request for help from the member who was wondering about the legality and ethicality of refusing to turn over the tapes, in Case 3, highlighted two different but salient issues: a question about ownership, yes—as one Committee member put it, "at the heart of the matter is who owns the data"—but also the equally important question about what the researcher did *up front* to get that question answered, arguably the responsibility of the researcher to work out with the institution funding the research. Ownership and eventual use of the data, and in what form, and how that would impact the participation and protection of the subjects: all of this should have been negotiated before the anthropologist signed the contract or began the work, and if none of these issues were satisfactorily resolved, the anthropologist should have walked away from the work.

In this instance, the anthropologist was complicit in the risk to the subjects of the work, since he/she didn't work these issues out in advance. In fact, though the anthropologist proposed the work, the Foundation funded it, paying for the time, the transcription, and the expenses incurred in conducting the research, and there was no contract and apparently not even a discussion about ownership or use of the data in any meaningful way. One of the comments made by a Committee member was about that very issue:

> An employer can assert a right to "ownership" of data if the researcher salary and expenses were paid by the employer during the time of the collection of data. The law might assume that the anthropologist was aware of these conditions when employment was secured.

As the anthropologist now notes:

> Anthropologists are increasingly bringing their skillset to other work terrains in corporate America and non-profit work. Whether we step into the Intels, Googles, Facebooks, or Relief Internationals and other foundations,[8] we have to come to terms with the fact that the standards regarding research materials may be very different from how we've been trained to think about our data. We need to become adept at negotiating contracts that explicitly spell out who owns the data and what information is being paid for before we engage in fieldwork. Every social scientist who conducts qualitative, ethnographic work with human subjects should legally establish (1) who owns the recordings, notes, and other data they produce, (2) to what degree they can or cannot use this data in their own publications, (3) that they are being paid to provide analyses and reports of their findings with all identifiers redacted, not the raw data, as part of our ethical guidelines to protect human subjects.

These concerns are not specific to anthropological practice, but rather are part of the way we as professionals craft our collaborative relationships. As anthropologists, we are particularly adept at negotiating with our subjects what the collaboration will look like—its limits, its benefits, its costs—but less so, in many instances, at taking the same clear-eyed proactive look at our professional collaborations, often with researchers from other disciplines who work within different (and perhaps foreign to us) professional contexts, who use different language and follow different customs, and perhaps have different expectations for outcomes. It is interesting and probably worthy of further questioning that our understanding of and sensitivity to the need to carefully co-create and nurture relationships in "the field" is often left there, in "the field," and we don't bring the same consideration to our professional relationships.

That said, it is important to recognize that the specifically anthropological and the generally professional arenas, as I've been describing them, are not always or necessarily discrete spheres of practice, and considerations of what it means to enter into ethically sensitive relationships in one will impact the other, as in both Case 2 and Case 3. The concerns in both of these cases about protection of the subjects in the research were a consequence in the first instance of a different interpretation of the contexts in which "confidentiality" of field-notes might be overridden in the service of another arguable good, and in the second case, the lack of a proactive engagement with the anthropologist's colleagues at the agency funding the research as it related to ownership of the data gathered. These concerns were only consequently related to the relationship between the anthropologist and the participants in the research, but nevertheless had implications for "the field." Changing practices of anthropology will continue to blur boundaries of "field" and "subject." Colleague Natalie Baloy notes:

> [I]n relation to my own work with the Centers for Collaborative Research for an Equitable California (CCREC), it's becoming apparent too that collaborative and activist anthropology can also underscore the relevance of RCR-type concerns even with our research interlocutors, as community organizations and community members become co-researchers/co-analysts/co-owners of data, etc., in ways that differ from past arrangements between anthropologists and subject communities. These relationships can often resemble collegial/professional relationships and attention to RCR ethics can perhaps help to address the limitations of human subject protection-type guidance that has dominated the code of ethics prior to the inclusion of this principle. (pers. communication, April 15, 2015)

Our facility with discussions about the work of the professional will only enhance our work as anthropologists, and will give us better tools to talk with our students about the need to pay sustained attention to all of our relationships, being mindful of how these relationships are often inextricably intertwined.

Educational Mandate

Since abolishing the adjudication process in 1995, the Committee on Ethics has had an educational mandate, and has, in my experience, done a good job. What we should strive for now is a broader integration into the Association of the discussions of cases taken up by the Committee on Ethics, and the AAA is making strides in that direction. The current Committee on Ethics has created a blog where the kinds of cases that have come before the committee, such as those described in the preceding section, can be posted for broader review, so that the membership will have the opportunity to engage with one another in examining the ethical dimensions of the issues presented there. While the Committee on Ethics has unique responsibilities to the Association, it is essential that active engagement in these discussions about the ambiguities of professional practice comes to be more fully recognized as a shared responsibility that we all have—to our students and to one another—and not simply the purview of a Committee wherein the concerns and responses are limited to the Committee members and the person bringing the concern.

Some concerns, especially those of our students, might never make it to the Committee on Ethics, leaving those who have those concerns uncertain about where to go for guidance. When the Task Force began its work in 2009, one of our first tasks was to convene a meeting of students at the 2009 Annual Meeting to talk with them about their concerns of practice, and what they hoped a new code might address. The following are some of the responses we received from several graduate students (Plemmons 2012):

> *How do graduate students address the multiple power dynamics involved in relationships between students, faculty, and administration (ex...sexual/social issues, ownership of research and publication credit)?*

> *A majority of students are unfamiliar with the process of research and publication and who the research 'belongs' to and who should/shouldn't receive credit during presentations and publication especially when the research overlaps with the interests of the advisor and/or committee chair.*

> *There is a lack of an effective, anonymous and safe mechanism to report and/or question when a student's research has been 'taken' by a faculty member and/or another student.*

> *Some academic advisors do not have the training necessary to guide graduate students through their programs.*

> *Academic advisor does not collaborate with the student in combining/synthesizing the theoretical and practical experience of the student in preparing them for the work force.*

These concerns are not dissimilar from ones expressed frequently in other areas of science and research, wherein graduate students and postdocs lament the stealing of their work by their primary mentor or the confusing and often-changing application of "rules" by mentors for assigning authorship, or claim that their mentor has no time/interest/experience to guide them.[9]

The mentoring relationship is crucial for the communication and modeling of ethical research and professionalism, and long the focus, though to varying degrees, of much attention across the sciences, and indeed currently, within our own discipline. Recently, the AAA's Mentoring Working Group posted their report to the AAA site (currently at www.aaanet.org/resources/researchers/upload/141028-AAA-Mentoring-Working-Group-Final-Report-Summary-Conclusions-2.pdf). This report explores the kinds of mentoring that are currently taking place across the various sections of the AAA, and offers some conclusions about how successful we are, and how we might improve, in integrating mentoring more fully into the Association. Some of the premier journals in the sciences—*Nature* and *Science* among them—have devoted several articles to these issues of mentoring specifically[10] (as well as to training in the ethical dimensions of research more broadly[11]). It might be beneficial for the Association to make use of some of this material in its conversations about mentoring, especially in thinking about adopting the use of individual development plans (IDPs)[12] with graduate students. These plans help students and mentors have a clearer picture of the student's skills and strengths, and most especially, these plans provide an excellent structure to begin a solid mentor/mentee training relationship. Many of the issues noted by the students described earlier in this chapter could begin to be addressed in the work of crafting these plans, which takes the student and the mentor through an assessment of several areas of professionalism, including the areas of RCR, where a student can assess whether or not s/he understands the data sharing and ownership issues of her/his work, conflicts of interest (including how a student might, as noted earlier, deal with "overlapping" research interests of student and advisor), and collaborative relationships with colleagues.

In facilitating Association-wide conversations about our professional relationships generally, the Committee on Ethics might make use of a range of helpful articles, blogs, and exercises from other disciplines that would assist us in being not just better mentors to our students, but in providing some much needed guidance to practitioners in *all* career stages about how to navigate through these issues of professional practice (cf. Chapter 8). Our conversations about these topics/practices don't necessarily need to be discipline-specific, either; in fact, in some ways, that kind of insularity prevents us from making use of the conversations long happening in other disciplines that could help us more successfully navigate these troubled waters, and these conversations offer different ways of thinking about, contextualizing, and responding to common issues across the sciences.

The relationships that we craft as professionals—with our students, colleagues, and peers and with other academics both in and outside our discipline and outside the academy—need careful and sustained attention. It was the intention of the Task Force that this final principle would affirm that importance, and lead the Association into the necessary work to facilitate that attention.

NOTES

1. Shortly after Levy's article was published, the AAA convened the Commission to Review the AAA Statements on Ethics. The Commission presented a draft of its report to the Section Assembly in May 1995, and the Executive Board unanimously accepted the report's recommendation that the AAA should "no longer seek to adjudicate claims of unethical behavior." The Commission went on to make substantial revisions to the PPR, and the AAA voted in 1998 to accept the revisions and adopt a revised Code of Ethics.
2. See http://ethics.aaanet.org/do-some-good-and-other-lessons-from-practice-for-a-new-aaa-code-of-ethics/ for a recent critique of the current PPR in this regard.
3. It is not the case, of course, that these are mutually exclusive or separable domains; the "specifically anthropological" and the more generally "professional" relationships overlap and engage one another at many turns, as discussed later in this chapter.

4. "Research ethics" in this instance is distinct from and more encompassing than its familiar usage in social science, when it refers almost exclusively to research with human subjects.
5. The NSF requirement at first applied only to those on Integrative Graduate Education and Research Traineeship Program (IGERT) grants.
6. Additionally, what I suspect is happening in anthropology, as in so many other disciplines, is a reliance on on-line modules as the vehicle for satisfying this requirement. But I would argue that learning in isolation about issues that come up in professional *relationships* doesn't make sense, because with such an approach the relevant context for making ethical sense of those relationships is too often missing.
7. A phrase attributed to Hugh Gusterson in Levy 2009.
8. These are not concerns simply for anthropologists working in corporate or non-profit settings. The limits of protection are clear in university settings, as well, when we think about promises of confidentiality.
9. Cf. www.the-scientist.com/?articles.view/articleNo/32287/title/Alls-Not-Fair-in-Science-and-Publishing/; http://sciencecareers.sciencemag.org/career_magazine/previous_issues/articles/2006_01_13/no-doi.9522592743045586763;www.the-scientist.com/?articles.view/articleNo/25328/title/How-to-resolve-authorship-disputes/; and www.asbmb.org/uploadedFiles/ProfessionalDevelopment/Enzymatics/An%20Open%20Letter%20to%20Mentors%20Everywhere.pdf.
10. Cf. www.nature.com/nature/journal/v447/n7146/full/447791a.html; www.nature.com/ncb/journal/v12/n2/full/ncb0210-101.html; and http://sciencecareers.sciencemag.org/career_magazine/previous_issues/articles/2012_02_03/caredit.a1200015.
11. http://sciencecareers.sciencemag.org/career_magazine/previous_issues/articles/2010_11_05/caredit.a1000108.
12. Since 2014, the use of IDPs for graduate and postdoctoral students on NIH funding has been "strongly encouraged" by NIH, and institutions must note in their progress reports whether the institution requires these to be completed.

REFERENCES

Commission on Research Integrity
1995 Integrity and Misconduct in Research. Department of Health and Human Services, Publication #1996-746-425. Washington DC: US Government Printing Office.

Hill, James N.
1987 Handbook on Ethical Issues in Anthropology. Joan Cassell and Sue-Ellen Jacobs, eds. AAA Special Publication #23. www.aaanet.org/committees/ethics/ch2.ht, accessed April 28, 2015.

Institution of Medicine (IOM)
1989 The Responsible Conduct of Research in the Health Sciences. Washington, DC: The National Academies Press.

Kalichman M.
2013 A Brief History of RCR Education. Accountability in Research 20(5-6):380-94.

Levy, Janet E.
1994 Anthropological Ethics, the PPR & the COE: Thoughts from the Front Line. Anthropology News, 35(2):5.
2009 Life is Full of Hard Choices: A Grievance Procedure for the AAA? Anthropology News 50(6):7-8.

Plemmons, Dena K.
2012 The Challenges for Research Ethics Education in the Social Sciences. Teaching Ethics 12(2):145-147.

Steneck N. H., and R. E. Bulger
2007 The History, Purpose, and Future of Instruction in the Responsible Conduct of Research. Academic Medicine 82(9):829–834.

CHAPTER ELEVEN

What's Different?

Alex W. Barker and Dena Plemmons

All codes or statements of professional responsibility are products of the times in which they were written, reflecting the peculiar contexts, concerns, and circumstances informing and in some respects constraining their creation. For the most part they are also contingent texts whose content relates in different ways to previous iterations or versions either by adding, revising, or removing sections. Because codes are products of their own times, they frequently reflect or seek to correct the problems most recently encountered, and are hence retrospective and aimed at preventing recurrence. They also serve as expressions of rectitude, as a way of distancing the profession from a previous scandal or problem by formally condemning or proscribing those actions. Previous chapters in this volume have provided background to the development of those earlier versions and the context in which the current principles were developed. Here we examine three salient areas in which the current principles differ from previous codes.

The main difference between past codes and the present PPR involves less of a change in what constitutes parameters of ethical practice than in the relationship of the code to how anthropologists assess and express those parameters. Through the Task Force's meetings and listening sessions it became increasingly clear that a longer and more specific set of principles was not always advantageous. The level of detail often reflected

Anthropological Ethics in Context: An Ongoing Dialogue, pp. 207-212. © 2016 Left Coast Press, Inc. All rights reserved.

an attempt to address a past difficulty in its particulars, and made the code a reactive and in some respects reactionary document, making it simpler to satisfy the letter of the code on the one hand while violating (or neatly avoiding) its spirit on the other. Actions were ethical unless specifically forbidden, making it harder to apply the code in novel situations. Another observation was that the longer code seemed to be used rarely by members in their daily professional lives. Instead, it seemed to be viewed as something applying exclusively to one's colleagues—who were presumably more subject to ethical transgression—since one's own ethical rectitude was rarely questioned.

The intent of the current principles was therefore different from the outset, and was designed to provide easily recalled principles that could inform and guide a range of decisions and choices in the daily lives of practicing anthropologists. While the term "educative code" has been used loosely to refer to any code without formal adjudication and enforcement provisions, here it has a more specific meaning. The new code replaces proscribed actions and "thou shalt nots" with a series of core expectations of ethical practice, which should be carefully considered in assessing the most appropriate course of action in any given setting. The seven principles are quite brief—one of us kept suggesting that the core principles should be able to fit on a coffee mug, so that they could be readily remembered and inform decision-making on a daily basis; the other (being perhaps more practically-minded) made up a set of such mugs and distributed them to the Task Force members when our work was completed. Each principle is a phrase—short and easily recalled. Each principle is supported by a longer discussion, making clear how these principles should be understood and how they might apply in different contexts, and are further supported by online resources and wide ranging examples. In many respects the present volume is a further extension of that progression; the structure and resulting chapters in this volume reflect the diversity of viewpoints and opinions represented on the Task Force, examining or illuminating aspects of the principles through more extended discussion and reflection. Going forward, the AAA Committee on Ethics has been charged with updating the resources, links, and discussions of the principles so that they remain relevant and meaningful as conditions change. And while we have framed the current principles carefully and developed them through extensive consultative and deliberative effort, we are under no illusions regarding their permanence. Codes can and should change, both to reflect changing needs or circumstances and because the systematic and far-reaching discussions involved in their revision offer important benefits to the profession.

But the changes were not merely didactic, as some elements of past codes were not specifically included in the new principles. The most important and (probably) most controversial element that was not carried forward from past statements is the assertion that the primary obligation of anthropologists is to the people they study. For many anthropologists this was (and remains) a cornerstone of ethical practice, and some were doubtless dismayed that it did not appear in the new principles in the same form as in previous codes. Its absence does not, in our view, reflect a change in anthropological values but instead a change in the dimensions of anthropological practice. Decades ago it may have been true—or at least broadly perceived as true—that anthropologists enjoyed a position of power and influence relative to the less developed people they studied, and that the role of anthropologists (especially cultural anthropologists) was to serve as interlocutors for marginalized or vulnerable populations, reflected in stereotypical anecdotes of anthropologists talking about "my" people. As Pels (1999) has argued, this ethical position arose from an understanding, during a particular period, that anthropology as a discipline and anthropologists as practitioners played an intermediary role between colonized peoples and colonizing powers. In recent decades, however, anthropologists have broadened the kinds of communities and individuals they study, and in many cases the presumption that an anthropologist's primary obligation is to those individuals being studied seems misplaced or inappropriate. As anthropologists "study up"—as we bring our disciplinary lenses to bear on the powerful rather than only the powerless, on those who exploit others rather than only those exploited—we must recognize that loyalties and ethical obligations cannot be assigned so simply. An anthropologist (in this instance probably a cultural, medical, or linguistic anthropologist) studying groups in conflict should not be expected to select whom to study based on whether or not they agree with that group's position; nor should the anthropologist be assumed to have an obligation to subsequently share or support that side's interests simply by virtue of studying them. Nor is it necessarily appropriate to promulgate ethical rules for the discipline as a whole predicated on the stereotypical image of the more advanced or advantaged (cultural) anthropologist studying "primitive" or subaltern peoples and serving as articulate spokesperson on their behalf.

For other kinds of anthropologists, the "primary obligation" rule presents other complexities. Biological anthropologists studying non-human primates can likely understand "Do No Harm" in context-specific ways, but the idea that they have differing obligations to the troop they studied as opposed to neighboring troops or groups seems problematic; nor would it seem ethical to privilege the species one studies over other sympatric species based on which species an anthropologist selected for study. Archaeologists or paleoanthropologists likewise must recast the dictum in complex and sometimes contradictory ways. Some archaeologists would argue that the obligation applies to descendant communities, but multiple communities or groups may claim descent from the same ancestral remains, and descent can be established through multiple lines of evidence; in many cases oral histories or traditional knowledge may differ from archaeological evidence, and archaeologists of good conscience can and do differ regarding where their primary obligations lie in such instances.

This question of primary responsibility was difficult and divisive, and members of the Task Force held differing opinions on this topic. While all agreed that there were many instances where an anthropologist's *primary* obligation was not, in fact, to those s/he studied, some felt nonetheless that it represented an aspirational or historical value that should be expressed even if it was not true in many circumstances. They pointed—with some justification—to principles like "do no harm," which established a general principle that could only be meaningfully understood with certain caveats.

There is an important distinction, however. "Do no harm" is not intended as a naïve exhortation to purity and universal beneficence, but as an expectation that anthropologists will deliberately weigh the consequences of their actions and the harms that might result from them. Within any social setting there may be a multiplicity of interests or agendas and little agreement regarding what course of action (or inaction) constitutes the most immediate harm or most desirable help. Anthropologists must therefore use their critical judgment to assess the likely consequences of their action (or inaction) and avoid creating or increasing harm, and the caveats make clear that this can and should take different forms in different circumstances. It does not intrinsically privilege one set of interests over another.

The issue, then, is not whether we owe obligations of appropriate protection, respect, and proper regard for the individuals or communities we study—we do, and this is clearly acknowledged in the new statement and reflected in multiple principles. It is, instead, whether study of a group *intrinsically obliges* an anthropologist to privilege that group's interests over those of other communities or individuals. In this set of principles the protections afforded research participants are maintained, but an explicit requirement to privilege their interests over those of other groups is not.

Also controversial is the notion that there may be cases in which restrictions on dissemination of data are appropriate. In the wake of the U.S. military's efforts to recruit anthropologists in its Human Terrain System program, the Association established the Commission on the Engagement of Anthropology with the U.S. Security and Intelligence Communities (CEAUSIC). The Commission's final report did not recommend prohibiting anthropological engagement with military or intelligence services, but instead focused on prohibiting anthropological work in contexts where informed consent could not be freely and fully obtained, specifically calling for clarifications to the existing code "notably the admonitions to do no harm, to require voluntary informed consent and to honestly and transparently inform all involved of activities undertaken" (CEAUSIC 2007:34).

Other anthropologists took a different approach, introducing a motion requiring the AAA to restore older language from the 1971 principles forbidding any research whose results could not be freely disseminated to the public and, where practical, to the people being studied. In response the then sitting AAA Committee on Ethics, augmented by additional members and nonvoting guests, was asked to review the existing code, propose revised language incorporating the principles of this motion, and identify when the ethical conduct of anthropology does and does not require specific forms of the public circulation of knowledge. The resulting recommendations incorporated some of the older language, revised to remove androcentric terms and to clarify the importance of reporting results to research participants.

This outcome did not satisfy all concerned. A minority report (see Chapter 3) was included in the committee's report, objecting to the insertion of the words "it is generally expected that" in the requirements that anthropologists should publicly disseminate their results, and the inclusion of an expectation that if dissemination is contraindicated and will not take place, the reasons why be explicitly stated. Both were deemed problematic, because the minority felt restricted distribution was never appropriate or ethical except in the narrow case of archaeological site locations. Notwithstanding this, the minority report did not call for the elimination of a separate section acknowledging the complexity of these issues and stating that decisions regarding whether dissemination was appropriate or ethical in any given instance must be decided on a case by case basis—which is why the phrase "it is generally expected that" had been added in the first place.

The call for prohibition of any anthropological work whose results could not be publicly disseminated was aimed largely at projects associated with the military and intelligence services, but it would also have disallowed work by applied anthropologists working for clients in many if not all cases. In part this focus reflected a sense that applied anthropological work was an unavoidable casualty of the need to eliminate gray areas that might be exploited to allow clandestine or covert research in some form, and in part it reflected a deep unease on the part of anthropologists in academia with the notion of anthropology serving corporate or capitalist interests.

As long as the work is openly and honestly described and fully informed consent is freely given (but see Chapter 7), the new principles do not presume such applied work is unethical in any respect, so long as other ethical expectations are fully satisfied. They do, however, reject clandestine work whose existence is not acknowledged and for which fully informed consent cannot be sought or secured.

While the format of the new principles differs rather significantly from past codes, the other elements and expectations are included or subsumed within these new principles. Certainly there were no other eliminations explicitly intended by the Task Force.

That does not mean, however, that the new principles are complete. They are explicitly intended to be dynamic and subject to regular reconsideration and revision. The AAA Committee on Ethics has been formally charged with updating the resources, links, and case studies accompanying these principles, and with recommending any revisions necessary—as will likely be needed—to address areas not discussed in the current principles or for which adequate guidance or direction is not provided. Such revisions will represent the success rather than the shortcomings of this new approach.

REFERENCES

AAA Commission on the Engagement of Anthropology with the US Security and Intelligence Communities
2007   Final Report, November 4, 2007. American Anthropological Association. www.aaanet.org/pdf/FINAL_Report_Complete.pdf.

Pels, Peter
1999   Professions of Duplexity: A Prehistory of Ethical Codes in Anthropology. Current Anthropology 40(2):101-136.

CHAPTER TWELVE

On Professional Diversity and the Future of Anthropology

Laura A. McNamara

As I am writing this chapter in late summer 2014, the United States faces yet another military engagement in the Persian Gulf. The rise of the self-titled Islamic State (IS) in Iraq and Syria may be driving the Global War on Terror into a new phase. At the risk of disciplinary navel-gazing, I wonder if policymakers in the Department of Defense and the United States' intelligence community will, once again, look to anthropologists for advice about countering transnational radicalism with soft power.

After all, this kind of overture is exactly what triggered nearly a decade of tumult in the American Anthropological Association. The preamble to the AAA's Principles of Professional Responsibility describes anthropology as "an irreducibly social enterprise" that seeks to build, disseminate, and apply anthropological knowledge to human problems (AAA 2012). What form that enterprise should take seems to be up for perennial debate, as we collectively try to maintain a coherent disciplinary identity, even as our research sites, sponsors, products, and practices are constantly evolving. Latent in most debates about ethics are tensions over what counts as legitimate anthropology and whether we can trust our peers to practice ethically responsible anthropology.

This chapter is not about ethics per se. Instead, I am using it as a springboard to explore the problem of professional and occupational diversity in the ranks of anthropology writ large, and in our professional associations

Anthropological Ethics in Context: An Ongoing Dialogue, pp. 213-230. © 2016 Left Coast Press, Inc. All rights reserved.

in particular. A number of trends are re-shaping the "normal" career path in anthropology, and it will not be long before the majority of anthropologists are working outside academia. If the past is any indication, we can expect that between one-third and three-quarters of these individuals will lose contact with anthropology's main professional institutions and organizations (CoPAPIA 2009: 44). This is a shame, since some of the most vibrant, creative, cross-disciplinary work in our field is being done outside the "normal" boundaries of applied and basic research. Anthropology, for all its professed openness to diversity, has a tendency to react somewhat allergically to new forms of practice. This is particularly the case for research activities that imply an alliance *with* institutions of power, as opposed to projects aimed at *deconstructing* institutions of power. However, for better or worse, anthropologists are taking their degrees into private and public sector institutions and building quite successful careers there. Considering how quickly this is happening, we should perhaps worry less whether these new forms are the "right" kind of anthropology, so that we can draw on their success to reinvigorate our discipline.

Whither the Anthropological Career?

Marietta Baba has written that a discipline's social legitimacy depends on public understanding about the role of that field in society (Baba 1986). Now, I expect that most of us would suggest anthropology as a viable career option for young people who want to make a difference in the lives of others. Others among us see a discipline entering an era of creative reinvention (I am one of those). Unfortunately, there are plenty of figures outside our discipline who are advising undergraduate students to run screaming from a degree in anthropology, who question the relevance of anthropological training, and who warn that an education in anthropology can cost more than the graduate will earn in their first working decade. So—who is right?

Actually, as it turns out, anthropology's social legitimacy is indeed under fire, even as our practices are moving into an ever widening range of professional niches. Let's begin with the bad news: Consider the cartoon series *Archer*, a favorite among America's Millennial generation (at least, those who can afford Netflix or cable television). A send-up of James Bond-type espionage thrillers, *Archer* is raunchy, raw, and politically incorrect in the extreme. Like all good satire, it also provides witty and cutting commentary on our social institutions, even anthropology.

In a 2011 episode entitled "Heart of Archness" (a play on Joseph Conrad's *Heart of Darkness*, which itself bears all kinds of complicated readings in relation to anthropological fieldwork), the hyper-masculine Sterling Archer is fighting his way out of an island prison with the help of another captive, Rip, and a scruffy, bespectacled graduate student named Noah. As they are escaping via a network of tunnels through a deep dungeon, Rip and Sterling ask Noah why he is living on a remote island populated with pirates. Noah's explanation—that he is a graduate student doing anthropological fieldwork—elicits derisive guffaws. "Anthropology?" exclaims Rip, pausing in their climb down a steep ladder into a dark pit. "Good luck with the job market!" Noah rather haughtily defends his career choice by insisting that anthropology is a *very* important field of study and that he plans to teach in a college or university. More laughter. "Anthropology? To, uh, other anthropology majors?" asks Rip. Sterling immediately follows with the *coup de grace*: "Thus continuing the *circle of why bother*!" Bah-da-Boom.

We can laugh off Archer's rapid-fire, take-no-prisoners satire. It's a cartoon, after all. However, it's a little harder to chuckle when *Forbes* magazine announces that undergraduate anthropology degrees are the "worst value" in today's job market (Goudreau 2012). In 2012, Georgetown University's Center on Education and the Workforce (CEW) published a study that identified anthropology (including archaeology) as the lowest-paying undergraduate degree field in the United States, with a projected unemployment rate of 10.5%—nearly twice the national average among all new college graduates at the time (Carnevale et al. 2013). *Forbes*, the *Huffington Post*, and *Time* were among the many publications that pounced on the study and warned parents to steer their children away from "low value" degrees, assuming that no family wanted its well-educated progeny returning to sleep on the basement couch. Although anthropology was front and center in a lot of the reporting, Georgetown's report was really about the changing valuation of humanities and arts degrees in a recovering job market and a shifting economy. For better or worse, that job market is not providing generous remuneration for arts and humanities degrees. These days, the market values STEM skills ("STEM" for science, technology, engineering and mathematics) over most everything else. It certainly seems shortsighted that the current job market fails to reward the skills and knowledge of young anthropologists, and at some point the pendulum will probably swing back. But considering the burden of educational debt, it is fair to question the economic value of an undergraduate degree in pretty much *anything* besides, say, statistics, pharmacology, or electrical engineering, among others.

Yet there is hope, friends! Other studies indicate that anthropology is actually a pretty decent career choice—under certain conditions, which I summarize here before elaborating upon them. First, career-seekers interested in anthropology must be willing to invest in at least a master's degree. They should consider augmenting their anthropological training with other research skills, including quantitative methodologies. They should seek opportunities to perform field studies before entering the job market, so they can demonstrate their ability to formulate, execute, and complete research projects. Lastly, they need to look for careers outside of academia.

Diversity of employers is an old story for archaeologists, for whom a terminal master's degree is often quite sufficient for a viable career in cultural resource management activities for federal, state, and local agencies, as well as private consulting firms. However, the rise of the terminal master's is a newer trend for us non-archaeologist anthropologists. Even though non-archaeologist anthropologists have comprised the majority of those with anthropology degrees awarded in the United States, as well as the majority membership in the American Anthropological Association, we have little information about the kinds of extra-academic careers that exist for these graduates. It behooves us to find out what these career paths look like.

This is exactly the question that the AAA's Commission on Practicing, Applied and Public Interest Anthropology (CoPAPIA) explored in a recent study of master's level anthropologists in the U.S. workforce (AAA 2009). As CoPAPIA pointed out in its final report, *three times* as many graduate students are electing terminal master's degrees over doctoral programs. These graduates are taking their degrees into industry, the public sector, nonprofit organizations, and museums. Some do find work in universities, primarily in research centers or think tanks rather than the academic departments that many graduate programs still prepare students to enter.

When asked to describe how they use anthropological training in their work, many of CoPAPIA's respondents referred to blending their ethnographic training with other research skills, such as survey methods, quantitative analysis, basic computer programming, or software design, in their work. This response is not surprising, considering how many positions are popping up for ethnographers who can perform consumer research in the tech industry. A master's level anthropologist is indeed quite hirable if the individual brings to the employer complementary skills in human-computer interaction, software design, or market research.

Importantly, CoPAPIA's survey is not the only source of information about the diffusion of anthropology careers outside academia. Every year, the United States Bureau of Labor Statistics publishes the *Occupational Outlook Handbook* (see www.bls.gov/ooh). The *Handbook* provides summary information about entry-level education, training requirements, median pay, and expected growth rates for several hundred occupations. Under the category "Anthropologists and Archaeologists," the *Handbook* describes a career studying the origin, development, and behavior of humans in various parts of the world. (Like the Georgetown study and *Forbes*, the BLS *Handbook* doesn't differentiate among our four fields; there is only archaeology and anthropology). Median pay for individuals with a master's degree hovers at about $58,000. Moreover, professional opportunities in our field are expected to grow at a brisk 19% through 2022.

Not bad news for novice anthropologists with master's degrees—under some conditions. First, our field is small. In 2012, the BLS estimated that the workforce included about 7200 jobs in anthropology in all sectors, which means that our strong 19% growth will yield only 1500 or so new positions, making this a competitive market for new graduates. Compare these figures to other professional sectors—in occupations related to computer science and engineering, for example, the BLS expects demand for *several hundred thousand* new hires, across roughly a half-dozen occupational categories.

That said, students who are interested in anthropology will be most successful if they take advantage of as many educational and training opportunities as they can to develop a portfolio of marketable skills. Admittedly, getting those skills can require significant financial investment on the part of the student. The BLS emphasizes that an undergraduate degree in anthropology is not likely to lead to a job in anthropology; instead, viable candidates will need at least a master's degree and in some cases a doctorate to have a chance at the jobs that are emerging in the market. Moreover, candidates are most hirable if they have practical experience in applying qualitative and quantitative research methods—that is, if they have done fieldwork.

Finally, and related to the preceding, students should prepare themselves for extra-academic careers. The brisk 19% growth rate is driven largely by demand for applied skills, not demand for postsecondary instructors or research professors. The BLS identifies two complementary trends that explain this shift: first, universities rely heavily on state and federal funding, both of which are at risk due to the country's increasingly dysfunctional discretionary budgeting process; and second, corporations appreciate anthropological insights into the global marketplace.

As the BLS points out, corporations are increasingly likely to invest in "…anthropological research to gain a better understanding of consumer demand within specific cultures or social groups…[and anthropologists] will also be needed to analyze markets, allowing business to serve their clients better or to target new customers or demographic groups."[1]

The Brave New World

Not all anthropologists will enthusiastically embrace a future in which their colleagues are respected for their skills in predictive market analytics. It is not just that Google, Facebook, or Uber might use ethnographic market research to increase profits. Instead, it touches on longstanding tensions between academic anthropology and its myriad forms of practice outside the academy. Historically, a vocal element of the discipline, primarily affiliated with academic institutions, has preferred that anthropology remain distant from institutions of power, under the strong assumption that distance is required to ensure the quality and independence of sociopolitical critique. A variation on this theme questions the influence of one's employer on one's professional autonomy, asking if anthropologists working for corporations or government are able to maintain the same epistemological, publication, and political freedom associated with academic anthropology.

The necessity of maintaining professional, political, and institutional distance is a strong trope in anthropology's disciplinary identity. Challenging this trope can be an intimidating experience. Indeed, the AAA has recently emerged from a prolonged period of internal turmoil that helps illustrate the vehemence with which Association members respond to perceived threats to the distance we value so strongly.

In the wake of the 9/11 events, as the United States' war activities escalated, anthropologists began debating the ethics of providing disciplinary expertise, when relevant, to government institutions prosecuting these wars. Some argued that we should take inspiration from the work of Ruth Benedict, Gregory Bateson, Margaret Mead and others who supported the Allied cause during World War II. Others reminded us about the social scientists who had supported covert operations in Vietnam, with horrific results to local populations. Some expressed more general concerns about the future of anthropology: ethical transgressions on the part of even a few anthropologists could have negative implications for field researchers throughout the world, for years to come. Still others opined that the very presumption of anthropologists aligned with intelligence and military activities represented a risk for our discipline's collective reputation, not to mention the safety of individual fieldworkers. Perhaps it was best to vocally disavow both wars? And, of course, underlying all these concerns was a fundamental fact of anthropology's disciplinary culture: we are, as Laura Nader once observed, most comfortable when squarely on the side of the underdog (1972).

There were plenty of opinion pieces, essays, and conference panels on these topics prior to 2006, but a more proximate series of events caused the AAA's Executive Board to take action on these matters. In 2004, journalist Seymour Hersh alleged (erroneously) that Raphael Patai's ethnography *The Arab Mind* played a role in the torture activities at Abu Ghraib (Hersh 2004; Patai 1973). Then, in 2005, Congress provided startup funding for the Pat Roberts Intelligence Scholars Program (PRISP), igniting debates about the desirability of having intelligence-oriented professionals in academic classrooms. The straw that broke the camel's back fell in 2006, when the United States Central Intelligence Agency expressed interest in placing a job ad in the Association's newsletter (Goodman 2006).

In response, the AAA's Executive Board established the Commission on the Engagement of Anthropology with the US Security and Intelligence Communities, or CEAUSSIC, to provide guidance and counsel on the Association's course of action for all matters related to anthropology in the Global War on Terror. I was an active member of the first incarnation of CEAUSSIC, was a supportive bystander during CEAUSSIC's second incarnation, and supported the Task Force on Ethics, whose members have authored this book. I want to emphasize that all these activities were extraordinarily collegial, leading to some of the best friendships and professional experiences of my career, despite the challenging problems and diversity of values we were asked to address.

That said, the early 2000s were *not* a comfortable time for anthropologists like myself, who were open about having careers inside the United States' national security community. Some number of anthropologists seemed to believe that career affiliations with the United States government represented a direct threat to the (moral? ethical? intellectual?) purity of anthropology. For example, when Gerald Sider asked, "Can Anthropology Ever Be Innocent?," he warned readers that any anthropology done in service to the state, in this era, is morally and ethically inexcusable, as "…the United States turns increasingly ugly and desperate in its processes of domination, openly flaunting [sic] basic human rights guarantees" (Sider 2009: 47). Sider was just one of many political intellectuals in our discipline who loudly insisted that even well-intentioned anthropologists working in military, intelligence, or even diplomatic functions were just deluding themselves. "Gateway drugs" was the analogy that historian David Price used to describe such entanglements, implying that naïve anthropologists were being lured into performing intellectual services they would later regret. Price urged his fellow anthropologists to take action, lest "...others determine how anthropology will be weaponized against those they study for the needs of American Hegemony" (Price 2006). Between 2006 and 2010, as an increasing number of anthropologists were vocally denouncing entanglements with the United States military-industrial-intelligence complex, I began feeling tremendously self-conscious at the annual meetings, to the point of hypersensitivity that the angry *they* might be talking about the culpable *me* (they weren't). At one point, I strongly considered resigning from the AAA.

But I did not, and writing this in 2014, I remain a happy member of the AAA, as well as the Society for Applied Anthropology. I am only describing this experience to underscore how utterly unwelcoming our professional associations can feel to anthropologists who do not practice, affiliate, publish, or receive remuneration in ways that maintain the particular distance that we are, apparently, expected to maintain. The collective can be ferocious on this point.

Yet the events of the past decade are best understood as expressing a much longer debate regarding anthropology's disciplinary identity, boundaries, and membership—particularly between anthropology as a *discipline* and anthropology as a suite of *professional occupations* (Baba 1986). As sociologist Penny Edgell Becker has pointed out, disagreements about "who we are and how we do things around here" underpin the very most divisive forms of institutional conflict (Becker 1999). Moral precepts and ethical principles are the strongest articulation of shared professional authority and identity, and challenges to moral and ethical axioms are bound to generate passionate debate. The past decade's uproar over anthropologists employed by the national security world are part of a much longer intergenerational, intra-disciplinary discussion about who does anthropology, where they do it, and how it is properly practiced (i.e., "applied").

Reinventing Anthropology, Revisited

Recently, I re-read the introduction to Dell Hymes' 1972 edited volume, *Reinventing Anthropology*. As Hymes points out, ever since Franz Boas successfully institutionalized anthropology as a university-based discipline, the standard anthropological career path consisted of graduate training with an experienced mentor, followed by fieldwork studying the non-Western Other, completion of one's dissertation, and a tenure-track academic career, with production of a monograph (or two, or six, or more) along the way.

At the time Hymes and his contributors assembled *Reinventing Anthropology*, the academic form of the anthropological career had ascended to the top of our disciplinary social structure, defining the norms, structures, products, and practices of anthropology *qua* Anthropology (Baba 1988). Until fairly recently, anthropology practiced *outside* the institutional funding and structure of U.S. academia—research aimed at addressing a particular social problem, informing policy or promoting a cause—was a far less respected form of the discipline. The very public involvement of prominent U.S. anthropologists in World War II notwithstanding, "applied" anthropology was treated as the discipline's unruly stepchild well into the 1980s and was widely treated as the "more dangerous, questionable, even unethical" form of the profession (Baba and Hill 2006:179). This disdain for applied anthropology can perhaps be explained by the discipline's intellectual aspirations in the postwar era of Big Science: to consciously align one's work with the interests of *any* particular group was inimical to the objectivity and neutrality of scientific research.

Yet Hymes and his contributors—many of whom were academic professionals—recognized that by the mid-1960s, post-colonial movements throughout the world had pretty much vitiated this model. Not only were anthropologists being kicked out of the countries they had previously studied, but the developing world was generating its own intellectual elite, members of whom were more than capable of articulating the historical, political, and epistemic problems of (white, male, mostly Western middle-class) anthropologists spending a year among the "the natives." An anthropology centered in Western academia, one focused on harvesting knowledge of the non-Western other for promulgation among other Western academics, *was* politically positioned, whether its practitioners wanted to acknowledge that or not. There was no use hiding behind scientific objectivity.

Accordingly, Hymes and his contributors instead grabbed the bull by the horns. They bravely argued that anthropology should acknowledge and embrace its position in the world, that anthropologists should look for opportunities to study "up, down, and sideways" (Nader 1972). Their essays amounted to a wholesale re-imagining of anthropological practice, a vision of anthropologists embracing the messiness of their place in the world, to ensure the discipline's continued relevance for the advancement of knowledge and human welfare.

Re-reading *Reinventing Anthropology* forty-some years after its publication, I am struck by how things have both changed and remain the same. Hymes and his contributors write about the need to re-think anthropological training, to break down intra-disciplinary barriers, to consider non-academic institutions as valid locations for professional practice, and to include all areas of Western society in our portfolio of research sites. Much of what they envisioned has indeed come to pass. For one thing, academia is no longer the dominant site for careers, practice, nor the production of anthropological knowledge. It is now normal for anthropologists to study "up" and "sideways," to borrow more terms from Laura Nader. I wrote my own upward dissertation, about the post-Cold war nuclear weapons programs at Los Alamos National Laboratory (McNamara 2001). By the time I was doing my doctoral work in the late 1990s, the ethnographic study of science and technology had become so mainstream that the AAA had established an interest group for the subfield: CASTAC, or the Committee for the Anthropology of Science, Technology and Computing. It remains active today.

Moreover, so-called "applied" anthropology is far less of a stepchild than it once was: at my last count, over thirty colleges and universities in the United States were either offering or beginning to develop programs in applied anthropology. We now laud anthropologists who deploy their skills to promote the interests of communities who lack access to social, political, and economic capital. The word "applied" is now one of many terms used to describe work outside traditional academia: we speak of anthropological practice and ethnographic praxis; we enthuse about design ethnography; we recognize anthropology for the public interest and advocate for anthropology in policymaking.

And so, just as Hymes predicted, anthropologists have spent the past four decades spinning off creative projects from the academic center. That centrifugal motion continues today. It perhaps quickens.

Ethics for a Centrifugal Discipline

Over the past decade, most of the AAA's members and its leadership have done an admirable job navigating some very difficult disciplinary tensions. The composition of the Principles of Professional Responsibility illustrates how much grace and forethought can be brought to bear on the problem of ethics, the discipline, and our changing landscape of practice.

In 2007, the Executive Board raised the issue of whether the 1998 Code of Ethics was up to the task of guiding anthropologists in the ethical challenges of their research activities, given the apparent diversity of practice. The fact that the existing Code of Ethics had become a source of some dispute among AAA members spoke to ongoing changes in the landscape of anthropological practice, including the rapid decentering of our discipline from academia into the public and private sector. To address this problem, the Executive Board appointed the Task Force for Comprehensive Ethics Review.

Thus began an effort to create a straightforward, clearly articulated set of guiding principles that we hoped would be more useful and accessible to the Association's constituency. Task Force members envisioned a set of statements, memorable but meaningful, that could carry an increasingly diverse discipline beyond the security-intelligence-and-military scandals consuming the AAA at the time. From the outset, the Association members who crafted the Principles acknowledged that anthropologists would continue to engage in new forms of research and practice across a dizzying array of institutional settings. Despite the furious debates raging about anthropologists working for military activities (specifically the U.S. Army's Human Terrain Systems), Task Force members agreed that the Principles could *not* be written to focus on a single moment, nor with an eye to delineating what counts as valid anthropological work and what does not. Instead, the principles were crafted with conscious attention to professional diversity, with the goal of providing all AAA members with clear and concise starting points for articulating the ethical requirements of good research in the broadening range of contexts of anthropological work. In late 2010, the draft Principles of Professional Responsibility were released over the course of several months via the American Anthropological Association's website, and were ratified soon after, in 2012.

Leaning In

We need an anthropology that embraces the bleeding edge. The economic shifts that will be opening the job market for anthropologists in the next eight to ten years are already changing the lives of human beings everywhere. These forces are extremely difficult to understand, and not just because we have incorporated them in so many areas of our lives, in such a short period of time. They are technically, mathematically, legally, and procedurally intricate, requiring a significant amount of domain knowledge before their implications can be appreciated. Ethnographers who develop fluency in a domain of practice, such as technology or finance, can become powerful interlocutors between individual citizens and the entities shaping our social worlds. In the next section I offer two examples to illustrate the creative and critical potential of our work, one from the tech industry and the other from capital markets.

Anthropology for, of, and in Technology

Anthropology gained a productive foothold in the tech industry back in the early 1980s, namely at Xerox PARC (Palo Alto Research Center), where John Seely Brown recruited a small group of anthropologists, including Lucy Suchman, Janette Blumberg, and Julian Orr, to encourage new ways of thinking about how humans relate to machines. Since that time, anthropologists have continued to develop productive careers in the tech industry, where a number of anthropologists including Bonnie Nardi, Edwin Hutchins, and Genevieve Bell are recognized as intellectual leaders in the field of human-information interaction.

Bell, for example, is an Australian-born cultural anthropologist who established the Intel Corporation's user experience research laboratory, which currently employs over one hundred social, behavioral, and computer scientists. Bell and her colleagues are using anthropology's methods, its epistemological tension and positioning, to understand how people around the world are integrating technology into the warp and weft of their daily lives. They are credited with broadening the Intel Corporation's focus on Moore's law to appreciating the design implications of human-technology relationships for next-generation microprocessors.

Over the past decade, Bell and her computer scientist colleague, Paul Dourish, have written extensively about the mythologies and realities of "ubiquitous computing" as humans increasingly rely on hardware and software technologies that collect, store, and exchange information for our world. As Dourish and Bell emphasize (2011), the computer scientists and software engineers who enthuse about ubiquitous computing live in the "proximate future." This is the future that technology is creating, the one that is just around the corner, as opposed to the one that is right in front of all of us. This forward-looking myopia keeps these developers from appreciating that ubiquitous computing has already arrived, and from recognizing the opportunities and constraints for human-computer relationships in the lived world, with all its shifting messiness. Computing, after all, is already everywhere, right now: consumers have purchased, appropriated, integrated, and normalized technology in their daily lives—just not in the way that proponents of ubiquitous computing have been imagining. Dourish and Bell emphasize the need to wake up and recognize the dynamic creativity of lived human experience as a source of inspiration for truly revolutionary and empowering technological systems.

Insights like this have established Bell as a well-respected ethnographer-futurist known for her keen observation powers, critical thinking, and skeptical assessments of technological determinism. As Bell recently told the *New York Times*, her job is to "…drag the future here and see if we want it" (Singer 2014).

The Culture of the Crash

The tech industry is not the only place where anthropologists are practicing ethnography, engaging in critique, and working to help people understand how structures of power actually function. Take the burgeoning field of "finance anthropology," whose practitioners include Karen Ho, Caitlin Zaloom, and Gillian Tett, among others. These individuals have developed careers alongside, even within, some very powerful financial institutions and have written compelling accounts about the sociocultural dynamics of international capitalism.

Gillian Tett is perhaps the best known of these finance anthropologists. She is an award-winning British financial journalist who holds a Ph.D. in Social Anthropology from Cambridge. As she moved into a career in journalism, Tett discovered that she had a knack for making sense of the *weltanschauung* of the professionals who run our international capital markets. By the early 2000s, Tett was a reporter for the London *Financial Times*: in other words, she had gone *completely native* in the world of financial capital. It was exactly this career decision that positioned her to develop a rich explanatory narrative for the financial crisis that broadsided all of us into recession.

In Tett's analysis, the capital experts who dominate the world's financial capitals, and particularly Wall Street and City of London, lived in a world of their own making, a world in which hyper-complex financial products beneficially distributed risk and maximized reward for the benefit of the worlds that they knew. An early siren of financial collapse, Tett emphasized that these products diluted risk in ways that created unprecedented separation among institutional lenders, security traders, and human borrowers. Warning signs that might have been clear in a less complex forest of financial instruments were simply drowned out by floods of new revenue. As it turned out, these complex securities were less secure than they seemed and were actually the Achilles' Heel of international capital markets. In 2009, within a few months after the crash of Lehman Brothers, Tett published *Fool's Gold*, considered one of the most lucid accounts of 2008's market meltdown (Tett 2009). She remains a powerful figure in the world of finance and financial journalism and in 2014 was appointed Managing Editor of the *Financial Times*.

Many of us, I think, enthusiastically applaud Tett's creative use of her ethnographic sensibility to understand how a rarified, professionally homogeneous social network can pursue thousands of small, acceptable, "rational" market decisions that collectively put the international economy on the brink of catastrophe. Yet Tett, like many anthropologists who have chosen careers working for institutions of power, has faced blunt rejection from her anthropological peer group. This is less of a problem for Tett, I think, than it is for anthropology—at least, that is one way to read the keynote speech she gave at the meeting of the American Anthropological Association in November 2010. In her talk, Tett spoke about former mentors and colleagues who asked that she stop calling herself an anthropologist and confessed to feeling like "an impostor" among her social scientist peers.

It is rather ironic that anthropology's professional networks can be so closed to new voices, considering what Tett has written about tight boundaries of the finance world: the markers, tribal affiliations, specialized languages, and worldview-constricting narratives that led the financial industry to divorce itself from the world around it. Tett suggests that anthropologists need to enter the domains they have traditionally sought to avoid: any discipline that sequesters itself from the most distasteful elements of political economy runs the risk of, in Tett's words, "intellectual suicide."

Back from the Brink

I do not believe that anthropology is on the brink of intellectual suicide. And unlike Sterling Archer, I believe in anthropology's ongoing relevance: read *Fool's Gold* or any of Genevieve Bell's articles and you will see what I mean. But we do need to redouble our efforts to embrace diversity within our ranks: to discover and engage the places where creative, vibrant, trans-disciplinary anthropology is recreating our landscape of practice.

I am optimistic that this will happen—that it is already happening, in fact. Over the past decade, we have seen a softening of attitudes toward anthropology in its applied form. The Society for Applied Anthropology gets huge credit for its decades' worth of leadership in this regard. SfAA has played a key role in maintaining a link between anthropology in the academic realm and practitioners in advocacy or problem-focused research. The National Association for the Practice of Anthropology has played a similar role within the AAA, which lately seems to be overcoming its historical ambivalence toward anthropologists pursuing careers in corporations, industry, or policy-making. To wit: in 2007, the Executive Board established a Practicing Anthropology Working Group (PAWG) to study and make recommendations for the AAA to provide better support for anthropologists in extra-academic careers. PAWG laid the foundation for CoPAPIA, which has done some good research around policies and activities to support practicing anthropologists—often working in partnership with the SfAA.

Anthropologists working in corporations, business, government, and industry have also established their own venues for knowledge exchange, increasingly with the encouragement and support of the AAA and the SfAA. For example, the Ethnographic Praxis in Industry Conference (EPIC), which began in 2005 as a small, industry-supported (Microsoft and the Intel Corporation provided startup funds) gathering of anthropologists and ethnographers working in, yes, industrial and corporate settings. EPIC is now a viable, independent non-profit conference whose attendance has quadrupled over the past nine years. Many of its founding members belonged to the National Association for the Practice of Anthropology (NAPA) and, by extension, the American Anthropological Association. A few years ago, EPIC and the AAA agreed to disseminate EPIC's conference proceedings through the AAA's AnthroSource online library.

Vibrant Novelty

The trend toward acceptance that I have described in the preceding several sections simply acknowledges a longstanding reality: anthropologists have been pursuing careers in business, industry, and government since the earliest days of our discipline in the United States, even if the visibility of those careers has waxed and waned over that period. Indeed, the market trends driving anthropologists into the arms of industry are part of a much larger shift that began in 1980s, as the idea of a "corporate anthropologist" gained traction in the public imagination (Marietta Baba has written extensively on this topic). I am glad these trends are continuing, even strengthening. Occupational diversity is not only inevitable; it is desirable as a sign of a vibrant, relevant field of study. I sincerely hope we can continue embracing disciplinary novelty, instead of shouting it down.

Of course, there is more to do. We need to prepare novice anthropologists with the methodological and topical knowledge required to thrive in a heterogeneous job market (Schensul et al. 2003). Those of us working outside academia, who have successful careers in interdisciplinary workplaces where anthropologists are a distinct minority, can bring valuable knowledge about what is required to prepare students for gainful, meaningful, impactful careers. If we are successful, novice anthropologists will feel excited and prepared to dive into boundary-breaking environments like the one that Genevieve Bell has created at Intel. We should encourage these anthropologists to return to us with tales of the field, so that we can engage in well-informed conversations about the possibility for ethical practice in the very institutions we have historically shunned. Eventually, maybe, we will collectively forget that a distinction between "applied" and "pure" practice ever existed.

NOTES

1. www.bls.gov/ooh/life-physical-and-social-science/anthropologists-and-archeologists.htm, accessed September 28, 2014.

REFERENCES

American Anthropological Association (AAA)
2009 The Changing Face of Anthropology: Anthropology Masters Reflect on Education, Careers, and Professional Organizations. Arlington, VA: American Anthropological Association.
2012 Principles of Professional Responsibility. http://ethics.aaanet.org/category/statement/, accessed September 28, 2014.

Baba, M.
1988 Anthropological Research in Major Corporations: Work Products of the Industrial Domain. Central Issues in Anthropology 7(2):1-17.
1986 Introduction. Annals of Anthropological Practice 2(1):1-46.

Baba, M. L. and C. Hill
2006 What's in the Name 'Applied Anthropology?' An Encounter with Global Practice. The Globalization of Anthropology NAPA Bulletin #25. Pp 176-207. Washington, DC: American Anthropological Association.

Becker, P. E.
1999 Congregations in Conflict: Cultural Models of Local Religious Life. New York: Cambridge University Press.

Carnevale, A.
2013 Hard Times: College Majors, Unemployment, and Earnings. Washington, DC: Georgetown University, Center for Education and the Workforce.

Dourish, P. and G. Bell
2011 Divining and Digital Future: Mess and Mythology in Ubiquitous Computing. Cambridge, MA: MIT Press.

Goodman, A.
2006 Engaging National Security. Anthropology News. www.aaanet.org/press/an/0206/goodman.html, accessed September 27, 2014.

Goudreau, Jenna
2012 The 10 Worst College Majors. Forbes Magazine. www.forbes.com/sites/jennagoudreau/2012/10/11/the-10-worst-college-majors/, accessed September 28, 2014.

Hersh, Seymour
2004 The Gray Zone. New Yorker 80 (13):38-44.

Hymes, Dell, ed.
1972 Reinventing Anthropology. New York: Pantheon.

McNamara, Laura
2001 Ways of Knowing about Weapons: The Cold War's End at Los Alamos National Laboratory. Ph.D. dissertation, Department of Anthropology, University of New Mexico.

Nader, Laura
1972. Up the Anthropologist: Perspectives Gained from Studying Up. *In* Reinventing Anthropology. Dell H. Hymes, ed. Pp. 284-311. New York: Vintage Books.

Patai, Raphael
1973. The Arab Mind. Tucson, AZ: Recovery Resource Press.

Price, David
2006 American Anthropologists Stand Up to Torture and the Invasion of Iraq. Counterpunch, November 20. www.counterpunch.org/2006/11/20/american-anthropologists-stand-up-against-torture-and-the-occupation-of-iraq/, accessed June 14, 2012.

Schensul, B., M. Baba, and S. Hyland
2003 Preparing Students for Work in Nonacademic Settings. Anthropology News 44, (3):21-23.

Sider, Gerald
2009 Can Anthropology Ever Be Innocent? Anthropology Now. 1(1): 43-50.

Singer, N.
2014 Intel's Sharp Eyed Social Scientist. New York Times. www.nytimes.com/2014/02/16/technology/intels-sharp-eyed-social-scientist.html?_r=0, accessed September 28, 2014.

Tett, G.
2009 Fool's Gold. The Inside Story of J. P. Morgan and How Wall Street Greed Corrupted its Bold Dream and Created a Financial Catastrophe. New York: Simon and Schuster.

AFTERWORD

Ethics as Institutional Process

Monica Heller

I write this in my capacity as a member of the elected, volunteer governance of the American Anthropological Association (AAA). In a variety of such roles, I have followed almost the full process of re-thinking the AAA's role in anthropological ethics, and notably the re-shaping of the Code of Ethics to a Statement on Ethics: Principles of Professional Responsibility. In this brief afterword I will trace my perspectives on that process, addressing some of the reasons why it is important for the AAA to provide spaces for reflection and discussion on anthropological ethics, and on why we shifted from "code" to "statement."

More broadly, I would like to frame this text as a specific contribution to the understanding of ethics as process, namely, as a description of the institutional process that shaped the text as it exists today, a frame inspired by the work of Aaron Cicourel (Briggs 2007; Cicourel 1980; Cicourel 1973). The idea is that our ideas about something (anthropological ethics, in this case) are always developed in interaction with other people and in connection to our experiences. Some are ephemeral, lasting a moment or two beyond specific conversations, while some are more widely shared and temporally more durable, getting sedimented into social structuration, and in particular, into social institutions—which then act as constraints on what can possibly come next (Giddens 1984). One result is that, in institutions, knowledge ends up inevitably being distributed such that no one person has the full picture of

Anthropological Ethics in Context: An Ongoing Dialogue, pp. 231-235. © 2016 Left Coast Press, Inc. All rights reserved.

what is going on. Rather, we have to rely on our networks and access to communicative resources to be able to navigate (and construct) institutional processes. What ends up being institutionalized (in this case, an academic association's Statement on Ethics) is only a sedimentation, or entextualization, of a moment in a process in which many people are involved, none of them with full control over (or knowledge of) what ends up happening. That text, of course, then does not get fixed forever in a unified interpretive process; as we shall see, this understanding of the Statement as an element (albeit a key one) of institutional process (as discursive process) underlies our institutionalization of it as a living document, and of its current foster home with its stewards, the standing Committee on Ethics.

As related elsewhere in this book, the re-thinking of the Code of Ethics began as an unintended consequence of a different institutional process altogether: the work of a Commission on the Engagement of Anthropology with the US Security and Intelligence Communities (CEAUSSIC), named in 2005 by then-President Alan Goodman. (In turn, that Commission was triggered, at least in part, by the most banal of institutional processes, a request by the CIA to place an ad in the AAA Job Centre.) I happened to be a member of the Executive Board at that time, and served as EB liaison to the Commission. As the Commission's reports explain, our work started out with an exploration of how best to address the question of what stance the AAA might (or should) take regarding such requests, which we learned quickly were merely forerunners of an increased interest in social science on the part of the Pentagon. (The matter of recruitment of social scientists to the "Human Terrain System" emerged only after we had begun our work.) We arrived fairly quickly at a consensus that our thinking should be driven not by politics, but by anthropological ethics. However, when we turned to the existing code, we did not feel that it gave us sufficient material to work with. As a result, one major recommendation was to begin a process of updating what the AAA has to say about ethics, with the results recounted in this volume.

I next picked up the story at the end of the Task Force's process, as Vice-President and President-Elect. At the request of then President Leith Mullings, I chaired a small committee made up of members of the Executive Board, which closely examined not only the texts the Task Force submitted but also the commentary on its drafts (members included Hugh Gusterson, Sandra López Varela, Deb Martin, Leith Mullings, Vilma Santiago Irizarry, Jay Schensul, and Ida Susser; Damon Dozier provided staff support). Consulting along the way with former Task Force members, we attended to it line by line, and simultaneously as a whole. I won't bore you with the details, some of which were editorial. Some rather interesting "editorial" debates, however, were really conceptual, as they concerned which bits went with which—confirming the Task Force's sense that, actually, all the threads are deeply intertwined.

More importantly, we accepted many of the Task Force's foundational ideas. The first two are that ethics *is* a discursive process, and that conditions are so variable that one size will never always fit all anyway. Both build on anthropological insights about morality and ethics as social process, and about the complexity of social life. It is therefore, we agreed, not possible, or even desirable, to provide hard and fast rules, but rather it is preferable to provide some means to engage in a discourse that might help each of us arrive at decisions in the concrete cases we face. We agreed that the AAA could, indeed should, participate in this process by providing anthropologists with principles to use to think through concrete cases, some examples of cases with which to compare our own, and some generous colleagues to help us do the thinking. (This is exactly what happened in the case of the AAA Statement on Human Terrain Systems.)

The third idea we accepted is that, as a result, having something to say about ethics is an appropriate and feasible thing for the AAA to do if we understand our text to be not a hard and fixed code, but a statement containing a set of principles. If we had a fixed code, we would have great difficulty in figuring out which elements apply when and to whom, given that over 20% of our members are based outside the United States, more and more work in settings other than academic ones, and the boundaries of disciplines and subdisciplines are getting quite blurred. It would make it difficult to foster the kind of discussion that understanding ethics as a discursive process supposes. This does not stop us from being clear about what is negotiable (say, paying a research participant) and what is not (say, forcing them to participate), nor, as we learned with HTS, does it stop us from saying so when something fails to correspond to the principles we won't negotiate, or when we feel the principles were unwisely applied in some specific case. More importantly, perhaps, the AAA is probably uniquely placed to provide the space for the discursive process that is ethics to unfold, precisely because its membership is so varied. What we re-discovered in the EB part of the process is that it turns out there *are* things that archeologists and linguists, Americans and Japanese, academics and marketing researchers, students and teachers, can agree on; and that being able to think with a wide range of conceptual tools and concrete examples is extremely helpful. This finding allowed us to come to an agreement to change what the text is called. (I should add, though, that the sub-committee spent a great deal of time debating the title of the first principle (Do No Harm) and its place at the top of the list. For many, critical research cannot guarantee that no harm will be done to anyone, and sometimes, frankly, harm to powerful oppressors is precisely what is desired).

The final point made by the Task Force is that the text needs to be understood as a living document. The Task Force provided several illustrative cases to be embedded through hyperlinks; the Executive Board did a little more homework on that front. Once the text was accepted, we asked the standing Committee on Ethics to be its steward, in a number of senses. First, it would take on the responsibility for making sure that links were still functional and relevant, adding and subtracting as new materials become available and older ones became out of date. Second, it would continue its practice of acting as a sounding board for members with questions, using the Statement as a set of tools to think with. That committee not only continues to respond itself to such requests, but continues to make use of an additional resource (usually known as the Friends of the Committee on Ethics, or just the Friends, and composed of past chairs willing to remain available) for consultation when needed. The challenge here is institutional memory, as chair and members have relatively short terms, and we have improvements to make in the socialization of new members to committees in general. It is worth noting how much support the Statement has received, and how little controversy it has generated. You know institutions are working well when you can't hear the gears.

The Statement as we now have it is thus the work of institutional process, including of course the individual Task Force and EB subcommittee members and AAA support staff, but, more centrally for my purposes here, these individuals all acted as part of institutional processes aimed at producing a text that has authority (in Bourdieu's sense) because it is an institutional voice. I think the other authors of this collection would agree with me though that, while the text is important, it signals a conversation, or rather a whole interconnected set of conversations linked up across both time and space. Those conversations did not, and must not, stop with the posting of the Statement on the AAA website, nor the publication of this book.

REFERENCES

AAA Commission on the Engagement of Anthropology with the US Security and Intelligence Communities
2007 Final Report, November 4, 2007. American Anthropological Association. www.aaanet.org/pdf/FINAL_Report_Complete.pdf.

Briggs, Charles L.
2007 Anthropology, Interviewing and Communicability in Contemporary Society. Current Anthropology 48(4):551-580.

Cicourel, Aaron V.
1980 Language and Social Interaction. Philosophical and Empirical Issues. Sociological Inquiry 50(3/4):1-30.
1973 Cognitive Sociology. London: Penguin.

Giddens, Anthony
1984 The Constitution of Society: Outline of the Theory of Structuration. Berkeley: University of California Press.

INDEX

A

"A Short History of American Anthropological Ethics, Codes, Principles, and Responsibilities"—Professional and Otherwise, 23nn
Aberle, David, 31, 35nn5
Aborigines Protection Society, 35nn1
Abu Ghraib, 219
accessibility of results, 62, 71–72, 107–18
Ad Hoc Committee (Committee of Concerned Anthropologists), 28–29, 31–32, 36nn7
Adams, Richard N., 35nn5
adjudication process, 62–64
Administrative Advisory Committee, 32–34
ADS. *see* Archaeological Data Service (ADS)
Albro, Robert, 119nn, 237
Altschul, Jeffery, 44
American Anthropological Association (AAA)
  and Code of Ethics revisions and language. see Code of Ethics (CoE)
  concerns over counterinsurgency and intelligence gathering. see clandestine research; military/intelligence agencies and research
  letter to members, 40–41
American Anthropological Association Code of Ethics. *see* Code of Ethics (CoE)
American Anthropologist (AA), 28–29
Anderson, D. C., 33nn8
Annual Business Meeting, Nov. 2007, 42–49
anthropological ethics, history of, 23–25
Anthropological Ethics in Context: An Ongoing, 231nn
Anthropological Ethics in Context: An Ongoing Dialogue, 9, 9nn, 23nn, 39nn, 75nn, 91nn, 107nn, 119nn, 145nn, 167nn, 207nn, 213nn
"Anthropological Ethics, the PPR & the COE: Thoughts from the Front Line", 185
"Anthropologists for the Boycott of Israeli Academic Institutions", 140nn6
anthropology, reinventing, 220–22
Anthropology Newsletter, 185
APA code of ethics, 57
The Arab Mind, 219
Archaeological Data Service (ADS), 114
Archer, 214–15
Australian Institute of Aboriginal and Torres Strait Islander Studies archive, 170

237

B

Baba, Marietta, 214, 228
"Background and Context to the Current Revisions", 39nn
Bainton, Barry, 36nn7
Baloy, Natalie, 200
Barker, Alex W. (Alec), 36nn11, 39nn, 44, 66, 85nn1, 103, 103nn1, 107nn, 207nn, 238
Bateson, Gregory, 218
"Be Open and Honest Regarding Your Work", 91nn
Beals, Ralph, 26–27, 35nn3
Beals Report, 27
Becker, Penny Edgell, 220
Behind Many Masks: Gerald Berreman and Berkeley Anthropology 1959-2001, 77
Bell, Genevieve, 224–25, 226–27
Bell, Kirsten, 131
The Belmont Report, 79–80, 82, 130, 139nn3
Benedict, Ruth, 218
Berreman, Gerald, 29, 103
Blakey, M. L., 33nn8
Blumberg, Janette, 224
Boas, Franz, 24, 170–71, 220–21
Briggs, Charles, 36nn11, 66
Briody, Elizabeth, 140nn9
Brown, John Seeley, 224
Brutes, Alice, 36nn7

C

CAAP. *see* Canadian Applied Anthropology Project (CAAP)
Canadian Applied Anthropology Project (CAAP), 175
Caplan, Patricia, 76
Career, anthropological, 214–18
CASPAR project, 172
CEAUSSIC. *see* Commission on the Engagement of Anthropology with the US Security and Intelligence Communities (CEAUSSIC)
Center on Education and the Workforce (CEW), Georgetown University, 215
Centers for Collaborative Research for an Equitable California (CCREC), 200
Chagnon, Napoleon, 32
Chrisman, Noel, 44, 55
Cicourel, Aaron, 231
clandestine research, 62, 101–3, 111, 184–86

clean money and lack of, 112
Code of Ethics (CoE). *see also* Principles of Professional Responsibility (PPR); Task Force principles
  1971 document, 19–20, 26–34
  1998 revisions, 42–44, 61, 120, 223
  accessibility of results. *see* accessibility of records
  consideration of issues, 184–86
  Do No Harm. *see* Do No Harm
  evolutions of, 207–12
  informed consent and necessary permissions. *see* informed consent and necessary permissions
  open and honest, as ethical principle. *see* open and honest, as ethical principle
  records, protect and preserve. *see* records, protect and preserve
  relationships, respectful and ethical. *see* relationships, respectful and ethical
  revisions, 104nn2, 121, 211
  and secrecy, 95–96
  and the Turner Motion, 39–58
Code of Ethics to a Statement on Ethics: Principles of Professional Responsibility, 231
collaborators, ethical considerations due. *see* competing ethical obligations, collaborators and affected parties
colleagues, engaging, 158
comfort zones, danger of, 9
Commission on Practicing, Applied and Public Interest Anthropology (CoPAPIA), 216
Commission on Research Integrity 1995, 192–94
Commission on the Engagement of Anthropology, 211
Commission on the Engagement of Anthropology with the US Security and Intelligence Communities (CEAUSSIC), 33–34, 39–40, 67, 122–24, 139nn1, 211, 219, 232
Commission to Review the AAA Statements on Ethics, 203nn1
Committee for the Anthropology of Science, Technology and Computing (CASTAC), 222

Index 239

Committee of Concerned
    Anthropologists, 35nn4, 35nn6
Committee on Ethics
    2007 dissemination of results, 49–58
    ad hoc committee, 28–29
    consideration of issues and language,
        184–86
    educational mandate, 201–3
    the Friends, 186–87
    queries responses, 194–200
    queries to, 186–91
    recommendations of, 45–48
    as stewards of the Code, 234
    Turner Resolution, 48–49
Common Rule, 130, 134–35
communities/group respondents,
    obligations to, 151
compartmented research, 97–99,
    104nn2
competing ethical obligations,
    collaborators and affected parties
    balancing competing obligations,
        146–47
    balancing context, judgments and
        obligations, 160–66
    competing obligations, 165–66
    complexity and engagement with
        populations, 148
    consideration of issues, 145–46
    as PPP principle, 71
    practical precursors, 154–59
    understanding and accounting for
        others, 148–54
Comprehensive Ethics Review, 18
confidentiality
    in the corporate setting, 204nn8
    field notes and records, 71
    obligations due collaborators, 54, 69
    regard to threatened populations and
        resources, 40–41, 45–46, 49
Conklin, Harold, 35nn4
context, judgments and obligations,
    balancing, 160–66
CoPAPIA. *see* Commission on
    Practicing, Applied and Public
    Interest Anthropology (CoPAPIA)
Cornell Medical School, 99
corporate anthropologist, 228
Council for the Preservation of
    Anthropological Records, 171
Crain, Cathleen, 145nn
Cushing, Frank Hamilton, 24

D
Darkness in El Dorado, 32
Darkness in El Dorado scandal, 32,
    120–21
data archives, 169–72
data destruction, 104nn4
data ownership and access, 156–57,
    163–64. *see also* accessibility of
    records
Department of Health and Human
    Services (HHS), 159
Derrida, Jacques, 12
Digital Curation Centre, 171
disciplinary boundaries, 177nn5
DNA collection misuse, 93, 99
"Do No Harm", 75nn
Do No Harm
    and ethics code revisions, 61
    as first principle, 77–79
    as primary obligation, 75–76
    and range of issues, 13–18
    responses from membership, 80–82
    summary remarks, 82–83
    and Task Force decisions, 76–77
    Task Force principles, 68–69
    Task Force Response, 83–85
"do some good vs. do no harm",
    140nn9
Dominguez, Virginia R., 9nn, 238
Dourish, Paul, 224–25
Dozier, Damon, 232–33

E
educational mandate, 201–3
El Dorado Task Force, 32
employers, obligations to, 153–54
EPIC. *see* Ethnographic Praxis in
    Industry Conference (EPIC)
ethical genealogy, 125
ethical principles from Task Force,
    68–74
"Ethics as Institutional Process", 231–
    34, 231nn
Ethics Committee. *see* Committee on
    Ethics
*Ethics in the Field: Contemporary
    Challenges*, 80
Ethnographic Praxis in Industry
    Conference (EPIC), 227
Evans-Pritchard, E. E., 128
Executive Board (EB), 33–34, 41–43

F

Federalwide Assurances (FWA), 159
Fellows Newsletter of the American Anthropological Association (FN), 29, 35nn4
Ferguson, T. J., 40
Fernea, Robert, 33nn8
finance anthropology, 225–26
Fleuhr-Lobban, Carolyn, 36nn10
FN. *see Fellows Newsletter of the American Anthropological Association* (FN)
Fool's Gold, 226–27
Forbes, 215
Fortune, Reo, 24–25
45 CFR 46 (Common Rule), 134–35
Frankel, Barbara, 36nn10
Fried, Morton, 35nn4
The Friends of the Committee on Ethics (the Friends), 63, 77, 186–87, 194, 234
Fuentes, Agustn, 44
funders, obligations to, 151–53
future of anthropology and professional diversity
   anthropologists outside academia, 218–20
   considerations of, 213–14
   ethics for a centrifugal discipline, 222–23
   and finance anthropology, 225–26
   reinventing anthropology, 220–22
   relevance of anthropology, 226–27
   technology and anthropology, 224–25
   Whither the anthropological career?, 214–18
FWA. *see* Federalwide Assurances (FWA)

G

Geertz, Clifford, 129
Genographic Project, 79
Gibson, Kathleen, 36nn10
Golbert, J., 33nn8
Goodman, Alan, 33–34
green open access/hybrid gold open access model, 114–15
Guatemala STD study, 79
Gusterson, Hugh, 50–51, 54, 204nn7, 231–33

H

Handbook on Ethical Issues in Anthropology, 184
Harris, Marvin, 35nn4
Havasupai Tribe, 173–74
Heider, Karl, 36nn7
Heller, Monica, 40, 103, 103nn1, 231–35, 231nn, 239
Hersh, Seymour, 219
Hill, James N., 184–85
Ho, Karen, 225
Hoeyer, Klaus, 126
Hogle, Linda F., 126
Holdren, John P., 177nn2
Huffington Post, 215
Hughes, C., 33nn8
Human Ecology Fund, 99
Human Genome Diversity Project, 79
Human Terrain System, 80, 211
Human Terrain Team, 102
Hutchins, Edwin, 224
Hymes, Dell, 35nn4, 220–22

I

"Improving the Management of and Access to Scientific Collections", 177nn2
individual respondents, obligations to, 149–51
informed consent and necessary permissions
   empower counterparts, 131–34
   ethical history of, 124–27
   informed consent as a phase, 129–31
   margins of the field, 127–29
   at present, 138–39
   professional obligations of anthropologists, 119–21
   risk and/or harm, 134–38
   Task Force principles, 70
Inside Higher Ed, 57
Institution of Medicine (IOM) Report 1989, 192
Institutional Review Board (IRB), 84, 130, 134–37, 159, 162
Integrity and Misconduct in Research, 192
intellectual suicide, 226–27
"Introduction: Ethics, Work, and Life—Individual Struggles, and Professional "Comfort Zones" in Anthropology", 9nn
IRB. *see* Institutional Review Board (IRB)
IRB-shopping, 104nn5
Irizarry, Vilma Santiago, 232–33
issues, range of. *see* range of issues

J

Jones, Delmos, 99
Jorgensen, Joseph, 35nn5

K

Keane, Webb, 131, 139–40nn4
Kelly, John, 40, 43
Kroeber Anthropological Society Papers, 77
Kubark Counterintelligence Interrogation manual 1963, 99
Kuhn, Thomas, 9

L

Lawless, Robert, 102
Leatherman, Tom, 40
LeCompte, Margaret D., 130
Lederman, Rena, 125, 127
Levy, Janet, 36nn10, 185, 203nn1
linguists and power abuse, 93
lives of anthropologists, 15–18
Lomawaima, Hartman, 173
Low, Setha, 40, 51
Lubicon Lake Cree, 112

M

MacKinnon, Katherine C., 36nn11, 44, 66, 75–85, 75nn, 77, 239
McNamara, Laura, 213nn
"Make Your Results Accessible", 107nn
Malinowski, Bronislaw Kasper, 128
Marks, Jonathan, 103, 103nn1, 104nn3
Martin, Deb, 232–33
McNamara, Laura A., 36nn11, 66, 213–30, 239–40
Mead, Margaret, 24–25, 218
Mentoring Working Group, 202
Mikell, Gwendolyn, 40
Milanich, Jerald, 36nn7
military ads, 28
military/intelligence agencies and research
  ads in *AA* and response to, 26–28
  and anthropological "innocence", 218–20
  CEAUSSIC report, 39–42, 211–12
  Code as response to, 96–99
  debates concerning, 119–11
  tensions by membership and use of data, 33–34
  an Turner resolution, 52
Mink, 24
Mooney, James, 24

"Moral Science: Protecting Participants in Human Subjects Research", 139nn3
moral turpitude, 17–18
Mullings, Leith, 232–33
Murphy, Robert, 35nn4
My Freshman Year: What a Professor Learned by Becoming a Student, 102

N

NADB. *see* National Archaeological Database (NADB)
Nader, Laura, 92, 131–32, 222
NAGPRA. *see* Native American Graves and Repatriation Act (NAGPRA)
NAPA. *see* National Association for the Practice of Anthropology (NAPA)
Nardi, Bonnie, 224
Nathan, Rebekah, 102
National Archaeological Database (NADB), 114
National Association for the Practice of Anthropology (NAPA), 277
National Institutes of Health, 192, 204nn12
Native American Graves and Repatriation Act (NAGPRA), 80
Nature, 202
New York Times, 35nn3
Nichols, Deborah, 40
Nuremberg Code, 1947, 25–26

O

object preservation, 170–71
"Obtain Informed Consent and Necessary Permissions", 119nn
Occupational Outlook Handbook, United States Bureau of Labor Statistics, 217
"On Professional Diversity and the Future of Anthropology", 213nn
online modules and education mandate, 204nn6
open and honest, as ethical principle
  clandestine research, 101–3
  compartmented research, 97–99
  impacts of anthropological writings, 96–97
  importance of, 91–94
  other approaches to disclosure, secrecy, deception and power, 99–102

secrecy and research, 94–96
Task Force recommendations, 69–70
orphaned collections, 177nn1
Orr, Julian, 224
"other" as object of study, 25
others, understanding and accounting for
  communities/group respondents, 151
  employers, 153–54
  funders, 151–53
  individual respondents, 149–51

P

participant observation/fieldwork
  issues of, 11–14
  privacy, importance of, 36, 48–49, 72
participants, protection of, 157–58
Pat Roberts Intelligence Scholars
  Program (PRISP), 219
Patai, Raphael, 219
PAWG. *see* Practicing Anthropology
  Working Group (PAWG)
Peacock, James, 36nn10
Peary, Robert, 24
Pels, Peter, 35nn1, 111–12, 115–16nn1
Pester, Tracy Meerwarth, 140nn9
Plemmons, Dena, 36nn11, 39nn, 44,
  66, 85nn1, 119nn, 207nn, 240
Pospisil, Leopold, 27
PPR. *see* Principles of Professional
  Responsibility (PPR)
Practicing Anthropology Working
  Group (PAWG), 227
precursors, practical
  avoid isolation, 158–59
  data ownership and access, 156–57
  engage with IRB, 159
  engaging colleagues, 158
  enumerate your stakeholders and
    promises, 155–56
  Federalwide Assurances (FWA), 159
  inventory of desires and benefits, 158
  know your ethics, 155
  protection of participants, 157–58
Presidential Commission for
  the Study of Bioethical Issues,
  124–25
Price, David, 23nn, 36nn11, 44,
  51, 65, 91nn, 220, 240
primary responsibility, of
  anthropologists, 61, 209–11

principles, communicating to
  membership, 64–65
Principles of Professional Responsibility
  (PPR)
  1971, 19–20, 29–32, 36nn12
  1990's and post 9/11, 32–34
  accessibility of results, 107–18,
    115–16nn1
  competing ethical obligations,
    collaborators and affected parties,
    145–66
  and Do No Harm principle, 75–88
  failure to revise, 1980's, 31–32
  informed consent and necessary
    permissions, 119–45
  open and honest, as ethical principle,
    91–104
professional diversity and future of
  anthropology
  anthropologists outside academia,
    218–20
  considerations of, 21–214
  ethics for a centrifugal discipline,
    222–23
  and finance anthropology, 225–26
  reinventing anthropology, 220–22
  relevance of anthropology, 226–27
  technology and anthropology,
    224–25
  Whither the anthropological career?,
    214–18
"Protect and Preserve Your Records",
  167nn

Q

questions for review, Task Force, 61–64

R

Raj, Dhooleka, 44
range of issues
  participant observation/fieldwork,
    10–15
  thought and responsibility, 16–17
  recommendations of, 64–65
records, accessibility and rights to,
  177nn4
records, making accessible. *see*
  accessibility of records
records, protect and preserve, 72–73,
  167–76, 177nn3

Index 243

Reinventing Anthropology, 220–22
relationships. *see also* competing ethical obligations, collaborators and affected parties
  CoE, 53–54
  collaborators and affected parties, 69–70, 145–66
  enpowering counterparts, 131–34
  informed consent and necessary permissions, 120–21, 134–38
  power in, 100–101
  researched and researchers, 11–12
relationships, respectful and ethical, 171
  7th Principle, 191–94
  clandestine research, 184–86
  Committee on Ethics queries, 186–91
  educational mandate, 201–3
  queries responses, 194–200
  Task Force principles, 35nn2, 73–74
research ethics, 23–25, 78, 192, 204nn4
research participant, use of, 35nn2
The Responsible Conduct of Research in the Health Sciences, 192
risk and/or harm and informed consent, 134–38
Roberts, John, 36nn7
Royal Anthropological Institute Archives, 169–70

S

Schensul, Jay, 232–33
Schensul, Jean J., 130
Scheper-Hughes, Nancy, 104nn5, 173–74
Schneider, David, 35nn5
Science, 202
secrecy and research, 94–96
  anti-secrecy clauses, Nov. 2007 meeting, 42–45
  and Code of Ethics language, 39–40
  and counterinsurgency work, 35nn3
  dual purpose of, 94–96
  as enemy of science, 92
  place in science, 28
  vs. proprietary work, 33
  and the Turner Motion, 50–55
secretive research. *see* clandestine research
SfAA. *see* Society for Applied Anthropology (SfAA)
Shack, William, 35nn5
Sider, Gerald, 219–20

Singer, Merrill, 44, 55
Small, Cathy, 102
social media, and ethical considerations, 164–65
social responsibilities of scientists, 139nn2
Society for Applied Anthropology (SfAA), 25, 175, 220, 227
SPARE. *see* Statement on Problems of Anthropological Research and Ethics (SPARE)
"spatially incarcerated", 128
The Spirit Sings: Artistic Traditions of Canada's First Peoples 1988, 112
Stark, Laura, 57
Statement on Government Involvement, 27
Statement on Problems of Anthropological Research and Ethics, 27
Statement on Problems of Anthropological Research and Ethics (SPARE), 27–28
STEM skills (science, engineering, technology and mathematics), 215
Stocking, George W., 128–29
The Structure of Scientific Revolutions, 9
Suchman, Lucy, 224
Susser, Ida, 232–33

T

Tashima, Nathaniel (Niel), 36nn11, 44, 66, 145nn, 240–41
Task Force for Comprehensive Ethics Review
  approach of, 58–61
  communicating principles, 64–65
  creation of, 55–58
  and ethics process, 232–34
  formation of code of ethics, 26
  policy on govt. advertising, 28–29
  questions for review, 61–64
  and range of issues, 10–11, 14–15, 17–18, 19–20
  response to Project Camelot, 26–27
Task Force on Ethics of the World Council of Anthropological Associations (WCAA), 20
Task Force principles
  accessibility of results, 107–18
  competing ethical obligations, collaborators and affected parties, 71
  Do No Harm, 68–69, 75–88
  informed consent and necessary

permissions, 70, 119–45
make results accessible, 71–72
open and honest, as ethical principle, 91–104
Preamble, 67–68
protect and preserve work, 71–72
respectful and ethical relationships, 73–74, 183–205
submitted principles, 74nn4
tDAR (the Digital Archaeological Record), 171
technology and anthropology, 224–25
Tett, Gillian, 225–26
"the field" descriptors, 127–29, 140nn5
Tierney, Patrick, 32
Time, 215
Treitler, Inga, 44
Turner, Terence, 33–34, 40–42, 50–51. *see also* Turner Motion; Turner Resolution
Turner Motion, 40–44, 48, 108
Turner Resolution, 44–45, 47–55, 122
Tuskegee Study, 79

U
UK Data Protection Act, 177nn6
UN Declaration on the Rights of Indigenous Peoples, 140nn7
university boards, 33, 36nn9
U.S. National Anthropological Archives, 170

U.S. Office of Science and Technology Policy, 177nn2
U.S. Public Health Service, 124–25

V
van Gennep, Arnold, 128–29
Varela, Sandra López, 232–33

W
Wax, Murray, 36nn10
WCAA. *see* Task Force on Ethics of the World Council of Anthropological Associations (WCAA)
"Weigh Competing Ethical Obligations to Collaborators and Affected Parties", 145nn
"we-they" attitude and anonymization data, 173
"What's Different?", 207nn
Wolf, Eric, 35nn4, 35nn5
writings, impact of, 96–97

Z
Zaloom, Caitlin, 225
Zeitlyn, David, 171

About the Editors and Contributors

Robert Albro (Ph.D., 1999, Chicago) has maintained long-term ethnographic research on urban indigenous politics in Bolivia, much of which is found in his book *Roosters at Midnight: Indigenous Signs and Stigma in Local Bolivian Politics* (2010). His present work seeks to understand the role of culture as a problem-solving resource in policy and in practice, in such contexts as national security, public diplomacy, humanitarian engagement, science, and technology, some of which is found in his two edited volumes *Anthropologists in the Securityscape* (2011) and *Cultural Awareness in the Military* (2014). He has been a Fulbright scholar, and has held fellowships at the John W. Kluge Center of the Library of Congress, the Carnegie Council for Ethics in International Affairs, and the Center for Folklife and Cultural Heritage at the Smithsonian Institution. Albro's research and writing has been supported over the years by the National Science Foundation, Rockefeller and Mellon foundations, and American Council of Learned Societies, among others. He has also held several leadership positions in the American Anthropological Association, including Chair of the Committee for Human Rights and of the Commission on the Engagement of Anthropology with the Security and Intelligence Communities. In 2009, he received the President's Award for outstanding contributions to the AAA. Albro currently serves as Vice-President of the Public Diplomacy Council and as a Research Associate Professor in American University's Center for Latin American & Latino Studies.

Alex W. Barker (Ph.D., 1999, University of Michigan) is Director of the University of Missouri's Museum of Art and Archaeology, an AAM-accredited, university-based museum. Barker has served as Treasurer of the Society for American Archaeology, President of the Council for Museum Anthropology, and Convenor of the forty professional societies comprising the Section Assembly of the American Anthropological Association. He chaired the Committee on Ethics of the AAA, as well as the SAA Committee on Ethics, and served on both the AAA Task Force for Comprehensive Ethics Review and the AAM Cultural Property Ethics Task Force. He has also chaired numerous museum accreditation and Museum Assessment Program visiting teams, and has received awards from the AAM for his work in museum assessment and from the SAA for his work in promoting archaeological ethics. Recent publications include the 2012 volume *All The Kings Horses: Essays on the Impact of Looting and the Illicit Antiquities Trade on our Knowledge of the Past* from the SAA Press, "Provenience, Provenance and Context" in *The Future of Our Pasts* from the School for Advanced Research, and "Exhibiting Archaeology: Archaeology in Museums" for *Annual Reviews in Anthropology*.

Virginia R. Dominguez (Ph.D., 1979, Yale) is the Edward William and Jane Marr Gutgsell Professor of Anthropology (and member of the Jewish Studies, Middle Eastern Studies, and Caribbean Studies faculty) at the University of Illinois-Urbana/Champaign. She is also Co-Founder and Consulting Director of The International Forum for U.S. Studies (established in 1995) and Co-Editor of its book series "Global Studies of the United States." A political and legal anthropologist, she was President of the AAA from 2009 to 2011, Editor of *American Ethnologist* from 2002 to 2007, and President of the AAA's Society for Cultural Anthropology from 1999 to 2001. In 2013, Dominguez helped the World Council of Anthropological Associations establish the Brazil-based Antropologos sem fronteiras (Anthropologists without Borders), of which she serves as Vice-President. She also currently serves as Chair of the WCAA's Task Force on Advocacy and Outreach Activities. Author, coauthor, editor, and coeditor of multiple books, she is perhaps best known for her work on the United States (especially in *White By Definition: Social Classification in Creole Louisiana*) and on Israel (especially in *People as Subject, People as Object: Selfhood and Peoplehood in Contemporary Israel*). Prior to joining the UIUC faculty in 2007, she taught at Duke University, the Hebrew University of Jerusalem, the University of California at Santa Cruz, the University of Iowa, and Eotvos Lorand University in Budapest. She has also been *Directeur d'Etudes* at the EHESS (the Ecole des Hautes Etudes en Sciences Sociales) in Paris, a Simon Professor at the University of

Manchester, a Mellon Fellow at the University of Cape Town, a Morgan Lecturer at the University of Rochester, a Research Fellow at the East-West Center in Honolulu, and a Junior Fellow at Harvard.

Monica Heller (Ph.D., 1982, University of California, Berkeley) is Professor at the Ontario Institute for Studies in Education and the Department of Anthropology, University of Toronto. She is a member of the Royal Society of Canada. A linguistic anthropologist, her work focusses on shifting ideologies of language, identity, and nation in the globalized new economy, with a focus on francophone Canada. Her recent publications include *Paths to Post-nationalism: A Critical Ethnography of Language and Identity* (2011, Oxford University Press) and *Language in Late Capitalism: Pride and Profit* (co-edited with Alexandre Duchêne, 2012, Routledge). From 2011 to 2015, Heller served as Vice-President/President-Elect and then President of the AAA. In that capacity she shepherded what became the "Statement on Ethics: Principles of Professional Responsibility" through AAA Executive Board revisions, and on to its current happy home as a living document with the AAA Committee on Ethics.

Katherine C. MacKinnon (Ph.D., 2002 University of California, Berkeley) is Associate Professor of Anthropology in the Department of Sociology and Anthropology at Saint Louis University; she also holds a secondary appointment in the Center for International Studies. She is President-Elect of the Biological Anthropology Section (BAS) of the AAA, co-founder and executive board member of the Midwest Primate Interest Group (MPIG), and a member of Friends of the Committee on Ethics (AAA). She has served on the AAA Committee on Ethics (2005-2008), was a member of the Task Force for Comprehensive Ethics Review (2008-2012) charged with overhauling the AAA Code of Ethics, and was Program Chair of BAS (2012-2014). MacKinnon has published on biological anthropology and primate behavior/ecology, and recently co-edited *Primates in Perspective* (2nd edition, Oxford University Press). She has done fieldwork in Costa Rica, Nicaragua, Panama, Suriname, Colombia, and Zambia, and her research interests include infant and juvenile social development, the evolution of social complexity, conservation/management issues, and ethics in field primatology.

Laura A. McNamara (Ph.D., 2001, University of New Mexico) is Principal Member of Technical Staff at Sandia National Laboratories in Albuquerque, NM. She holds a Ph.D. in cultural anthropology from the

University of New Mexico. Dr. McNamara has worked in the Department of Energy's national laboratory environment since 1997, when she started her career as a graduate student at Los Alamos National Laboratory. Since joining Sandia in 2003, McNamara has contributed to a wide range of research and design projects in the area of human-information interaction. She currently leads an interdisciplinary behavioral science research team that applies quantitative and qualitative methods to study visual cognition "in the wild," with consumers of complex, heterogeneous scientific and remote sensing data.

Dena Plemmons (Ph.D., 1996, University of North Carolina), an anthropologist at UC San Diego, is a research ethicist with both the Research Ethics Program at UC San Diego and the San Diego Research Ethics Consortium, and is growing a research ethics program at the University of California, Riverside, in its Graduate Division. Her research and writing, in the areas of research ethics and research ethics education, has long been supported by NIH and NSF. She was a member of the AAA's Committee on Ethics from 2007-2010, serving as interim chair in 2008, chair in 2009, and co-chair in 2010. She chaired the Task Force for Comprehensive Ethics Review, 2008-2011. In 2011 she received the President's Award for outstanding contributions to the AAA, and she was elected an AAAS Fellow in 2012 for her work in the area of research ethics across the sciences.

David Price (Ph.D., 1993, University of Florida) is a Professor of Anthropology in St. Martin's University's Department of Society and Social Justice. He has written a three volume series of books using documents released under the Freedom of Information Act and archival sources to examine American anthropologists' interactions with intelligence agencies: *Threatening Anthropology* (2004, Duke); *Anthropological Intelligence* (2008, Duke); and *Dual Use Anthropology: The CIA, Pentagon, Universities, and the Enticements of Cold War Anthropology* (Duke, in press).

Natahaniel (Niel) Tashima (Ph.D., 1985, Northwestern University) and **Cathleen Crain** (M.A., 1978, McMaster University) are the founding and Managing Partners of LTG Associates, the oldest anthropologically based consulting firm in North America. Their wide-ranging topical work has focused on: refugee resettlement; HIV/AIDS/STD prevention and treatment; intimate partner violence prevention; early childhood wellness; food security; and interfaith relations. The majority of their work has employed the methods of monitoring, evaluation, and assessment, always informed and guided by the tools, skills, and ethics of anthropology. Under their direction, LTG has conducted work in all fifty states, all Freely Associated States and Territories and more than fifty countries. LTG has worked with more than thirty-five ethnic and cultural communities in the United States. LTG's work has been conducted with local government and community based organizations, local and national foundations, universities, international non-governmental organizations and with a wide range of agencies in the federal Department of Health and Human Services, the Department of the Interior, and the U.S. Agency for International Development, as well as with the World Health Organization. Niel co-authored the original National Association for the Practice of Anthropology's (NAPA) Ethical Guidelines and has been engaged in the last two revisions of the AAA's Code of Ethics. Cathleen co-designed the NAPA Mentor Program, which has continued to support the development of new professional anthropologists for the past twenty-five years. Cathleen has led the annual NAPA/AAA co-sponsored Careers Expo at the annual AAA meetings, which is the largest gathering of professional anthropologists within the AAA.